MW00423893

Mints

Mints

A FAMILY OF

HERBS AND ORNAMENTALS

Barbara Perry Lawton

Foreword by Steven Still

TIMBER PRESS
Portland, Oregon

Copyright © 2002 by Barbara Perry Lawton. All rights reserved.
All photographs by Barbara Perry Lawton unless otherwise stated.

Published in 2002 by
Timber Press, Inc.
The Haseltine Building
133 S.W. Second Avenue, Suite 450
Portland, Oregon 97204, U.S.A.

Printed in Hong Kong

Library of Congress Cataloging-in-Publication Data

Lawton, Barbara Perry.
Mints : family of herbs and ornamentals / Barbara Perry Lawton; foreword by Steven Still.
p. cm.
Includes bibliographical references (p.).
ISBN 0-88192-524-1
1. Mints (Plants) I. Title.

SB295.M5 L39 2002
633.8′2—dc21

2001035808

To Cindy and Doug

with thanks for their interest and encouragement

Contents

Foreword 9
Preface 11

CHAPTER 1 Mints in History and Lore 17
CHAPTER 2 Mints in Health and Home 43
CHAPTER 3 Herbal Mints 59
CHAPTER 4 Ornamental Mints 85
CHAPTER 5 Weedy Mints 99
CHAPTER 6 Pests and Diseases 105
CHAPTER 7 Botany of Mints 111
CHAPTER 8 Catalog of Mints 115

USDA Hardiness Zone Map 216
Further Reading 217
Glossary 221
Index of Plant Names 225

Color plates follow page 64

Foreword

The mint family is an extensive one that finds economic use in both the ornamental and culinary worlds. Many of us experience mints on a daily basis, especially where flavoring of food is involved. They embellish our food and drink and often provide highly ornamental plants for our gardens.

In her newest work, Barbara Perry Lawton has skillfully combined her love of gardening, knowledge of plants, and writing expertise to compile the first ever review of the mint family. Though books on individual genera have been written, such as Betsy Clebsch's *A Book of Salvias,* none has surveyed the entire family. *Mints: A Family of Herbs and Ornamentals* is also the first book to pack information regarding which plants can be used as ornamentals in the landscape with discussion of the perfect herbs for flavoring that special recipe.

Readers will find Barbara's writing style to be concise, factual, and very informative. She has been polishing this skill since 1960, during which time she has written several gardening books including *Magic of Irises,* which was nominated for an American Horticultural Society Award. She has served as editor and manager of publications at the Missouri Botanical Garden, president of the Garden Writers Association of America, and has written weekly garden columns for the *St. Louis Post-Dispatch.* In short, Barbara is a professional who combines her knowledge with thorough research to create informative material.

Mints: A Family of Herbs and Ornamentals is a complete text that provides readers with information on the classification, use, and care of mints. Amateurs and professionals alike will benefit from acquiring this thorough treatment of the mint family, which is sure to prove popular with the gardener in all of us.

Steven Still, Ph.D.
Department of Horticulture
Ohio State University

Preface

The mint family, the family Lamiaceae or Labiatae, has long been a favorite of mine in both the garden and the kitchen. I have enjoyed growing members of this group ever since I can remember, and I continue to use mint family herbs in salads, soups, stews, and other dishes. Some mints are, in my mind, closely associated with holidays. What would Thanksgiving be without the marvelous, pungent fragrance of sage (*Salvia officinalis*)?

The mint family is loaded with useful plants, including the majority of important culinary and household herbs. These herbs are, without a doubt, among the most engaging plants I know. Their history and lore are intriguing. They have the marvelous ability to enhance the best as well as the most humble foods. Their fragrances and tastes are inimitable. There is definitely something special about these plants that has endeared them to me. Horehound (*Marrubium vulgare*), lavender (*Lavandula*), lemon balm (*Melissa officinalis*), oregano (*Origanum vulgare*), rosemary (*Rosmarinus officinalis*), sage (*Salvia officinalis*), savory (*Satureja hortensis* and *S. montana*), sweet basil (*Ocimum basilicum*), sweet marjoram (*Origanum majorana*), thyme (*Thymus*), and of course the true mints (*Mentha*) are just a few of the many meritorious herbal mints.

As if that weren't enough for one family to brag about, the mints also include many handsome ornamentals. Bee balm (*Monarda*), obedience plant (*Physostegia virginiana*), and Russian sage (*Perovskia atriplicifolia*) are just a few of the wonderful garden perennials that come to mind.

In contrast to the more popular members of the mint family, some mints seem to be universally disliked by both gardeners and farmers. This is the case with certain dead nettles (*Lamium*). Although they may color the spring and early summer fields with their pinkish lavender flowers, I don't know of a soul who wants weedy dead nettles in garden beds and borders. Yet just about every gardener can find a spot for *L. maculatum* 'White Nancy' or other handsome cultivars. Indeed, some lamiums are very popular in today's gardens.

Other weedy mints enjoy similarly mixed reputations. True mints are often so successful that they become the scourges of ornamental gardens. I myself grow some that have to be pulled by the bucketful, although there is nothing like them for flavor and fragrance. Catmint (*Nepeta* ×*faassenii*), catnip (*N. cataria*), and lemon balm (*Melissa officinalis*) may all jump garden boundaries and become a nuisance; yet all of these are shallow-rooted and, when handled with perseverance, easily controllable.

I have wanted to write extensively on the mint family for a long time. It is an interest that began when I worked for the Missouri Botanical Garden from 1967 to 1972. That enjoyable tour of duty led to my becoming a more avid gardener with a great interest in horticultural botany. Up until that point my background had been in zoology, not botany, but there is nothing like working with experts to whet the appetite. Although I had always been interested in gardening and plants, this experience sharpened my curiosity and expanded my knowledge of the plant world. In recent years I have returned to the garden as a volunteer and continue to learn from the many experts there.

I learned quite a bit about plant taxonomy from my associations with staff botanists generous enough to share their knowledge with me. Many plant families, like human families, have obvious distinguishing characteristics. The mint family is one of these. The attributes shared by mints are often enough to make their relatives easily recognizable. Whenever I see equal and opposite leaves, square stems, and lipped flowers, I am quite sure that I'm meeting another mint cousin. For example, at one point I was looking at a Swedish ivy (*Plectranthus verticillatus*) in my living room, and although it was not in flower I noticed that the foliage displayed the characteristic look of the mint family. Looking it up I found that, sure enough, Swedish ivy is a mint that originated in South Africa. As I discovered soon after, coleus (*Solenostemon scutellarioides*), that colorful annual plant that provides bright foliage accents in many gardens, is also a member of the mint family.

Many years of garden writing have strengthened my curiosity about the relationships of plants to each other and to mankind. In many cases the ties between people and plants reach way beyond written history so that we can only guess how some plant associations began. I hope that these pages expand your appreciation of the mint family as I share my discoveries and insights.

The words *herb* and *herbal* have different meanings that may be confusing in some of the chapters ahead. In the strictest botanical sense *herb* refers to herbaceous plants, those that die down when cold weather arrives and grow again from the roots in spring. Another meaning, the one I use in this book, refers to plants with herbal qualities (culinary, medicinal, aromatic, or other). The word *mint* also has different meanings. All the plants in the mint family are loosely referred to as *mints,* while the term *true mints* describes only those that belong to *Mentha,* a single genus of the family.

Chapters 1 and 2 describe the many ways in which mints have been used, both historically and in present time. Chapters 3, 4, and 5 survey the better-known herbal, ornamental, and weedy mints, while chapter 8 serves as a general catalog to a more extensive list of plants. A comprehensive list of common names and synonyms as well as USDA hardiness zone and basic habit information can be found in chapter 8.

ACKNOWLEDGMENTS

My thanks for both encouragement and valuable information go to many people, especially those associated with the Missouri Botanical Garden. Director Peter Raven pointed the way toward previously unknown (to me) species, while June Hutson and Chip Tynan were always able to provide horticultural information whenever I ran into a blank wall. Special thanks to Connie Wolf and her staff at the Missouri Botanical Garden Library for their generosity and research assistance. I am lucky to live only twenty minutes from this great botanical garden—what a treat to have immediate access to the living collections and research facilities there. I also appreciate the research of Suldan Khan of the Islamic Foundation of Greater St. Louis, who found the Koran reference for me. And special thanks go to Steven Still—author, photographer, and professor of horticulture at Ohio State University—for writing the foreword for this book. Sincere thanks also to the staff of Timber Press, all of whom have been supportive throughout this project and seem always able to point the way out of the mazes and traps of writing.

ABOUT THE ILLUSTRATIONS

The illustrations in chapter 1 are borrowed from the rare book collections of the Missouri Botanical Garden or, more specifically, from the Missouri Botanical Garden Library Sturtevant Pre-Linnaean Collection, which includes botanical works dating from 1474 to 1753. The collection is named for E. Lewis Sturtevant, a botanist and agriculturist who donated his personal collection of 463 volumes to the garden in 1892. The collection is important because it contains many herbals and other works that are among early attempts to classify plants systematically. It is called pre-Linnaean because the books were published before Carl Linnaeus' *Species Plantarum* (1753), the first publication ever to use binomial nomenclature consistently. The Sturtevant Collection has grown to include more than eleven hundred volumes. Many figures found in chapter 8 are from volumes in the Missouri Botanical Garden Post-1753 Rare Book Collection. See Further Reading for additional details about any of these works.

Other illustrations have been generously provided by Cindy Gilberg, Ken Miller, and Andrew Van Hevelingen. I very much appreciate their interest in the book.

556 THE SECOND BOOKE OF THE

The temperature.

Water Mint is hot and drie as is the garden Mint, but it is of a stronger smell and operation.

The vertues.

A It is commended to haue the like vertues that the garden Mint hath: and also to be good against the stinging of Bees and Waspes, if the place be rubbed therewith.

B The sauour or smell of the water Mint reioiceth the hart of man, for which cause they strowe it in chambers and places of recreation, pleasure, and repose, and where feasts and banquets are made.

C There is no vse heereof in Phisicke, whilest we may haue the garden Mint, which is sweeter, and more agreeing to the nature of man.

Of mountaine Mint, or Calamint. Chap. 218.

The kindes.

There be three Calamints, as *Dioscorides* teacheth. The later writers haue found more.

1 *Calamintha montana vulgaris.* Calamint, or mountaine Mint.

2 *Calamintha montana præstantior.* The more excellent Calamint.

The description.

1 Mountaine Calamint is a lowe herbe, seldome aboue a foote high, parted into many branches: the stalkes are fower square, and haue ioints as it were, out of euerie one whereof growe foorth leaues something rounde, lesser then those of Basill, couered with a verie thinne hairie downe, as are also the stalkes, somewhat whitish, and of a sweete smell: the toppes of the branches are gallantly deckt with flowers, somewhat of a purple colour, then groweth the seede which is blacke: the rootes are full of strings, and continue.

2 This most excellent kinde of Calamint hath vpright stalkes a cubite high, couered ouer with a woolley mossines, beset with rough leaues like a nettle, somewhat notched about the edges; among the leaues come foorth blewish or skie coloured flowers; the roote is woodie, and the whole plant is of a very good smell.

There

Two calamints from John Gerard's *Herball* (1597). Missouri Botanical Garden Library Sturtevant Pre-Linnaean Collection.

CHAPTER 1

Mints in History and Lore

Our relationship with mints is long and tangled, stretching back into prehistoric times. Though we can only conjecture, it is highly likely that prehistoric people valued the strongly scented and flavored members of this family. Who, after all, would not be curious about plants whose fragrances rise up to greet you as you brush through the foliage?

Since written history goes back to about 5000 B.C. in China, or 3000 B.C. in Europe, we can only imagine that men and women of the Paleolithic period gathered herbs along with other edibles. This would have happened during the hunter-gatherer period—the same era as the last Ice Age, which ended about 8000 B.C.—and most likely would have taken place in the eastern Mediterranean region where many of the major herbs originally grew. In all likelihood the gatherers foraged on the hillsides along the great sea, seeking edible plants. They might discover an herb such as garden thyme (*Thymus vulgaris*), rosemary (*Rosmarinus officinalis*), or sage (*Salvia officinalis*), sniff its leaves, and perhaps even take a small bite of a tender leaf. Experimentation would follow. One person might try adding some bits of leaves to a stew. Another might try moving a plant to a more convenient spot.

Those who discovered new ways to use and grow these herbs would undoubtedly have earned special places of honor in their tribes. Holy men, holy women, or shamans might have known the most about herbs, learning ways to use the plants for the purposes of healing or magic and then passing along the knowledge in the oral tradition. In this way the knowledge and experience of honored tribesmen would pass from one generation to another.

Some experts claim that cultivation began no less than twenty thousand years ago. But surely farming, as opposed to simply gathering, became a major activity among early mankind during the Neolithic period, some six thousand years ago. During this period, pottery and weaving developed into useful arts, and people lived in villages rather than existing as nomads. Grain crops were scratched into the soil outside the village proper. One can imagine that the valuable herbs of the mint family were kept closer to home.

Perhaps these early people grew herbs in a penned-in area close to their shelters where the plants would be protected from animals and children and conveniently located for the cook and the medicine man. The kitchen garden so traditional in Western gardens probably originated in these prehistoric times. Over many hundreds of years herbal traditions and lore would have developed as people learned and grew through experience and experimentation —religion, magic, early medicine, and culinary styles all becoming bound into the warp and woof of herbal lore. Ceremonies and ceremonial procedures would have become overlaid and interwoven with one another.

All in all, we really know very little about the prehistory of the Lamiaceae. We can only refer to anthropological texts and draw vague, if logical, conclusions based on what we know about plants, gardens, and people.

But in early historical times, when written language began to hold sway over oral customs, people developed the rich written tradition of herbal lore and knowledge. Some of the earliest writings can be found in herbals—books about herbs and other plants, especially those useful to mankind.

Recorded texts on herbs from Sumeria, written about 2200 B.C., still exist. Consisting of inscriptions on tablets, these herbals list some one thousand plants. The Sumerians developed a successful agricultural economy, living in the region of lower Mesopotamia that is now Iran. They invented a system of writing called cuneiform or wedge-form earlier than 3000 B.C. The thousands of clay tablets that have been found prove that these highly civilized people knew of not only herbal and medical traditions but also mathematical and astronomical concepts.

Texts that record the medicinal uses of herbs in ancient Egypt have also survived the centuries, written on traditional papyrus scrolls that date to 2800 B.C. During this, their early period of history, Egyptians not only perfected the writing and recording of manuscripts, they also learned how to irrigate fields and use a plow for cultivation. It was the Bronze Age. After learning to use copper and tin, and after discovering how to blend these materials into bronze, craftsmen began to fashion metal tools. Excavations of Egyptian tombs have provided additional proof of the use of mints in ancient Egypt. A sprig of a form of wild thyme, for instance, was found in the tomb of King Tutankhamen, and peppermint was discovered in a wreath that dates back perhaps as far as the Twentieth Dynasty (1570–525 B.C.).

MINTS AND SACRED TEXTS

The first written information about herbs to become well known in the Western world can be found in the Bible, which dates its Old Testament writings back to the time of Moses or even earlier. The tale of Moses and the escape of the Israelites from Egypt is told in the Old Testament book of Exodus. This eloquent saga is thought to have taken place during the reign of Ramses II (1304–1237 B.C.) in the period known as the New Kingdom (1580–1100 B.C.). This period coincided with the Iron Age, the era when alphabets were developed, empires were built, and iron became the preferred metal for tools.

Marjoram and sage are two of the major herbal mints referred to in the Bible. Experts have argued that the hyssop mentioned in the Old Testament is *Hyssopus officinalis,* but most biblical scholars believe it to be Syrian marjoram (*Origanum maru*). The semantics of different translations often make it hard to deal with biblical specifics. Syrian marjoram has a pungent, fragrant smell and tastes much like peppermint (*Mentha ×piperita*). Like others of the same genus, this herb was used to treat colds, colic, rheumatism, sprains, and swellings.

To this day, Syrian marjoram is used as a Passover symbol, recalling when the Israelites were directed to paint the blood of a lamb on door frames to save their children from the Egyptian Pharaoh's death sentence. In Exodus 12:22 Moses tells the elders of Israel how to save their children by using the herb and lamb's blood in a religious ceremony: "And ye shall take a bunch of hyssop, and dip it into the blood that is in the basin, and strike the lintel and the two side posts with the blood that is in the basin." In Numbers 19:6 Jehovah speaks to Moses and Aaron: "The priest shall take cedarwood, and hyssop, and scarlet, and cast it into the midst of the burning of the heifer." And again, in Numbers 19:18, it is said that "a clean person shall take hyssop, and dip it in the water, and sprinkle it upon the tent, and upon all the vessels, and upon the persons that were there, and upon him that touched the bone, or the slain, or the dead, or the grave."

In I Kings 4:33 God gave Solomon wisdom, "And he [Solomon] spake of trees, from the cedar that is in Lebanon even unto hyssop that springeth out of the wall." Psalms 51:7 also refers to this plant: "Purify me with hyssop, and I shall be clean: Wash me, and I shall be whiter than snow." Syrian marjoram does seem to fit well with these quotes. It was used to cleanse homes defiled by leprosy or death and came to symbolize cleanliness. Its fragrance and taste led it to be prized by the ancient Romans and the Greeks before them. Brides and grooms wore crowns made of marjoram. It was also quite likely prized in the kitchen, as it is now.

According to biblical scholars, Judean sage (*Salvia judaica*) may have inspired the creation of the menorah, the traditional seven-branched candlestick of Chanukah. Exodus 37:17–19 tells of Bezalel of the tribe of Judah, one of Moses' Israelites, who made an ark, altar, and table of acacia wood:

> And he made the candlestick of pure gold: of beaten work made he the candlestick, even its base, and its shaft, its cups, its knops, and its flowers were of one piece with it. And there were six branches going out of the sides thereof; three branches of the candlestick out of the one side thereof, and three branches out of the other side thereof: three cups made like almond-blossoms in one branch, a knop and a flower; and three cups made like almond-blossoms in the other branch, a knop and a flower.

Sage had already proven its value as both a flavoring and a medicine, so it is hardly surprising that it appeared in religious symbolism. The Israelites, like many ancient peoples before them, took inspiration for their artwork from plants and animals. The Judean sage described in Exodus grows about 36 inches (90 cm) tall and displays the mint family's typically square stems and leaves that are equal and opposite, growing in pairs. When the plant is pressed it has a look similar to the menorah, revealing spikes of buds that may have inspired the artist's knops on that first golden candlestick.

With the help of Suldan Kahn, a Koran scholar and member of the religious committee of the Islamic Foundation of Greater St. Louis, I learned of an herbal reference in Surah II of the Koran—a section called "The Cow" (*Al-Baqarah*), named after its story of the sacrifice of a yellow heifer. Verse 61 reads, "And when ye said: O Moses! We are weary of one kind of food: so call upon thy Lord for us that he bring forth for us of that which the earth groweth—of its herbs and its cucumbers and its corn and its lentils and its onions." This reference to herbs, we agreed, most likely implied members of the mint family. Still, it was the only herbal reference we could find in the Koran.

MINTS AND SHAKESPEARE

William Shakespeare, arguably the world's greatest dramatist, referred to many plants in his works, not the least of which were members of the mint family. He lived from 1564 to 1616, a time of great discovery, world exploration, and literary brilliance, as well as a time devastated by epidemics of plague and other fearful diseases. During this time the great European herbalists enjoyed success as healers.

Shakespeare's *The Winter's Tale* contains a multitude of plant references. "For you there's rosemary and rue," says Perdita, daughter of the king of Sicily, as the assembled characters gather at a shepherd's cottage for sheep shearing (Act IV, Scene 3). A bit later she adds, "Here's flowers for you; hot lavender, mints, savory, marjoram." This represents one of Shakespeare's typical gatherings of herbal mints—all except the rue, of course.

Rosemary was even more highly prized in Shakespeare's time than it is now. The herb was used in medicine, cooking, perfumery, and as a garnish. Shakespeare referred to rosemary twice in *Romeo and Juliet* (Act II, Scene 4) as an herb to improve memory and once as a funeral decoration symbolizing remembrance (Act IV, Scene 5). Rosemary again appears as a sign of remembrance in *Hamlet* (Act II, Scene 5) and is associated with madness in *King Lear* (Act II, Scene 3).

In Act I, Scene 3, of *Othello,* Iago speaks to Roderigo, who has been gulled and is contemplating suicide:

> Our bodies are our gardens, to which our wills are gardeners; so that if we plant nettles or sow lettuce, set hyssop and weed up thyme, supply it with one gender of herbs or distract it with many, wither to have it sterile with idleness or manured with industry, why the power and corrigible authority of this lies in our wills.

Both hyssop and thyme are notable mints.

Finally, in Act IV, Scene 6, of *King Lear,* the mad king is wandering on the heath near Dover with the Earl of Gloucester's son, Edgar, as his guide. King Lear is rambling in his talk when suddenly he asks for the watchword or password. "Give the word," he demands. "Sweet marjoram," Edgar replies. Interestingly, this is the herb that was used to treat mental disorders.

THE LANGUAGE OF HERBS

The origin of the language of flowers goes back many centuries to the Middle East, where it first became customary to send floral messages with hidden meanings. When someone sent a bunch of flowers, each flower might represent a particular verse of classical poetry or might contain one or more other meanings. In some cases the symbolism came from the medicinal uses of the plants.

Although the crusaders carried this custom back to Europe during the Middle Ages, the practice of sending floral messages didn't reach its peak until the Victorian Age, a time when sending dried arrangements and nosegays was also popular. When the meanings attached to the flowers were contradictory, as was sometimes the case, the results must have been confusing, to say the least. For this reason it would have been important to include a translation of the intended meaning along with such a bouquet.

Many mint family herbs were traditionally accorded these kinds of meanings. The more common meanings are listed first.

Balm (*Melissa*)	Sympathy, pleasantry, don't misuse me
Garden thyme (*Thymus vulgaris*)	Courage, activity
Lavender (*Lavandula*)	Distrust, you are difficult to understand
Pennyroyal (*Mentha pulegium*)	Flee, run away
Peppermint (*Mentha* ×*piperita*)	Warmth of feeling
Rosemary (*Rosmarinus officinalis*)	Remembrance and fidelity
Sage (*Salvia officinalis*)	Esteem, domestic virtue and happiness, immortality, wisdom, I will suffer all for you
Salvia, blue (*Salvia*)	I think of you
Salvia, red (*Salvia*)	Forever thine
Spearmint (*Mentha spicata*)	Warmth of sentiment
Sweet basil (*Ocimum basilicum*)	Best wishes, love or serious intentions, hatred or an enemy is near

Sweet marjoram (*Origanum majorana*)	Happiness and joy, innocence and blushes, charm against witchcraft, don't you love anyone?
True mints (*Mentha*)	Homely virtue, wisdom, find someone your own age, don't make such a to-do about small things
Winter savory (*Satureja montana*)	The truth may be bitter

Although the practice has dwindled since the Victorian Age, this herbal language may have a place in our modern times. Plant an herb garden featuring sweet marjoram, sage, and garden thyme to celebrate a happy home. Plant sweet basil and rosemary to honor a friendship. Add peppermint and spearmint to a birthday bouquet as a symbol of affection.

Be thoughtful when making a selection, though. Sprigs of winter savory and pennyroyal in a small arrangement might mean that the receiver should run away because the truth will be bitter. Similarly, a bouquet of sweet basil, garden thyme, and true mints might mean that the receiver had better have courage because enemies are near, but also that he or she shouldn't make mountains out of molehills.

HISTORY OF HERB GARDENS

From the earliest of times useful plants were collected and carried home by explorers and warriors. Rulers directed their minions to gather these plants, often from faraway places. In about 1100 B.C. the Assyrian king known as Tiglath-pileser I bragged that he had carried many plants, including cedars and box, from countries he had conquered. The conquering routes of Alexander the Great (356–323 B.C.) and his army brought the influence of Greece to most of the civilized Western world and in turn brought the plants of those conquered lands back to Greece. (Incidentally, it was Aristotle who taught Alexander to take a keen interest in other countries and their plants and animals.) The crusaders collected plants to take back to Europe during their expeditions to conquer the Moslems in the Holy Land from about A.D. 1100 to 1300.

Once new plants were brought home they were planted in gardens where they could be admired, appreciated, and perhaps even protected. These gardens developed in ways that reflected both the sites and the owners. In ancient Egypt, for example, the shape of a garden reflected the desert environment. The rectangular shapes and straight lines indicated that irrigation was an important aspect of gardening in such a dry climate. The walled European gardens of later times showed the need for protection from invaders and were often a sign that the contemporary constructions had been built upon Roman ruins.

The concept of an herb garden probably developed from early Egyptian gardens as well as from Islamic and Christian religious and medical traditions. Evidence of herb gardening in ancient Egypt can be found in the wall paintings and relics of tombs created about four thousand years ago. Herbs were associated with temples, rituals, and worship of the gods. Garden thyme (*Thymus vulgaris*) was used by the Egyptians as well as the Etruscans and Greeks as both an embalming herb and perfume; and sweet basil (*Ocimum basilicum*), which was thought to help transport the dead into the world beyond, has been found in ancient Egyptian and Hindu tombs.

What little can be said about gardening in Europe before the Renaissance comes from a few surviving descriptions of ancient gardens, particularly those descriptions included in the letters of Pliny the Younger (A.D. 61–113), nephew of Pliny the Elder. Gathered into ten books, these letters illustrate the life and interests of this scholarly Roman gentleman. Pliny owned a number of villas in Italy and wrote of his gardens, describing how they added pleasure to his life. The gardens featured long colonnades and walkways lined with lawns, dwarf trees, boxwood hedges, and topiary shrubs. Roses grew in sunlit spots, and apple trees stood interspersed with small obelisks. A favorite site included a half circle of open lawn surrounded by plane trees covered in ivy.

An especially popular plant of these times was rosemary (*Rosmarinus officinalis*), grown not only for its medicinal and culinary uses but also for its fragrance and beauty. Rosemary undoubtedly grew in the gardens used by well-to-do Romans, gardens not tied to religious rites or to the art of healing as the gardens of ancient Egypt had been or as the monastery gardens of future centuries would be, but which were created instead for the purposes of strolling and contemplation. These gardens consisted of a series of rooms or courtyards, and the walls often featured murals of garden scenes, as evidenced by the excavated ruins of Pompeii.

Pliny the Elder, a civil servant and contemporary of the Greek physician Pedanius Dioscorides, had written *Natural History,* an important work that included volumes about medical botany. He invited Pliny the Younger to visit Pompeii with him to view the eruptions at Mount Vesuvius. Pliny the Younger declined because of his studies—fortunate for him as Pliny the Elder was killed in the eruption that buried Pompeii. The Younger Pliny went on to write descriptions of the gardens of his day, which constituted the majority of historical documentation until Pompeii was excavated.

Christian monasteries, largely based on the designs of early Roman villas, were the major sites of herb gardens for many centuries. They would, in fact, be a major influence on herb gardening until their dissolution in the mid-sixteenth century by Henry VIII, who established the Church of England and overthrew the authority of the pope in England in order to divorce his first wife, Catherine of Aragon.

The first monastery, which represented the start of the Roman Catholic monastic system, was founded near Memphis in northern Egypt in A.D. 305 by Anthony of Thebes, a hermit who was later to become one of the greatest saints of the early Roman Catholic Church. Monastic gardens were designed with geometric formality, quite in keeping with the walls within which they were sited. These geometric patterns would later evolve into intricate formal patterns, into knot gardens and parterres with many small beds within a larger design. Since monasteries were self-sufficient, growing all of their own fruits and vegetables, gardening was a major occupation.

Saint Benedict of Nursia (c. 480–543) first established a monastery in Italy at Subiaco, then founded the famous Benedictine order at Monte Cassino in 529. The order spread throughout western Europe, becoming a bastion of strength for Christianity throughout the Middle Ages. Benedictine monasteries grew herbs in many beds of their rectangular gardens, especially to heal those with injuries and illnesses. Healing herbs, including major herbs of the mint family, were grown in the compounds of hospitals and infirmaries run by nuns of various orders.

By the sixteenth century herbs were also grown to support the teachings of medicine and botany in universities. Called physic gardens, these were the ancestors of the botanical gardens of today. The first physic garden was established in the mid-sixteenth century at the University of Padua in Italy. Plants were arranged in ways to support the teachings. They might be grouped alphabetically according to related uses or according to the relationships of the plants. The Chelsea Physic Garden in London is one of the few remaining gardens of this old style.

Herb gardens have gone through many fads and styles since the monastery gardens were destroyed and the walls torn down. The formal styles, with their knot gardens and intricate patterns of herbs, are reminiscent of the heritage of garden design from the Egyptians to the monasteries. The informal, more naturalistic designs owe some of their inspiration to the great designers of England, especially Lancelot "Capability" Brown (1715–1783), who helped to radically change the traditional look of estates by tossing out formality in favor of parks and grounds in the natural or landscape style. The grounds of Blenheim Palace in England—with their rolling hillsides, placid stretches of water, and artfully placed clumps of trees—remain a shining example of Brown's work. Informal herb gardens are also indebted to English cottage gardens, where plants were often placed where they were handy or wherever there was space, creating a sort of undesigned design.

DOCTRINE OF SIGNATURES

In early times, probably before written records, a practice developed whereby the medicinal uses of herbs were identified by noting the similarities of certain aspects of plants to certain ailments. Practitioners of herbal medicine, for instance, used plants with red signatures—with red sap, in other words—such as St. John's wort (*Hypericum*), to treat blood disorders. Similarly, because the dark lines on the petals of foxglove (*Digitalis purpurea*) look like blood vessels this plant was used to treat blood and heart disorders. As it turned out, foxglove contained digitalis, a substance that proved valuable in treating heart disorders, so that the doctrine of signatures appeared to work. In most cases, however, this system of using the appearances of plants as clues to nature's healing powers proved scientifically valueless.

The doctrine of signatures—also known as the doctrine of similars and the doctrine of contraries—had a resurgence of popularity in the sixteenth and seventeenth centuries when its reasoning was carried to extreme lengths by certain herbalists. Some said that if patients were treated with plants that had short lives, the patients' lives would also be short. The doctrine of contraries stated that plants with opposite characters should be used to treat certain conditions. For instance, mints and other herbs with cool qualities would cure fevers. Some believers in homeopathic medicine are now reviving aspects of these earlier doctrines.

While much of the doctrine of signatures has been proven to be nonsense, scientists and medical researchers are renewing their studies of plants—including the traditional herbs of the mint family—with the knowledge that many treatments and cures for human conditions remain to be found. The general public also increasingly looks to herbal dietary supplements in the hopes that these plants will make them healthier and keep them younger. In China, herbal medicine coexists with modern medicine, a phenomenon also beginning to take place in the Western world. It is important to point out, however, that one should always be wary of using herbs as dietary supplements, learning as much as possible about possible side effects and potential dangers.

MINTS IN OLD HERBALS

The story of mints in the kitchen and the home, in maintaining health, and in healing disease, is in a sense the story of the old herbals. True mints and their relatives occupy major portions of these masterpieces, which aimed to identify and describe such plants and record the details of their usage. Herbals made it easier to classify plants used for medicinal purposes. Although most of the usage was based more on myth, magic, and tradition than on scientific fact, some herbs continue to be used in exactly the same ways today.

Before printing was invented in the middle of the fifteenth century, herbals had to be written individually and illustrated by hand. Errors crept in and were perpetuated. Drawings were copied from copies, each one looking less like the original plant. The earliest known herbal was supposedly written by the mythical Chinese emperor Shên-nung some five thousand years ago. Unfortunately, most of it was lost. Only parts of it survived long enough to be noted by other Chinese herbalists.

The first written herbal of the Western world was produced in about 300 B.C. by Theophrastus, a Greek and a pupil of both Aristotle and Plato. Theophrastus' *Enquiry into Plants* addressed the structure of plants and made the first systematized attempt to sort the plant world into logical classifications.

For more than fifteen hundred years the recognized authority on medicinal plants was *De Materia Medica,* one of the greatest herbals of the Western world. It was written by Dioscorides during the first century, about A.D. 60, in the time of Nero's rule. Theophrastus had studied the plants, but Dioscorides studied the plants in relationship to their healing virtues. *De Materia Medica* described some six hundred herbs, about three hundred of which were native to the eastern Mediterranean region.

Dioscorides dedicated *De Materia Medica* to his friend and fellow physician Areius. The original Greek manuscript, however, was lost. The oldest known version, now housed in the Austrian National Library in Vienna, is the *Codex Dioscorides* created for Princess Anicia Juliana (circa A.D. 512). The grateful citizens of Honoratae, now part of Istanbul, commissioned the codex and presented it to Anicia Juliana in thanks for her donation of a church to their town. It contains the oldest surviving plant illustrations, which are hand-colored and surprisingly sophisticated. Showing the plants from flowers to roots, the illustrations are quite accurate and appear to be drawn from life. Although the generic and specific identification are not always evident, the look of the mint family is obvious.

Although *Circa Instans* (A.D. 1130–1150) is a collective work by the School of Salerno, the famous medical center of the early Middle Ages, credit for this herbal is usually given to Matthaeus Platearius, a leading physician and teacher in his time. It included treatises on the simples, those primary ingredients used to make medical prescriptions, and remained a leading medical authority until the appearance of comprehensive printed herbals some three hundred years later. Only fourteen copies of *Circa Instans* remain in the United States.

Peter Schöffer's *Herbarius Latinus,* which first appeared in Mainz in 1484, is a collection of works by many authors, probably from manuscripts written before 1300. Schöffer, a contemporary of Gutenberg, intended the book for those without access to physicians. Book collectors and botanists alike consider this book dear, in part because of its 150 handsome woodcuts of plants arranged in alphabetical order, but also because it was reprinted in several locations so that there are interesting variations. The first of two major sections of the book contains descriptions and medicinal uses of plants that grow in Germany. The second half explains the uses of medicinal herbs as described in other herbals including *Circa Instans*. There appear to be two copies of *Herbarius Latinus* in the United States: a 1484 copy kept at the Missouri Botanical Garden and a 1482 copy kept, according to Stanley H. Johnston Jr. in *The Cleveland Herbal, Botanical, and Horticultural Collections* (1992), in a library in the Cleveland area. The 1484 copy includes the original animal-skin binding. The hand-colored woodcuts are drawn and colored crudely, making the illustrations decorative but not botanically accurate. Even though the work is strongly stylized, however, it is possible to identify a mint family herb here and there.

Schöffer's second book, *Der Gart der Gesundheit,* printed just one year after *Herbarius Latinus,* showed great advances over other herbals. Written in German rather than Greek or Latin, it contained many illustrations executed from nature rather than copied from other herbals. Some 65 of the 379 woodcuts are obviously drawn directly from the plants themselves. *Der Gart der Gesundheit* also reached a wider audience, since it was written in the local tongue, and included the first comprehensive indices of human diseases with references to the chapters as well as an alphabetical listing of the medicinal simples.

In 1530 former monk and theologian Otto Brunfels pointed the way toward the study of botany as we know it with the publication of *Herbarum Vivae Eicones*. Though written by Brunfels, the herbal included superb woodcuts by Hans von Weiditz, an artist whose work equaled that of Albrecht Dürer. It was, in fact, the artwork that distinguished Brunfels' herbal from previous works. The illustrations are lively and botanically accurate. A handsome depiction of lemon balm (*Melissa officinalis*), for example, represents the entire plant including the root system, with the virtues and medicinal uses of the plant listed on the overleaf. The text, however, merely follows the order in which the woodcuts were completed, in some cases not even matching up with the illustrations. Brunfels clearly needed a proofreader; indeed, he did not even know the botanical names or medicinal uses for all the plants depicted in *Herbarum Vivae Eicones*.

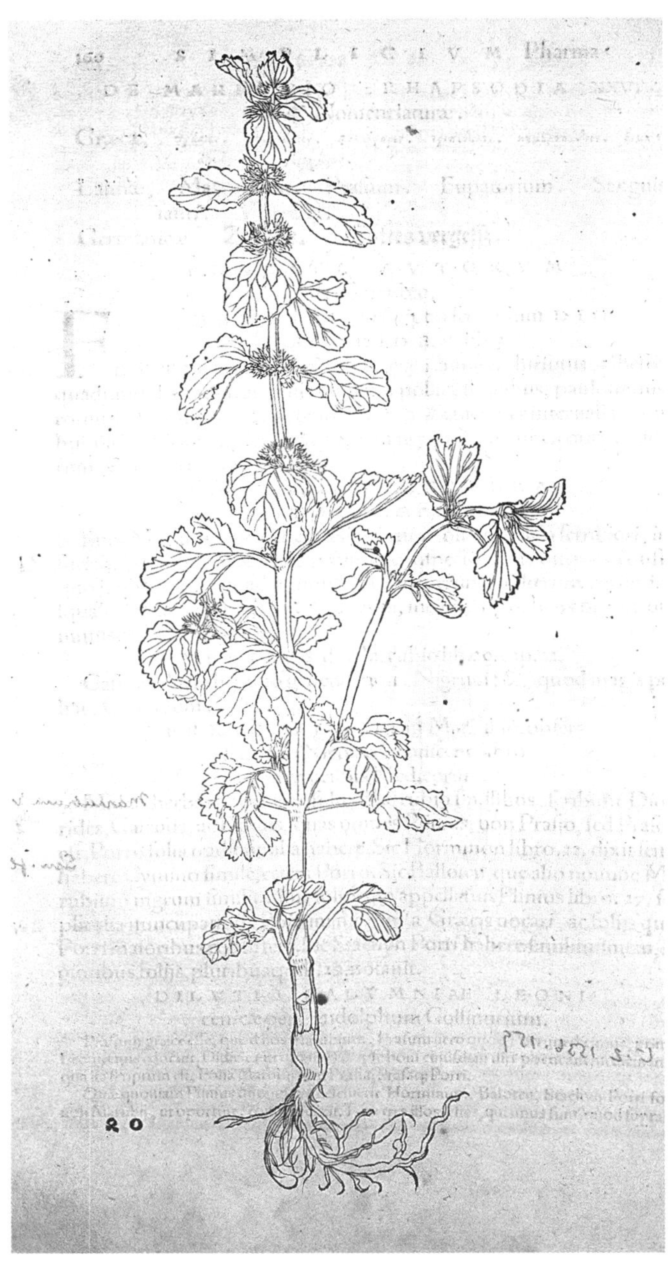

Mint plant from Otto Brunfels' *Herbarum Vivae Eicones* (1530). Missouri Botanical Garden Library Sturtevant Pre-Linnaean Collection.

Hieronymus Bock's *Kreuter Buch* was the first of the great herbals to go beyond mere identification by also including firsthand information on the characteristics and effects of plants that grew in Germany. Born in 1498, Bock had studied medicine near Strassburg and undoubtedly gained his botanical education while serving as superintendent of Count Palatine Ludwig's garden. Having little money for illustrations, he was the first to describe plants in such a detailed and accurate manner that they could be identified from text alone. *Kreuter Buch* does, however, include some delightful illustrations. The drawing of wild thyme, *Gundelreben* in the old German, is excellent even if the coloring is poorly executed (this particular woodcut looks a bit more like creeping Charlie than thyme). In addition, and more importantly to the emerging science of botany, Bock arranged the plant descriptions according to their similarities in appearance and relationships.

The next of the great herbals was Leonhart Fuchs' *De Historia Stirpium,* published in Basel in 1542 (Plate 1). Fuchs was a medical doctor and took his authorship seriously, producing a work that was learned for its time. He contracted with the best of Basel's artists for the 509 illustrations included in the book, closely overseeing designers as they executed each woodcut directly from a living model. Identification of the herbs is possible with the aid of both the illustrations and the Latin text. Woodcuts of *Salvia major* and *S. minor,* shown on the same page, are typical examples. Vertically rectangular, presumably to better fit the wood blocks, the illustrations are attractive as well as botanically true. Some later editions of *De Historia Stirpium* appear reversed because the art was traced directly onto a new woodblock. Most of the better-known botanical works from the next hundred years copied the artwork. Admirers of the old herbals remain divided in their praise for the illustrations of both *De Historia Stirpium* and *Herbarum Vivae Eicones.*

Up to this point all the great herbals had been produced in continental Europe. A new focus on England, however, developed with the publication of William Turner's *A New Herball,* the only original botanical work written in the sixteenth century. Born in

Northumberland in about 1515, Turner has often been referred to as the father of English botany. He wrote the herbal in English for the sake of British apothecaries who were not fluent in Latin or Greek but who needed more information on the plants necessary for their medicines. Published in three parts, beginning in 1551, sections of *A New Herball* were dedicated to Turner's patrons, the Duke of Somerset and Lord Thomas Wentworth, while the entire work was dedicated to Queen Elizabeth. Although about a third of the illustrations were taken from Fuchs' work, many of the woodcuts were made under Turner's direction.

Born in Siena in 1501, Pietro Andrea Mattioli was among the most eminent herbalists of his century. During his education and career as a physician he developed a great interest in Dioscorides and *De Materia Medica*. He hoped to consolidate Dioscorides' work with the botanical studies and botanical discoveries that had occurred since that earlier time. The resulting book, *Commentarij,* was published in Venice in 1544. The first Latin edition of the book was published in 1554, also in Venice. It was this edition, illustrated with 562 woodcuts, that earned Mattioli recognition throughout Europe. The illustration of lavender (*Lavandula*) is typical of the artwork, stylized yet delicately drawn and accurate enough for identification purposes. Like many botanical illustrations of the time, the artwork appears to have been adapted to fit the wood blocks on which the cuts were made. Aiming to become the world expert on Dioscorides, Mattioli continued to revise his work, and in 1565 another edition was released by the famous Valgrisi Press of Venice. In spite of his prestige and fame Mattioli was not a knowledgeable botanist and did not check the accuracy of the plant illustrations and descriptions. Some forty-five editions of *Commentarij* were published prior to Mattioli's death at the age of seventy-five.

John Gerard's *Herball* is probably the best-known of the old herbals because it was reproduced in such large numbers during the late twentieth century. Gerard was born in Cheshire in 1545 and came to London in his thirties following his education and apprenticeship to a member of the Barber-Surgeon's Company. Soon,

Teucrium alterum from Pietro Andrea Mattioli's *Commentarij* (1583). Missouri Botanical Garden Library Sturtevant Pre-Linnaean Collection.

through influential friends and associates, he came to be occupied in the care of three major gardens where he raised not only native plants but also new discoveries from the Americas and the rest of the world. Additional facts of his life are little known as many of the records have disappeared.

Though his name appears on *The Herball,* first printed in 1597 in London, the exact amount of work Gerard actually put into the text and illustrations is unknown. The Queen's printer, John Norton, hired Dr. Robert Priest to translate the esteemed *Pemptades,* an herbal by Rembert Dodoens. When Priest suddenly died, Norton, having heard of Gerard's knowledge of plants, hired him to help in putting the work together. As a result, Gerard's herbal is best described as the Anglicized version of *Pemptades,* which grew out of Dodoens' *Cruydeboeck,* originally published in Antwerp in 1554.

With its wonderful descriptions and rich language, *The Herball* is a joy regardless of its history and authorship. Nearly fifty pages are devoted to illustrations and descriptions of various mints. The artwork is also delicately and accurately accomplished. Mint family plants are easy to recognize. Each woodcut is obviously drawn to fit its wooden block, and the delicacy of the lines and hatchings is superb. Writing in Old English, Gerard describes basil in a most appealing way.

> Garden basill is of two sorts, differing one from another in bigness. The first hath broad, thicke, and fat leaves, of a pleasant sweet smell, and of which some one here and there are of a black reddish colour, somewhat snipped about the edges, not unlike the leaves of French Mercurie. The stalke groweth to a height of halfe a cubit, dividing itself into diverse branches, whereupon doe stand small and base floures sometimes whitish, and often tending to a darke purple. The root is threddie, and dieth at the approch of Winter.
>
> The middle Basill is very like unto the former, but it is altogether lesser. The whole plant is of a most odoriferous smell, not unlike the smell of a Limon, or Citron, whereof it tooke his surname.

The Old English is difficult at first but soon becomes clear as the antiquated expressions clarify themselves in the context of the writ-

Mentha cruciata from John Gerard's *Herball* (1597). Missouri Botanical Garden Library Sturtevant Pre-Linnaean Collection.

ing. Gerard goes on to describe what he calls *Ocimum Indicum,* also listed as bush basil, explaining how to grow the herb and discussing its medicinal virtues. It is difficult to place this basil into modern taxonomic form, but it might be a botanical name formerly applied to *O. basilicum.*

A Dioscorides saith that if Basil be much eaten, it dulleth the fight, mollifieth the belly, breedeth winde, provoketh urine, drieth up milke, and is of a hard digestion.
B The juice mixed with fine meale of parched Barly, oile of roses and Vinegar, is good against inflammations, and the stinging of venomous beasts.
C The juice drunke in wine of Chios or strong Sacke, is good against head ache.
D The juice clenseth away the dimmenesse of the eyes, and drieth up the humour that falleth into them.
E The seede drunke is a remedie for melancholicke people, for those that are short winded, and them that can hardly make water.
F If the same be shift up in the nose, it causeth often sneesing: also the herbe it self does the same.
G There be that shunne Basill and will not eat thereof, because that if it be chewed and laid in the Sun, it ingendreth wormes.
H They of Africke do also affirme, that they who are stung of the Scorpion and have eaten of it, shall feele no paine at all.
I The Later writers among whom Simon Zethy is one, doe teach, that the smell of Basill is good for the heart and the head. That the seeds cureth the informities of the heart, taketh away sorrowfulness which commeth of melancholy, and make a man merry and glad.

John Parkinson (1567–1650) is sometimes called the last of the great English herbalists. He was born in Nottinghamshire and became, by the age of nineteen, an apothecary with his own garden in the heart of London. He was chosen as the official apothecary to King James I and was later named Botanicus Regius Primarius by King Charles I. His first book, published in 1629, was *Paradisi in Sole Paradisus Terrestris.* Not truly an herbal, it was rather an excellent tome on gardening with 109 woodcuts of nearly eight hundred

Salvia Romana from John Gerard's *Herball* (1597). Missouri Botanical Garden Sturtevant Pre-Linnaean Collection.

plants. Parkinson's second and most important book was *Theatrum Botanicum,* which he dedicated to Charles I. It is probably the largest herbal in the English language, containing descriptions of nearly four thousand plants in a folio edition of 1755 pages. *Theatrum Botanicum* also includes folklore and recipes for certain cosmetic concoctions.

Elizabeth Blackwell, the engraver and artist of *A Curious Herbal* (1737–1739), was the only woman of her time to produce a notable herbal (Plate 2). Her husband, former physician Alexander Blackwell, became a successful printer but was jailed after his fellow printers learned that he had not served an apprenticeship. He landed in debtors' prison, where he might have remained if it had not been for his wife.

Elizabeth learned that there were plans to publish an herbal about medicinal plants from the New World. Although her knowledge of botany was slim, she was a skilled artist. She arranged to work with Isaac Rand, curator and botanist at the Chelsea Physic Garden, where many of the plants were growing. At Rand's insistence, she relocated to lodgings near the garden so that she would be able to conveniently draw the plants for the herbal. She worked on the engravings and drawings from life while her husband assisted with the text from his jail cell.

The resulting two volumes, which included five hundred of Elizabeth's illustrations, were acclaimed by England's Royal College of Surgeons. This guaranteed the work's financial success, and Elizabeth was able to use her royalties to purchase her husband's release. In spite of her loyalty, however, Alexander deserted his wife and their child a few years later, moving to Sweden where he was named court physician to the king. Elizabeth apparently continued to support him, though he was later accused of treason and beheaded.

In order to support herself and her child, Elizabeth gradually sold the rights to *A Curious Herbal,* which continued to be popular and was reissued in an enlarged form. She died in 1758. While many, including those in the medical professions, admired and respected her drawings and engravings, some critics labeled her work that of an industrious amateur. Still, the herbal continues to be admired today.

I, for one, think her plant illustrations are simply gorgeous. Her horehound (*Marrubium album*) shows foliage, stem, and flowers along the stem with lovely and true color, detail, and shading that would be hard to match. Alongside the main illustration are small insets of the florets, seeds, and other flower parts. An illustration of catnip (*Nepeta cataria*) is likewise both botanically accurate and beautiful.

CHAPTER 2

Mints in Health and Home

Consider the scope of the medicinal, culinary, and household uses of mints—there are few more valuable groups of plants. The leaves of many of these plants hold pungent volatile oils that are of great economical value. The majority of important culinary herbs are mints. Some of these plants have long been known for their special fragrances, which are often the major essences of soaps, colognes, and other personal products. Others are noted for fragrances featured in household products.

A trip to a health food store underscores the importance of the mint family in dietary additives, cosmetic substances, and medicinals. Rosemary (*Rosmarinus officinalis*) is an ingredient in a nasal decongestant, and horehound (*Marrubium vulgare*) is found in a capsule for decongestion and cough suppression. Lemon balm (*Melissa officinalis*) and skullcap (*Scutellaria*) are nervine products that promise to encourage relaxation, calm anxiety, and ease premenstrual tension. Hyssop (*Hyssopus officinalis*) vows to ease bronchitis and relieve anxiety. A dietary supplement features rosemary.

In the personal products section is a hair and scalp rinse listing rosemary (*Rosmarinus officinalis*) and sage (*Salvia officinalis*) as major ingredients. A facial cleanser also features rosemary and sage, along with the addition of true mints. Peppermint (*Mentha* ×*piperita*) and lavender (*Lavandula*) are primary ingredients of an antistress pulse point cream. Toothpastes and mouthwashes include true mints, peppermint, and spearmint (*M. spicata*). And in the household products area air freshener is scented with lavender.

MINTS IN HEALTH CARE

The mint family has, since ancient times, played a major role in matters of health and healing. Mints have long been used to treat such conditions as flatulence, headaches, nervous conditions, burns, coughs, and colds. They have also been used as expectorants and carminatives. The ancients treated a multitude of conditions and diseases with these plants. Poultices, for example, were made of fresh or dried herbs either powdered or chopped and mixed with water to make a paste, then applied hot to affected areas of the body. Oils were distilled from fresh herbs and used in treatments. Tinctures called for steeping crushed herbs in a mixture of alcohol and water at room temperature for twelve hours. Fluid extracts were concentrated materials made from herbs and alcohol. Infusions were made by pouring boiling water over herbs and letting the mix sit for five to ten minutes. Teas were also taken medicinally. The resulting concoctions were used in various ways, both externally and internally, depending upon the conditions and the desired result.

Many of these treatments remain in use. Something as simple as a soothing mint tea can be a grand way of taking a break and calming down after work or exercise. Still, while there are no poisonous mints, and while many are used in herbal and homeopathic medicine, it is always wise to use caution when using herbs to treat disease, injury, or other health conditions. When in doubt, consult a physician.

While much of the medicinal use of mints comes to us from Europe, some of these plants have traditional uses among the native peoples of the New World. One such mint, *Salvia divinorum,* was discovered in the 1950s by ethnobotanists in the state of Oaxaca, Mexico, and named in the early 1960s. The Mazatec Indians of that region use this unusual salvia, which is said to be psychotropic, in their folk medicine and divinatory rites.

MINTS IN THE HOME

As increasing numbers of people begin to grow herbs, and as more of these people want to use organic products to make their own household and cosmetic preparations, many traditional uses of herbs are once again gaining popularity. Herbal recipes for household and cosmetic mixes can be found in books, magazines, herb societies, and botanical gardens. It may be helpful to begin with an overview of some favorite applications.

Many herbs of the mint family are useful as insect repellants. Savvy gardeners will rub a few crushed leaves of lemon balm (*Melissa officinalis*), lemon thyme (*Thymus* ×*citriodorus*), pennyroyal (*Mentha pulegium*), rosemary (*Rosmarinus officinalis*), sweet basil (*Ocimum basilicum*), or sweet marjoram (*Origanum majorana*) on their hands, arms, and face to repel mosquitoes and biting flies. Strewing leaves of these strong-smelling plants will also repel ants and other insect pests from pantry shelves, bureau drawers, and closets.

Strewn herbs were used during medieval times to cut down on unpleasant smells in the home. In great halls, where diners might throw bones to the dogs lazing about, the fragrant herbs would cover the odor of putrid meat. Although this is not a modern problem, there are times when the smells of cooking foods linger unpleasantly. Bouquets of aromatic herbs such as lavender (*Lavandula*), lemon balm (*Melissa officinalis*), lemon thyme (*Thymus* ×*citriodorus*), pennyroyal (*Mentha pulegium*), rosemary (*Rosmarinus officinalis*), sweet basil (*Ocimum basilicum*), and sweet marjoram (*Origanum majorana*) are not only attractive but also serve to cover the odors of cabbage, liver, and other strong-smelling foods.

Similarly, herbs added to summer bouquets give freshness to the air. During hot, humid periods herbs in bunches or bouquets are especially effective. An easy way to make the kitchen smell wonderful is to simmer a small pan of water with a few favorite herbs. Spices such as cloves and cinnamon add another pleasing touch to the mix.

Sachets are another popular application of herbal mints. These are simply small bags of insect-repellent herbs. Dry and crush the herbs, placing a combination of them into small cloth bags closed with ribbon or colorful twine. The bags can be easily made from pieces of lightweight cotton. Lavender (*Lavandula*) is a traditional favorite for sachets. Orris root, a fixative made from the Florentine iris, is another common additive. Without fixative the sachet will have to be renewed more often, although that would be a small amount of work for such a pleasant return. Directions for making sachets often recommend adding spices as well. When finished, place the sachets in linen closets and bureau drawers to repel moths and other insects and to add a pleasant fragrance to linens and clothing.

Herb pillows offer another use for fragrant mints. Simply dry the herbs before using them to stuff small pillows. Like balsam pillows that bring memories of vacations at wooded lakes, herb pillows can fill the long winter months with the scent of a summer garden. The mint family might even be a soothing cure for cabin fever.

Fragrant herbs can also be used as additives to rinse water for linens, homemade furniture polish, potpourri, and candles. Essential oils of herbs such as lavender are useful in adding herbal qualities to household preparations.

Lavender (*Lavandula*), lemon balm (*Melissa officinalis*), peppermint (*Mentha* ×*piperita*), rosemary (*Rosmarinus officinalis*), spearmint (*Mentha spicata*), and thyme (*Thymus*) are among the mints more commonly used cosmetically. The easiest way to use them is in a hot bath. Simply tear up a handful of favorite herbs and spread them over the water. The fragrance will rise, making a common bath into a special treat.

True mints are wonderful additives as well. Add them fresh or dried to unscented soaps, lotions, skin bracers, or bath oils, and let them sit for a couple of weeks to allow the products to soak up the special qualities of the herbs. Lavender (*Lavandula*) is especially good for this purpose.

Rosemary (*Rosmarinus officinalis*) has been traditionally popular in hair treatments. One recipe involves making a rosemary tea with crushed leaves in a couple of cups of water. Simply heat the water, let it cool to a comfortable temperature, and use it as a hair rinse.

Many other recipes can be found for shampoos, oil treatments for hair, soaps, lotions, and other cosmetics. These are just a few inspirational ideas for those who love herbs and want to use them in new ways.

MINTS IN THE KITCHEN

The art of cooking stirs the senses and often inspires both the cook and those who partake of the food. Herbal traditions are strong in many kitchens, and there is no doubt that the major culinary herbs belong to the Lamiaceae. Popular culinary herbs include oregano (*Origanum vulgare*), rosemary (*Rosmarinus officinalis*), sage (*Salvia officinalis*), savory (*Satureja hortensis* and *S. montana*), sweet basil (*Ocimum basilicum*), sweet marjoram (*Origanum majorana*), thyme (*Thymus*), and the true mints. People even cook with lavender (*Lavandula*).

The true mints come in a number of varieties named for their flavors and fragrances. They are best known in the kitchen as cool, refreshing components of hot or iced teas and as flavoring for candies and jellies. Spearmint (*Mentha spicata*), probably the best-known of the true mints, is a favorite garnish and component of iced tea, mint juleps, steamed garden peas, and those elegant accompaniments of lamb—mint sauce and mint jelly. Peppermint (*M.* ×*piperita*) has a sharper taste and is often used in candies and frostings. Apple mint (*M. suaveolens*) makes a delightful tea or addition to tea and is especially good for making candied mint leaves. Pineapple mint (*M. suaveolens* 'Variegata') is a variation of apple mint and is similarly used. Water mint (*M. aquatica*) has a fruitier scent and taste than the other true mints.

Use rosemary (*Rosmarinus officinalis*) in its several forms, whether fresh or dried, to flavor soups, stews, vegetables, chicken, and meats. This herb is especially effective in enhancing lamb. Sprigs of rosemary will flavor fish while it's baking. Sprigs or finely chopped rosemary can also be used to flavor vinegar and olive oils for use in salad dressing. It is also good with spinach, peas, or broccoli and excellent in sauces, salads, biscuits, and egg dishes. Rosemary has a strong flavor, however, and should be used sparingly in all recipes.

Sage (*Salvia officinalis*) is an important seasoning herb for pork, veal, chicken, duck, stuffing, tomatoes, and green beans. To my way of thinking, dressing for turkeys or roasting chickens should be rich with it. The fresh leaves are also good as garnish or chopped and added to cream cheese or cottage cheese.

Savory (*Satureja*), including the strong-flavored, perennial winter savory (*S. montana*) and the milder summer savory (*S. hortensis*), has a flavor and aroma somewhat similar to sage but not as strong. Use winter savory in soups, sausages, and poultry stuffing as well as with veal, pork, beef, chicken, gamy meats, and liver patés. The annual summer savory is often called the green bean herb because of the wonderful way it enhances the fresh green beans of summer. Use the delicate flavor of summer savory to make soups, peas, beans, eggplant, squash, fish, liver, and rice dishes more special.

The genus *Origanum* is often confusing, mainly because so many gardeners grow an oregano expecting it to smell and taste like the commercial oregano used to flavor pizza, spaghetti sauces, and other dishes. In truth, commercial oregano consists of a variety of plants including oregano (*O. vulgare*), sweet marjoram (*O. majorana*), pennyroyal (*Mentha pulegium*), spearmint (*M. spicata*), and others. Consider it a flavor rather than a specific plant. That will eliminate the confusion that occurs when buying an oregano plant that doesn't smell or taste as expected. The herb nearest to what most people think of as the fragrance and taste of pizza or spaghetti is actually sweet marjoram. This tender perennial has a wonderful pungent flavor and aroma that blends well with just about everything. It is popularly used with poultry and in poultry stuffing. It is equally delicious in meat dishes as it is in soups and stews, will enhance many vegetables, and is great with mushrooms.

Oregano (*Origanum*) is used in other dishes as well. The milder Greek mountain oregano (*O. vulgare* subsp. *hirtum*) is a good choice for minestrone, stew, meatloaf, seafood, or cheese and egg dishes. And oregano (*O. vulgare*) is an ingredient in chili powder.

Thyme (*Thymus*), in several of its species and varieties, is a wonderful herb to use in soups, chowders, stews, and sauces. It should be used sparingly, however, because it is strong in flavor. Many fine cooks consider it one of the best herbs to blend with other herbs. Caraway thyme (*T. herba-barona*), creeping thyme (*T. praecox*), silver-edged lemon thyme (*T.* ×*citriodorus* 'Silver Queen'), mother of thyme (*T. serpyllum*), and woolly thyme (*T. pseudolanuginosus*) are just a few of the many thymes commonly found in the marketplace.

Sweet basil (*Ocimum basilicum*) is often associated with tomatoes because it blends so well with them, whether fresh or in soups and sauces. It is also, of course, a necessity when making pesto. A spicy herb, sweet basil goes well with salads, fish, meats, eggs, and cheese. Quite a few attractive and tasty varieties are available as well (see chapter 3). Some are named for their characteristics, such as 'Purple Ruffles'; others are named for their place of origin, as is the case with 'True Thai'.

Though perhaps not used in cooking as much as other major mints, lavender (*Lavandula*) can in fact give certain dishes a unique zest. Add a few small corollas of lavender flowers to iced or hot teas, white wines, or a favorite martini for a special touch. Include a few chopped leaves with salads, dressings, vinegars, fruit, breads, or poultry dishes.

Many fine cooks use blends of herbs, a practice especially notable in French cuisine. Bouquets garnis are combinations of fresh or dried herbs either tied in a bouquet or put into a small cheesecloth herb bag. They are used in stews, soups, and gravies and discarded before serving. The herbs in a bouquet garni may include bay leaf (*Laurus nobilis*, Lauraceae), chervil (*Anthriscus cereifolium*, Apiaceae or Umbelliferae), garden thyme (*Thymus vulgaris*), parsley (*Petroselinum crispum*, Apiaceae), and sweet marjoram (*Origanum majorana*). Fines herbes are finely chopped blends of several kinds of freshly harvested herbs. These are added to dishes just before serving. A typical fines herbes blend includes chervil, chives (*Allium schoenopra-*

sum, Alliaceae or Liliaceae), garden thyme, rosemary (*Rosmarinus officinalis*), sweet basil (*Ocimum basilicum*), sweet marjoram, and tarragon (*Artemisia dracunculus*, Compositae).

Harvesting and storing herbs is also important. It is best, of course, to use fresh herbs, but they can also be used dried or frozen when they are off season. More in-depth information and advice can be obtained through herb societies and clubs dedicated solely to growing herbs for culinary purposes. Organizations such as these produce more capable cooks, tastier dishes, and last but not least a great deal of enjoyable camaraderie.

Cooking with herbs, however, can be a very individual thing. My suggestions are only that: suggestions, plus a nod to the traditional culinary uses of these wonderful plants. After learning a few of the basics, it is time to experiment and use one's own individuality and imagination in cooking with herbs.

MINTS IN AMERICAN GARDENS

Herb gardens, which were out of favor for many years during and following the Great Depression and World War II, are again gaining popularity with gardeners of all sorts. American herb gardens now come in all shapes and sizes. Try visiting a few of them to learn more about herbs and to see how many different ways there are to use them—as culinaries, cosmetics, utilitarian household products, and ornamentals. As the neophyte soon discovers, the major herbs are easy to grow and will enhance many dishes.

Public gardens, where the herbs are usually fairly well labeled, are great places to learn more about the uses of herbs. The Ozark Folk Center, a state park in Mountain View, Arkansas, is such a place. This park is dedicated to preserving folklore, folk music, and traditional crafts. It not only includes wonderful herb beds and plantings but also features special weekends that focus on herb traditions and usage. Herbs can be seen growing in containers, raised beds, and hillside gardens (Plate 3).

Historical societies often include herbs and herb gardens as integral parts of their historic preservation programs. Local herb societies popping up all over the country are also good places to learn more. In many cases herb societies and historical societies cooperate in the development of herb gardens that reflect the past.

Williamsburg Herb Gardens

The formal and informal gardens of the Historic Area of Williamsburg, Virginia, both reflect history and provide inspiration to herb gardeners with a leaning toward nostalgia. The gardens of the outdoor living history museum called Colonial Williamsburg are true to the colonial period, defined as 1776 to about 1820, when plant collectors shifted their sights westward. Exchanges of plants between Europe and eastern North America were extensive during this period.

Most of the herbs in Williamsburg gardens came from the Old World, introduced by early settlers who also brought fruit trees, vegetables, and ornamentals. While the settlers were adventurous in spirit, not always knowing what the New World held for them, they also wanted to preserve certain well-established ways of life, including their eating habits. Important herbal mints such as garden thyme (*Thymus vulgaris*), lavender (*Lavandula*), lemon balm (*Melissa officinalis*), mint (*Mentha*), rosemary (*Rosmarinus officinalis*), sage (*Salvia officinalis*), savory (*Satureja hortensis* and *S. montana*), and sweet marjoram (*Origanum majorana*) were brought to the New World in this way and are commonly found in Williamsburg herb gardens.

Missouri Botanical Garden

The herb gardens at Missouri Botanical Garden in St. Louis come in both formal and informal designs. The formal herb garden maintained by the St. Louis Herb Society lies behind Tower Grove House (Plate 4), the restored home of the botanical garden's founder, Henry Shaw. This garden accurately reflects aspects of the Victorian Age, when Shaw was alive. A black wrought iron fence surrounds the garden, defining it handsomely. Brick paths delineate rectangular beds and borders where a wide variety of herbs thrive. The focal point is the thyme (*Thymus*) garden, a square set on an angle with a sundial and four triangles of thyme set inside the brick paths (Plate 5). Each quadrant is planted with a different species or cultivar of thyme, making it easy to compare different forms of this favorite herb.

A number of other herb plantings can be found at the Missouri Botanical Garden. The garden, fondly called Shaw's Garden after its founder, is my favorite hangout. I spend hours there almost every week. Among the demonstration gardens are areas featuring modern informal plantings of herbs, including many mints (Plate 6).

National Herb Garden

One of America's great treasures, the National Herb Garden is located on two and a half acres in the U.S. National Arboretum in Washington, D.C. A visit is not only a treat but also an education. The Herb Society of America first proposed the garden in 1965 and, after years of fundraising and working with the federal government, dedicated it in June 1980. Thousands of useful and beautiful plants are on display, all well labeled so that one can learn more about herbs while enjoying a tour of this magnificent garden.

The National Herb Garden is divided into three main sections. The Knot Garden, a contemporary version about 50 feet (15 m) long and 25 feet (7.5 m) wide, includes chains of dwarf evergreens in intricate patterns. The Historic and Species Rose Garden includes roses cultivated before 1867, the date when the first hybrid tea rose, 'La France', was introduced.

Most marvelous of all are ten Specialty Gardens, each one worthy of attention. The Dioscorides Garden, for example, includes more than four dozen herbs described in *De Materia Medica*. The mint family is represented by such plants as black horehound (*Ballota nigra*), used to treat dog bites, ulcers, and venereal warts; bluebeard (*Salvia viridis*), believed to lessen edema and draw out splinters; dittany of Crete (*Origanum dictamnus*), used to hasten childbirth and repel poisonous beasts; germander (*Teucrium polium*), a treatment for those bitten by venomous beasts; Greek mountain oregano (*Origanum vulgare* subsp. *hirtum*), used as an antidote to poison hemlock; Jerusalem sage (*Phlomis fruticosa*), used to treat inflamed eyes; sage (*Salvia officinalis*), used to treat wounds and ulcers; and wall germander (*T. chamaedrys*), used to treat convulsions and coughs.

The Dye Garden highlights an important and useful part of the arts and rites of people. For thousands of years people have dyed and painted their hair, bodies, clothing, pottery, baskets, and religious and living spaces. This garden includes one member of the mint family used for these purposes: *Perovskia atriplicifolia* (Russian sage, Plate 7). When this plant is in flower the aboveground parts can be used to dye wool. Depending on the mordant used, the result may be one of several shades. An iron mordant produces a soft gray-green effect while dyeing with the flowers alone results in a beautiful blue color.

The Colonial Garden salutes the importance of herbs in colonial America, where they were used in foods, medicines, dyes, repellents, and home fragrances. Mints comprise nearly a fifth of the plants in this garden. Included are bee balm (*Monarda didyma*), used in colonial times as a medicinal tea; catnip (*Nepeta cataria*), a medicinal herb; clary (*Salvia sclarea*), a culinary and medicinal herb; common betony (*Stachys officinalis*), a medicinal herb; creeping thyme (*Thymus praecox* subsp. *arcticus*), a seasoning and medicinal herb; garden thyme (*T. vulgaris*), a culinary and medicinal herb; hyssop (*Hyssopus officinalis*), a seasoning, medicinal, and strewing herb; oregano (*Origanum vulgare*), a medicinal herb; pennyroyal (*Mentha pulegium*), a medicinal herb and insect repellent; rosemary (*Rosmarinus officinalis*), a culinary, medicinal, and strewing herb; sage (*Salvia officinalis*); self-heal (*Prunella vulgaris*), a medicinal herb; spearmint (*Mentha spicata*), a seasoning and strewing herb; sweet marjoram (*Origanum majorana*), a culinary and strewing herb; and winter savory (*Satureja montana*), a culinary and medicinal herb.

The Native American Garden contains herbs that were gathered by native people for foods, medicines, dyes, smoking materials, and even amulets. Nearly 10 percent of the herbs in this garden are mints including medicinals such as American dittany (*Cunila origanoides*), American pennyroyal (*Hedeoma pulegioides*), cancerweed (*Salvia lyrata*), horsemint (*Monarda punctata*), wild bergamot (*M. fistulosa*), and wood mint (*Blephilia hirsuta*). Also included is prairie hyssop (*Pycnanthemum virginianum*), a culinary herb. European colonists learned how to use these herbs through the teachings of Native Americans.

The Medicinal Garden includes five dozen herbs traditionally used in treating diseases and injuries. Until the nineteenth century nearly all medicines included herbs, and according to some estimates slightly less than half of modern medicines include plant products. Although synthesized medicinal products have been extremely successful, scientists still search the world for new medicinal uses of plants. The Medicinal Garden displays several mints including creeping thyme (*Thymus praecox* subsp. *arcticus*), garden thyme (*T. vulgaris*), horehound (*Marrubium vulgare*), motherwort (*Leonurus cardiaca*), peppermint (*Mentha* ×*piperita*), and sage (*Salvia officinalis*).

Not surprisingly twenty-one of the seventy-two herbs found in the Culinary Garden belong to the mint family including Cuban oregano (*Plectranthus amboinicus*), English lavender (*Lavandula angustifolia*), garden thyme (*Thymus vulgaris*), hyssop (*Hyssopus officinalis*), Italian oregano (*Origanum* ×*majoricum*), lemon balm (*Melissa officinalis*), lemon thyme (*Thymus* ×*citriodorus*), oregano-scented thyme (*T. pulegioides* 'Oregano-scented'), pineapple sage (*Salvia elegans*), pot marjoram (*Origanum onites*), rosemary (*Rosmarinus officinalis*), sage (*Salvia officinalis*), spearmint (*Mentha spicata*), summer savory (*Satureja hortensis*), sweet basil (*Ocimum basilicum*), sweet marjoram (*Origanum majorana*), water mint (*Mentha aquatica*), and winter savory (*Satureja montana*).

Besides the National Herb Garden, there are many other herb gardens throughout the United States that offer design and care themes and ideas. The best of these keep their plants well labeled so that visitors can learn to identify them. I add only two or three new varieties to my mint collections at a time. In doing so I get to know the new ones well, avoiding the confusion caused by too many new plants. Novice and experienced herb gardeners alike will learn a lot from taking advantage of any resources available to them. Countless books and magazines also provide useful design ideas and inspiration.

MINTS IN GARDEN DESIGN

As the popularity of herbs continues to grow, gardeners increasingly plant true mints and other mint family herbs in mixed beds and borders, among vegetables, and among ornamental annuals and perennials (Plate 8). In the past, gardeners tended to create segregated sites—keeping vegetables among vegetables, herbs among herbs, and even annuals and perennials in their own separate places.

Although the old-fashioned vegetable garden with regimented rows and divisions is still with us, more flexible and daring gardeners will make vegetable gardens as decorative and attractive as their flower beds. To give a vegetable garden a more ornamental look and to increase its beauty and value, add mints to it and plant the vegetables in amebalike shapes rather than in rigid rows. Use mints in containers as focal points or mix a few annuals in with the mints to provide color, contrast, and texture.

Some gardeners like to plant their herbs near the kitchen door, a wonderful and convenient plan if the area has full sun. Others, myself included, mix herbs in with plantings of perennials and annuals. Garden thyme (*Thymus vulgaris*), for example, whether variegated or in solid colors, makes handsome ground cover to border a mixed bed. Herbs can be used in the flower garden as well. Plants such as lavender (*Lavandula*), rosemary (*Rosmarinus officinalis*), and sage (*Salvia officinalis*) offer gray-green foliage with interesting texture and growth patterns and provide good contrast and transition to bright-colored flowering annuals and perennials. Plants with gray-green foliage, like plants with white flowers, are valuable design tools for separating flowers that would clash if planted side by side. Gray-green foliage also makes a handsome contrast to green foliage.

Fragrance is an added bonus any time herbs are added to garden beds and borders. Placing some of the more aromatic mints at the edge of beds offers opportunities for brushing against them or reaching out to stroke the oil-bearing leaves. Add the true mints to gardens with filtered shade, whether in containers or directly in the ground. They perform well and help create an impression of coolness on hot afternoons.

Lemon thyme (*Thymus* ×*citriodorus*) works well as short borders at the edges of gardens. The plants spill out into paths where passersby can brush by them, creating a heavenly fragrance. Lemon thyme can also handle a small amount of traffic. Plant it in between stepping stones for another sort of fragrant path. Other aromatic herbs that can take some traffic include Corsican mint (*Mentha requienii*) and mother of thyme (*T. serpyllum*).

With their propensity for leaping tall mountains, the true mints are excellent prospects for container gardening (Plate 9). When planted in a container, mints cannot spread throughout the garden beds. Mix a few bright annuals into a large container featuring the true mints for a good contrast of textures and colors. Choose a handsome container that will hold the plants both summer and winter, outdoors and indoors. For the most pleasing effect, use containers of different sizes and place them at different levels. Group some together and use others as accents beside a bench, at a bend in a path, or wherever the eye is meant to travel. Some tender mints, such as most rosemary (*Rosmarinus officinalis*) and lavender (*Lavandula*) cultivars, need to come indoors during the hard winters of more northern climes.

Another way to use mints in the garden is as living wreaths. Begin by placing a wire wreath frame into a container of appropriate size, sinking the base 1 to 2 inches (2.5 to 5 cm) into the soil. Plant true mints or creeping rosemary (*Rosmarinus officinalis*) by each side of the metal frame, and train the plants around the frame as they grow, using soft twine or garden ties. Prune as necessary to keep the living wreath in its desired shape.

Some mints lend themselves to topiary training. The aim is to develop a trunk on top of which there is bushy growth so that the plant looks like a miniature tree. Upright rosemary (*Rosmarinus officinalis*), dwarf sage (*Salvia officinalis* 'Nana'), and lavender (*Lavandula*) are good choices for topiary projects. Choose a young plant with a long stem. Tender stems will probably have to be tied to a small dowel while they are being trained. Trim off any side shoots and allow growth to develop at the top. Through periodic pruning the tiny tree will develop, becoming a handsome conversation piece for outdoor or windowsill gardens. These same plants can be trained into patterns and shapes that resemble Japanese bonsai. Prostrate rosemary is especially good for training as a bonsai-type plant.

Designs for herb plantings can take many forms, depending upon not only the physical traits of the site but also on the way that the herbs will be used. Generally speaking, a site with moderately decent soil that receives four to six hours of sun or more is a good choice for growing most mints. Choose whatever is most pleasing and whatever fits best with the roles the plants might play ornamentally and in the kitchen.

Whether designing and planting formal or informal gardens, herb gardens or mixed beds and borders, the important thing is to include herbs (Plate 10). Personally, while I admire formal plantings in many ways, I favor informal designs for my own use. They are easier to work with and require less maintenance. My experience with hedges and other formal design elements is that shortly after the plant design matures and looks healthy and beautiful, a plant in the middle dies.

CHAPTER 3

Herbal Mints

Herbal mints are simply mints that possess herbal properties, meaning they have culinary, medicinal, cosmetic, or other uses. It is astounding that so many of our most popular and valuable herbs, including what I would consider the majority of the finest culinary herbs, are in the mint family.

The best-known of the herbal mints are the true mints, which comprise the genus *Mentha*. True mint species and their cultivars have long been used in both culinary recipes and medicinal remedies. They have also been used as strewing herbs to improve the atmosphere of places polluted by animal odors, unwanted cooking smells, and other unpleasant scents. True mints have, in fact, been used in more ways than can easily be imagined. Evidence of their medicinal virtues has been found in Egyptian papyrus scrolls dating from 2800 B.C. The Arabs offered cups of mint tea as gestures of hospitality. The English herbalist Nicholas Culpeper (1616–1654) wrote that "Mint Juice taken in Vinegar, stirreth up venery, or bodily lust." During Prohibition spearmint (*M. spicata*) was so strongly linked with the bourbon drink called mint julep that mint beds were dug up and ripped out in several southern states including Virginia.

Although minty tastes and fragrances can be found in many modern products, from room fresheners to toothpastes to breath fresheners, not all true mints are so useful. Corsican mint (*M. requienii*), Japanese mint (*Mentha arvensis* var. *piperascens*), and the pennyroyals (*M. cervina, M. pulegium*) all contain a toxic oil that can cause convulsions and coma. Obviously then, unlike most mints, these should not be eaten or consumed as food additives or teas, at least in any quantity. As physicians often say, "The severity of the poison lies in the size of the dose." A small amount of these mints would probably not harm a person, but why bother with potentially harmful herbs when there are so many varieties that are both tasty and safe?

The true mints are vigorous and enthusiastic, often to a fault, spreading quickly by means of surface runners and underground rhizomes. Curly mint (*Mentha spicata* 'Crispa'), peppermint (*M.* ×*piperita*), and spearmint (*M. spicata*) are especially notorious for their ability to colonize entire flower beds. These plants, however, are shallow rooted and easy to pull. Weeding true mints from a flower bed can also be a rather heady experience, surrounding a gardener with that wonderful, indescribable minty fragrance.

Although I can't imagine having a garden without at least a couple of true mints, many gardeners find it easier to grow these energetic plants in containers or in other places that will keep them from leaping into unwanted areas. Beds confined by railroad ties or at the edge of decks, patios, or walkways are ideal for rampant plants. Of course, the tendency of true mints to roam can be a virtue where attractive, fragrant, useful ground cover is desired. Corn mint (*Mentha arvensis*), Corsican mint (*M. requienii*), pennyroyal (*M. pulegium*), and peppermint (*M.* ×*piperita*) make good ground covers. Mowing them whenever they look straggly will encourage thick, bushy growth.

Another mixed blessing is the ability of true mints to survive just about any conditions. I have pulled one of these plants and thrown it onto a compost heap only to have it take root and thrive there. One summer a friend gave me a plant of her favorite true mint, and after putting the pot at the edge of the property I forgot about it for several weeks. Following a period of typical St. Louis summer—day after day of hot sun and no rain—the plant looked totally dead. I soaked the dried root ball and planted it without hope that it had survived. Sure enough, true to the mint legend, it survived. Indeed, it seemed none the worse for its droughty ordeal.

The true mints are hardy throughout the United States although they may be difficult to grow in the mild, humid climate of the Gulf Coast. In regions with severe winter cold or swift and severe weather contrasts, light winter mulches of leaves or hay may help ensure survival. Pennyroyal (*Mentha pulegium*), a bit more tender, will probably not survive temperatures below 5°F (−15°C). Although true mints will grow in shade and wet soil, they develop the fullest fragrance and taste in full sun with a well-draining, moderately fertile soil that has a pH of 6 to 7. Special soil amendments or any other special treatments are unnecessary as these plants are not fussy. The majority of true mints are hardy well into Zone 5 or even colder regions. Some, including Corsican mint (*M. requienii*) and English pennyroyal (*M. pulegium*), generally must be treated as annuals in regions north of Zone 7. They may reseed themselves for the following spring.

According to current wisdom, the genus *Mentha* includes eighteen to nineteen true species (species that are fertile and are not hybrids) plus dozens of subspecies, cultivars, and variations since the plants are basically variable and also readily hybridize and produce sports. Economically, the most important species include *M. aquatica, M. arvensis, M. spicata,* and *M. suaveolens.* Many true mints readily hybridize both naturally and in cultivation, which makes them a complex group that is often difficult to specifically identify. This fact is made apparent by the synonymous names often applied to true mints and by the sometimes incorrect or misleading labeling on nursery plants. Since different environments may result in different characteristics in the true mints, growers and botanists have occasionally believed they have discovered a new species only to find that the "new" plant is an already familiar one that has simply responded to specific environmental conditions in some unusual way. For this reason the best way to propagate true mints is by cuttings rather than by seeds. Make 6-inch (15-cm) cuttings of rooted stems and plant them horizontally, or make 3- to 6-inch (7.5- to 15-cm) cuttings, strip the leaves from the lower half, and place in a rooting medium.

To keep true mints looking good in the garden renew them every three years or so by dividing the roots and resetting strong young clumps in the spring or fall. Peppermint (*Mentha ×piperita*) should be periodically moved to a new place since it has a tendency to dwindle if kept in one spot too long. Be sure to pick the tender tips often for use in drinks or as decorative touches. If the top few inches are regularly pruned the plants are less inclined to become straggly. Pruning to prevent flowering also encourages greater leaf production.

Although any of the true mints can be grown indoors, apple mint (*Mentha suaveolens*) is the easiest. With five to six or more hours of direct sunlight each day and regular pinching back, apple mint grows into a compact bushy plant. The other true mints tend to become scrawny when grown indoors. Just as with outdoor mints, regularly cutting back a plant will increase its branching and thus its bushiness.

I have included a list of varieties most desired and most commonly available for growing in herb gardens. Note that the taxonomy may not match certain botanical resources since there is still disagreement as to the exact classification of some of these plants. The true mints are listed first, followed by other well-known herbal mints.

TRUE MINTS

Mentha aquatica. The taxonomic complexity of the true mints is clearly seen in the case of *M. aquatica* (water mint), which has been known by a number of scientific and common names (see chapter 8). Traditionally it was used as an internal medicine to improve digestion, treat painful menstruation, and relieve spasms, although a large dose can cause nausea. Growing in marshy places, water mint is the most common wild mint of temperate zones.

Mentha arvensis. Grown commercially in Japan, Brazil, and other countries for its essential oils, which are used in toothpastes, pharmaceutical products, and colognes, *M. arvensis* (corn mint) is also a natural, commercial source of menthol. Propagation is by cuttings, divisions, stolons, or runners. The lanceolate leaves are often hairy and have a strong mint fragrance and flavor. *Mentha arvensis* prefers a drier situation than most mints. Early European settlers liked it because it reminded them of peppermint (*M. ×piperita*) and spearmint (*M. spicata*), herbs with which they were already familiar. *Mentha arvensis* var. *piperascens* (Japanese mint) was for many centuries the major mint in Asian usage, both as medicine and as flavoring. The toothed leaves are lanceolate, and the flowers are pale lavender. The Japanese grow this plant from runners or stem cuttings in deep soil that is rich in humus. *Mentha arvensis* 'Banana' has a scent similar to banana peels, while *M. arvensis* 'Coconut', which is mostly used in potpourris, does not smell very much like coconut to most people. *Mentha arvensis* 'Variegata', often called ginger mint, has green and gold leaves and is most useful in potpourris and as an ornamental in bouquets. Some forms of *M. arvensis* are sold as basil mint although the scent is not particularly like true basil.

Mentha ×piperita. A hybrid between water mint (*M. aquatica*) and spearmint (*M. spicata*), *M. ×piperita* (peppermint) does not set viable seeds. Its cool, spicy, clean menthol flavor and fragrance are strong and distinctive. It is a vigorous perennial, growing 18 to 36 inches (45 to 90 cm) tall and about 24 inches (60 cm) wide. Two strains of peppermint are commonly recognized: black peppermint, which has purplish stems, and white peppermint, which has leaves of a paler green, more slender stems, and a milder fragrance and taste. The common forms tend to creep and have elongated, acuminate leaves with spikes of pink to lavender flowers. Peppermint prefers sun to partial shade and moist, organic, well-draining soil. As with all true mints, propagation is recommended by divisions, cuttings, stolons, or ground layering. Use dried or fresh peppermint leaves and flowers as garnishes or in teas, cosmetics, potpourris, and sachets. The herb has also traditionally been eaten to settle indigestion and applied to the forehead and temples to ease headaches. Its strong odor can even clear the sinuses. Since the essential oil is not water soluble, its curative powers are stronger if tincture of peppermint is used instead of the leaves. Peppermint oil is produced by specialized cells on the undersides of the leaves. Although most gardeners pick peppermint leaves as needed, the absolutely best time to harvest is on a sunny day as flowering is just beginning, when menthol is at its peak.

'Citrata' (bergamot mint, eau de cologne mint, lemon mint) is a form of *Mentha* ×*piperita* and can be distinguished from the original peppermint by its smooth leaves. The roundish leaves are dark, often tinged with purple, and may appear somewhat bronzy. Flowers are lilac. This cultivar prefers moist organic soil in sun to semishade. Propagation is recommended by cuttings, divisions, or runners. With its strong citruslike aroma and flavor, 'Citrata' is a favorite for use with fresh fruits and other desserts and a favorite component of refreshing teas that might also include spearmint (*M. spicata*) and lemon balm (*Melissa officinalis*). In fact many true mints are used in blends to make tasty teas that may be either stimulating or soothing. Indeed, books have been written on using these herbs in teas and other beverages and foods. *Mentha* ×*piperita* 'Crispa' (curly mint) has bright green leaves that are crinkled. Because of its trailing habit, this is a good subject for container growing. A popular cultivar is *M.* ×*piperita* 'Lime', which has a citrus fragrance many find cool and refreshing. Try it in iced tea.

Some confusion exists between *Mentha* ×*piperita* and *M. aquatica.* The National Herb Garden lists *M.* ×*piperita* var. *citrata* as a synonym for water mint while other resources do not. Black peppermint (*M.* ×*piperita* var. *piperita*), including various forms of the cultivar 'Micham', is a good choice for candies and beverages. White peppermint (*M.* ×*piperita* var. *officinalis*) has a more mellow fragrance and flavor than black peppermint. A wonderful variety of *M.* ×*piperita* is 'Chocolate Mint' (Plate 11), a treat when its chocolate-scented leaves are added to tea, coffee, or hot chocolate. Oddly, some people cannot detect the chocolate fragrance.

Plate 1. Mint plant from Leonhart Fuchs' *De Historia Stirpium* (1542). Missouri Botanical Garden Library Sturtevant Pre-Linnaean Collection.

Plate 2. *Mentha* from Elizabeth Blackwell's *A Curious Herbal* (1737). Missouri Botanical Garden Sturtevant Pre-Linnaean Collection.

Plate 3. True mints do well in containers such as these half barrels at the Ozark Folk Center, Mountain View, Arkansas.

Plate 4. A bed of *Rosmarinus officinalis* (rosemary) grows near a bed of *Lavandula dentata* (French lavender) at Tower Grove House, Missouri Botanical Garden. PHOTO BY CINDY GILBERG.

Plate 5. Various forms of *Thymus* (thyme) encircle a sundial in a formal herb garden at the Missouri Botanical Garden.

Plate 6. *Stachys byzantina* (lamb's ear) grows in front of containerized true mints at the Missouri Botanical Garden. PHOTO BY CINDY GILBERG.

Plate 7. *Perovskia atriplicifolia* (Russian sage).

Plate 8. *Physostegia virginiana* 'Vivid' provides a splash of pink to a mixed bed. PHOTO BY KEN MILLER.

Plate 9. Culinary herbs make good choices for ornamental containerized plantings. Here *Mentha suaveolens* 'Variegata' (pineapple mint) tumbles out of a pot while *Salvia officinalis* 'Purpurescens' grows neatly in a container behind it. PHOTO BY CINDY GILBERG.

Plate 10. A mixed bed of mints includes the golden, variegated *Salvia officinalis* 'Icterina', *Teucrium chamaedrys* (wall germander), and *S. farinacea* 'Victoria'. PHOTO BY CINDY GILBERG.

Plate 11. *Mentha* ×*piperita* 'Chocolate Mint'. PHOTO BY ANDREW VAN HEVELINGEN.

Plate 12. *Mentha spicata* (spearmint). PHOTO BY KEN MILLER.

Plate 13. *Mentha suaveolens* 'Variegata' (pineapple mint). PHOTO BY ANDREW VAN HEVELINGEN.

Plate 14. *Lavandula angustifolia* 'Hidcote'. PHOTO BY ANDREW VAN HEVELINGEN.

Plate 15. *Lavandula angustifolia* 'Jean Davis'. PHOTO BY ANDREW VAN HEVELINGEN.

Plate 16. *Lavandula angustifolia* 'Munstead'.

Plate 17. *Lavandula dentata* (French lavender).

Plate 18. *Melissa officinalis* (lemon balm).

Plate 19. *Melissa officinalis* 'Aurea' (golden lemon balm). PHOTO BY KEN MILLER.

Plate 20. *Ocimum basilicum* 'Cinnamon' (cinnamon basil). PHOTO BY CINDY GILBERG.

Plate 21. *Ocimum basilicum* 'Dark Opal' grows with scented geranium (*Pelargonium*). PHOTO BY CINDY GILBERG.

Plate 22. *Ocimum basilicum* 'Purple Ruffles'. PHOTO BY CINDY GILBERG.

Plate 23. *Ocimum basilicum* 'True Thai'.

Plate 24. *Origanum dictamnus* (dittany of Crete). PHOTO BY ANDREW VAN HEVELINGEN.

Plate 25. *Salvia elegans* (pineapple sage). PHOTO BY CINDY GILBERG.

Plate 26. *Salvia officinalis* (sage) in bloom. PHOTO BY CINDY GILBERG.

Plate 27. *Salvia officinalis* 'Nana'.

Plate 28. *Salvia officinalis* 'Berggarten'.

Plate 29. *Salvia officinalis* 'Icterina'. PHOTO BY CINDY GILBERG.

Plate 30. *Salvia officinalis* 'Purpurescens'. PHOTO BY CINDY GILBERG.

Plate 31. *Salvia officinalis* 'Tricolor'. PHOTO BY CINDY GILBERG.

Plate 32. *Teucrium chamaedrys* (wall germander). PHOTO BY KEN MILLER.

Plate 33. A hedge of *Teucrium chamaedrys* (wall germander) surrounds a formal bed of sages including *Salvia officinalis* 'Berggarten' and the golden *S. officinalis* 'Aurea'.

Plate 34. Various forms of *Thymus* (thyme) make a handsome tapestry in a bed at Sissinghurst Gardens, England. PHOTO BY KEN MILLER.

Plate 35. *Thymus ×citriodorus* 'Silver Queen'. PHOTO BY CINDY GILBERG.

Plate 36. *Thymus herba-barona* (caraway thyme). PHOTO BY KEN MILLER.

Plate 37. *Thymus praecox* (creeping thyme).

Plate 38. *Thymus pseudolanuginosus* (woolly thyme).

Plate 39. *Thymus serpyllum* (mother of thyme).

Plate 40. *Orthosiphon stamineus* (cat's whiskers).

Plate 41. *Agastache foeniculum* (anise hyssop). PHOTO BY ANDREW VAN HEVELINGEN.

Plate 42. *Ajuga reptans* (carpet bugleweed) borders a path that will help contain it. PHOTO BY KEN MILLER.

Plate 43. *Ajuga reptans* 'Purple Brocade'.

Plate 44. *Calamintha nepeta* (lesser calamint).

Plate 45. *Lamium galeobdolon* (yellow archangel). PHOTO BY CINDY GILBERG.

Plate 46. *Lamium maculatum* 'White Nancy'.

Plate 47. *Monarda didyma* 'Marshall's Delight'. PHOTO BY ANDREW VAN HEVELINGEN.

Plate 48. *Nepeta* ×*faassenii* (catmint). PHOTO BY KEN MILLER.

Plate 49. *Perilla frutescens* (beefsteak plant). PHOTO BY ANDREW VAN HEVELINGEN.

Plate 50. *Perovskia atriplicifolia* (Russian sage) with *Echinacea* (Compositae). PHOTO BY CINDY GILBERG.

Plate 51. *Physostegia virginiana* (obedience plant).

Plate 52. *Salvia coccinea* (tropical sage).

Plate 53. *Salvia farinacea* 'Cirrus'.

Plate 54. *Salvia farinacea* 'Victoria' adds color to a mixed bed. PHOTO BY CINDY GILBERG.

Plate 55. The violet-purple spikes of *Salvia nemorosa* 'East Friesland' blend well in this garden. PHOTO BY CINDY GILBERG.

Plate 56. A bed filled with varieties of *Solenostemon scutellarioides* (coleus) displays the great diversity in color, size, and form. Note that this bed is in a sunny location.

Plate 57. *Solenostemon scutellarioides* 'Rusty'.

Plate 58. *Stachys byzantina* (lamb's ear). PHOTO BY CINDY GILBERG.

Plate 59. *Stachys macrantha* (big betony). PHOTO BY CINDY GILBERG.

Plate 60. *Glechoma hederacea* (creeping Charlie).

Plate 61. *Lamium purpureum* (red dead nettle).

Mentha pulegium. A rather bitter herb, *M. pulegium* (pennyroyal) has long been known as an effective insect repellent. In fact its species name refers to the fleas that it wards off so nicely. The 0.5- to 1.5-inch (1.25- to 3.75-cm) leaves are typically smooth, oval, and covered with tiny hairs. The plants grow to a height of about 12 inches (30 cm) and in midsummer bear lilac flowers in tiers on flower spikes 6 to 12 inches (15 to 30 cm) in length. Pennyroyal enjoys moist soil and rather shady locations. Its prostrate habit and tolerance of shade make it a good choice as a ground cover under trees where grass will not grow. Mow it if flower stalks are bothersome or if it becomes straggly. Ingesting the essential oil can be lethal, eating the leaves or tea can be irritating to the genitourinary tract, and it has even been reported to induce abortions. Yet John Gerard suggested it for purifying the blood, and the herbalist Nicholas Culpeper reported that pennyroyal would heal venomous bites and cure fainting. Although some people may want to wash their dogs with a tea of pennyroyal to repel fleas and ticks, they should be aware of its toxicity. Propagation is by cuttings or root divisions.

Mentha requienii. A prostrate herb that grows only 1 to 4 inches (2.5 to 10 cm) in height, *M. requienii* (Corsican mint) has tiny oval to round 0.25-inch (0.6-cm) leaves. It has a strong, pungent peppermint smell and has been used to flavor liqueurs. Its best use, however, is as an aromatic ground cover, especially in small areas such as parts of a rock garden where there is perfect drainage. Corsican mint requires a moist, shady, protected location. It forms dense mats with its thin rooting stems. Protect it during severe cold spells with a loose mulch such as hay or straw.

Mentha spicata. Unquestionably the best-known member of the mint family, *M. spicata* (spearmint, Plate 12) has a strong scent and taste that are universally recognizable. It is also one of the greenest and an old favorite for lemonades, iced teas, mint juleps, chewing gum, candies, or mint sauces. Spearmint has many culinary and medicinal uses. Plants may grow more than 36 inches (90 cm) tall with narrow, pointed, serrate leaves with prominent veining. The stems may have a tint of red. White to pale pink to violet flowers grow in close-set spikes that rise above the foliage on a central stem in midsummer. Spearmint includes many varieties, hybrids, and cultivars. The best-known and most widely grown form is 'Kentucky Colonel', a cultivar with outstanding fragrance and flavor and larger, more crinkly, more attractive leaves than the species. 'Crispa' has round, very crinkled leaves and is excellent both fresh and candied. Propagate spearmint by cuttings, divisions, runners, or stolons. Like many true mints, it won't reliably come true from seeds.

Mentha suaveolens. Easy to grow and a great favorite of many herb gardeners, *M. suaveolens* (apple mint) has rounded, woolly bright green leaves 1 to 4 inches (2.5 to 10 cm) long and a pleasing apple-mint fragrance. The plant grows 6 to 36 inches (15 to 90 cm) tall. In midsummer it bears 2- to 4-inch (5- to 10-cm) spikes of whitish flowers that turn pink or violet as they mature. Apple mint is less popular than some other true mints because of the woolly quality of its leaves. The flowers and foliage do, however, make attractive additions to floral arrangements. The cultivar 'Variegata' (Plate 13) is known as pineapple mint and has a more fruity scent than the species. It is not only zestfully tasty as an herb but also highly decorative with its green and white foliage.

OTHER HERBAL MINTS

Hyssopus. Due in great part to its strong, camphorlike scent, *H. officinalis* (hyssop) used to be a valuable culinary, strewing, and medicinal herb. As a strewing herb in medieval times it was fragrant to walk on, and its strong flavor was used to season gamy meats, soups, and sauces. The Romans even made a wine from hyssop. Throughout early times it was also used externally to treat rheumatism, cuts, and bruises and was used by herbalists in preparations prescribed internally for coughs and inflammation of the chest and throat. Although some herbalists still use hyssop in this way, it is better known as an ornamental (see chapter 4).

Lavandula. The history and lore surrounding the genus *Lavandula* (lavender) have been entwined with the course of mankind for thousands of years. The Egyptians used essential oils of lavender to help mummify their dead. The Phoenicians and other people of Middle Eastern regions used lavenders for cooking, bathing, and making their homes smell fresher.

The English and Latin names for this herb come from the Latin word *Lavare,* meaning "to wash." Not surprisingly, lavender was mixed into bath water by the soldiers of the Roman Empire, who knew of it from where it grew wild in the Mediterranean region. Not only did the herb give a fresh yet pungent fragrance to the water, it also may have had a repellent effect on lice, bedbugs, and fleas, those pestiferous animals that traveled with the armies.

Many experts believe Roman soldiers brought lavender to the British Isles during an invasion. Once there, lavender soon became associated with soaps, laundry washing, baths, perfumes, sachets, and potpourris—essentially with all ways of making day-to-day life cleaner and more fragrant. Lavender is still used for these purposes and is also a culinary herb (see chapter 2).

The zesty fragrance of lavender arises from the plant's essential oils and varies slightly, depending on the species. The scent has long been associated with love and the libido, a theory that has been scientifically proven in recent years. Oil distilled from the flowers of *Lavandula angustifolia* and *L. stoechas* is used in perfumes and other toiletry products. One of the traditional sources of lavenders and their essential oils remains the Provence region of France where, during the right season, visitors will find fields of lavender in full bloom.

Lavandula angustifolia (English lavender) is the most commonly grown lavender in American gardens. There are a number of well-known cultivars including 'Alba' with white flowers, 'Hidcote' with purple flowers (Plate 14), 'Jean Davis' with pale lavender flowers (Plate 15), 'Munstead' (Plate 16), one of the hardiest members of the genus, with striking flowers of soft lavender-blue, the dwarf 'Nana', 'Rosea', and 'Vera' with lavender flowers.

Lavandula dentata (French lavender, Plate 17) is a tender perennial hardy only to Zones 8 to 9. It has unusual texture and is well worth growing as a containerized patio plant in areas with severe winters. Another tender lavender is *L. stoechas* (French lavender), which usually has purple flowers. It has been developed into several cultivars including 'Alba' and the bright purple-flowered 'Papillon'.

Marrubium. A woody perennial herb with a scent similar to thyme, *M. vulgare* (horehound) has long been used in sweet confections as well as cough and throat medicines. Its flavor may be musky and bitter, but its high content of mucilage is soothing to the mucous membranes of the throat. Horehound is also said to be a traditional bitter herb of the Jewish Passover. Plants are erect and grow 18 to 24 inches (45 to 60 cm) tall with a spreading growth habit. The leaves are woolly and wrinkled, characteristics that led to its common name. Full sun and poor soil are required for growing vigorous horehound plants. Propagation is recommended by seeds, cuttings, or divisions. Plants are easy to grow and may become invasive. Small white flowers are borne in summer in dense whorls at intervals along the stems. The flowers are good attractors of honey bees.

Melissa. The species *M. officinalis* (lemon balm, Plate 18) has been used as a medicinal herb since at least the times of the ancient Greeks and Romans. It is currently most valued as a tea, garnish, perfume ingredient, and seasoning for veal and poultry. The lemon character of the plant is more citruslike in fragrance than in taste. *Melissa* means "honey bee" in Greek, an appropriate reference for an herb that attracts bees.

Lemon balm grew in many colonial gardens including those at Williamsburg and Jefferson's Monticello. It has a rather coarse texture and may flop over as it gets tall. Pruning regularly will encourage bushier growth. The hairy leaves are oval and toothed, and white to pale yellow flowers appear toward the end of summer. As is the case with many other mints, the flavor and taste of this herb is more intense if the plant is grown under less fertile conditions. Lemon balm prefers full sun to light shade and a comparatively poor soil with a pH of 6 to 8. Lemon balm can be grown from seeds or cuttings. Seeds germinate better when left uncovered. Root divisions and stem cuttings result in the same genetic composition, so choose a favorite lemon balm to propagate in this way. Spring and summer are the best times to take cuttings. Variegated forms of lemon balm, such as 'All Gold' and 'Aurea' (golden lemon balm, Plate 19), generally scorch or turn green unless sheltered from hot afternoon sun.

Nepeta. The genus *Nepeta* is best known for catnip (*N. cataria*), a coarse gray-green perennial noted for driving some cats to joyous distraction. An Old World native, catnip naturalized so rapidly after being introduced by immigrant Europeans that Native Americans included it in their pharmacopoeia and did not even associate it with the early settlers. The lemony, minty taste lends itself well to teas that are said to ease the symptoms of colds. Like many mints, catnip also served as a medicinal in early times.

Although it is a good plant for the herb garden, catnip is not a particularly good choice for an ornamental planting because of its coarse habit and comparatively inconsequential flowers. Cats may also roll in it, knocking down the plants. It may, however, also be grown in containers or window boxes. The flowering tops are the most potent parts of the plant. Though especially pungent if grown in full sun and sandy soil, catnip also tolerates partial shade and ordinary garden soil with a pH of 5 to 7.5. It is easily propagated from seeds, divisions, or cuttings. Catmint (*Nepeta ×faassenii*) is a close relative with good ornamental value (see chapter 4).

Ocimum. Known mostly as an essential element of the kitchen, where it is both an ingredient and a seasoning, *Ocimum* (basil) also has a long history of medicinal and mystical usage. It has long been regarded a sacred herb in India. It is often considered an herb of love—although, paradoxically, it may also be used to represent hatred for an enemy. Basil was thought in ancient times to be a witches' herb used for evil deeds as well as an herb of love that would attract the loveliest of ladies with its aroma. These sorts of contradictions are common among plants that have journeyed through several civilizations with mankind. The gardeners of ancient Greece and Rome even believed basil would thrive only if the gardener cursed and shouted when sowing the seeds.

The basils are tender plants and so must be treated and grown as annuals. They come in many sizes, from dwarf to 36 inches (90 cm) or more. They are also available in several colors and a number of growing patterns. Many basils are attractive enough to use as ornamentals in mixed beds as well as in herb gardens.

Basil seeds sprout easily and quickly in warm, sunny locations as long as the soil has a pH of about 6 and is rich and evenly moist. Basil may be started indoors in the spring and later transplanted. It will also grow easily from cuttings, which may be taken late in the growing season and grown indoors for a supply of fresh basil during cold months. Smaller basils, such as *Ocimum basilicum* × *O. americanum* 'Spicy Globe', work better for indoor plants than the large-leafed, tall-growing sweet basil (*O. basilicum*). Pinch basil regularly, pinching out the flower buds and one or more pairs of leaves, both for use in salads and pestos and to make the plants bushier.

The extremely variable *Ocimum basilicum* (sweet basil) and its selected varieties are the most widely grown plants of the genus. Gardeners quickly discover that some varieties combine the original basil flavor and fragrance with overtones that may be quite different. Since there are many subtle taste variations, it may be best to grow several varieties and then choose your favorites. The species itself is one of the best-known culinary herbs, appreciated for its tangy flavor, whether added to a dish or enjoyed by itself. The aroma is equally wonderful. It grows up to 36 inches (90 cm) in height with bright green leaves that are large, broad, and smooth. White flowers grow in terminal spikes.

Ocimum basilicum 'Anise' (licorice basil) is a rather lanky 30-inch (75-cm) plant with pinkish whorls of flowers and a distinctive sweet licorice flavor.

Ocimum basilicum 'Cinnamon' (cinnamon basil, Plate 20) is a 30-inch (75-cm) vigorous plant with a strong flavor of cinnamon combined with the typical basil taste. Terminal spikes of purple flowers rise above glossy green foliage.

Ocimum basilicum var. *citriodorum* (lemon basil) has a delightful lemony basil flavor that is good in teas, chicken dishes, and pestos. The 18- to 24-inch (45- to 60-cm) plants have light green, pointed leaves. This basil has a tendency to flower early, so be sure to pinch out the flower buds. There are also a number of cultivars including 'Sweet Dani', noted for its especially sweet lemon flavor, and 'Mrs. Burns', a favorite New Mexican basil for more than sixty years said to have the most lemony flavor of all. 'Mrs. Burns' also reliably self-seeds.

Ocimum basilicum var. *crispum* (lettuce leaf basil) is a classic form that has large, bright green, heavily crinkled leaves up to 4 inches (10 cm) long and wide. This herb grows up to 24 inches (60 cm) tall and has excellent flavor and aroma.

Ocimum basilicum 'Dark Opal' (Plate 21) is one of the original purple-leafed basils. It grows about 24 inches (60 cm) tall. The foliage is deep red to purple. All of the purple-leafed basils are wonderful for making pink-toned basil vinegar. Simply add some leaves to a good-quality white vinegar for a few days and store in a cool, dark place.

Ocimum basilicum 'Fino Verde Compatto' is a 12- to 15-inch (30- to 37.5-cm) Italian basil with small, fine 1-inch (2.5-cm) leaves. The plant, which looks like a leafy shrub, is a favorite with Italian cooks who prefer its sweet, pungent flavor.

Ocimum basilicum var. *minimum* 'Fine Leaf' (Greek basil) is a small basil, reaching only about 12 inches (30 cm) in height. Its small size lends it to growing as a border or container plant, and it has a marvelous pungent fragrance and flavor.

Ocimum basilicum 'Napoletano' is an Italian basil with large, round, deeply crinkled leaves. The leafy plant forms as dense canopy that is almost tropical in appearance. Lush leaves are light green, sweetly fragrant, and have a rich flavor.

Ocimum basilicum 'Purple Ruffles' (Plate 22) has fluted leaves of dark purple often used to color and flavor salad vinegars. Plants grow to 24 inches (60 cm) with pink to lavender flowers.

Ocimum basilicum 'Red Rubin' is a selection of 'Dark Opal' that is more uniform and holds its rich purple color more reliably. The lush plants are about 24 inches (60 cm) tall with garnet-colored foliage that makes a great contrast for herb gardens and mixed borders.

Ocimum basilicum 'Sweet Thai' has small green leaves, purple stems, and purple blossoms on 12- to 18-inch (30- to 45-cm) plants. Noted for its very strong, spicy, anise-clove scent, this basil is most commonly used for cooking in Thailand. It is, however, gaining popularity in the United States.

Ocimum basilicum 'True Thai' (Plate 23) is a 24-inch (60-cm) plant with attractive, terminal, spiky whorls of purple flowers. It is noted for its spicy licorice flavor and fragrance.

Ocimum basilicum × *O. americanum* 'Spicy Globe' is both tasty and ornamental. Only 12 inches (30 cm) tall, it forms a handsome globe shape that makes it a good addition to mixed beds and borders as well as herb gardens. It is also a great container plant. The tiny leaves are bright green.

Ocimum tenuiflorum (holy basil) is revered by Hindus. It grows 18 to 24 inches (45 to 60 cm) tall with medium-sized, slender, slightly hairy green leaves that have a unique musky fragrance with hints of mint. The purplish stems are hairy, and the flowers are pink or white. The plant is bushy and makes a good ornamental for the garden. It may reseed itself. 'Red and Green' is a distinctive variety of holy basil named for its red and green leaves. It has a spicy, pungent scent with overtones of clove.

Origanum. The members of the genus *Origanum* (oregano) were traditionally ascribed certain attributes. *Origanum majorana* (sweet marjoram), for example, offered mankind good luck and good health. *Origanum vulgare* (oregano) was thought to give protection from poisons by withdrawing them from the body. Another tradition held that oregano contained mystical secrets for a potent Black Magic, but since it was a crime for one to write about those secrets they have unfortunately been lost in time. *Oregano,* derived from Greek, translates to "joy on the mountain."

Oregano requires a sunny site with rich, well-draining soil. Since these plants can be quite variable in taste and aroma, try to sample before making a purchase. Rub a leaf and sniff, but remember that the ability to discriminate is diminished once several have been sniffed.

The leaves of dittany of Crete (*Origanum dictamnus,* Plate 24) have a mild oregano fragrance and taste. Though grown mainly for its ornamental value, some people make a tea of the flowers and use the leaves in salads. The flowers are also used fresh or dried in arrangements. Best grown in containers north of Zone 8, this tender perennial grows into a low mound and in the late summer bears clusters of dainty pink flowers within large bright purple bracts. Leaves are covered with soft hairs, giving it a grayish appearance. Dittany of Crete requires excellent drainage and a sunny site.

Sweet marjoram (*Origanum majorana*) is a tender plant that must be treated as an annual throughout much of the northern United States. Since its fragrance was said to be able to revive the spirits of anyone inhaling it, this herb took on the attributes of both happiness and protection. Sweet marjoram thrives in sunny sites with well-draining alkaline soil. The plant forms a dense 12-inch (30-cm) mound and in warmer climates, where it can be perennial, it may reach 24 inches (60 cm) in height. Pinch it back to encourage bushiness, then enjoy cooking with the clippings. Sweet marjoram is a good candidate for container growing. Unlike most herbs, it has a stronger flavor and aroma when grown in fertile soil. The small oval leaves are pubescent and make a valuable seasoning, fresh or dry, to many dishes, from meats to soups to stuffings. Sweet marjoram is also grown for its essential oil.

Some use the leaves and flowers of pot marjoram (*Origanum onites*) in potpourris. The taste of the leaves is somewhat bitter and the leaves smell a bit like thyme. 'Aureum' is a gold-leafed cultivar.

Italian oregano (*Origanum ×majoricum*) is a sterile hybrid. It resembles sweet marjoram (*O. majorana*) and is likely a cross between it and *O. vulgare*. In taste and fragrance Italian oregano is much like sweet marjoram, though less strong.

Origanum vulgare (oregano) is a hardy perennial with a sprawling growth habit. It requires full sun and well-draining soil. A number of cultivars belong to *O. vulgare* including the golden oregano known as 'Aurea' (golden marjoram). 'Aureum Crispum' is noted for its yellowish, wrinkled, round leaves. It is inclined to scorch in full sun and is not as tough as 'Aurea'. 'Alba' is somewhat smaller with white flowers and paler green leaves than the species. 'Compactum' is a smaller, more compact plant, which makes it a good prospect for rock gardens and container growing.

Other varieties vary from the original species in color, size, or growth habit. As is true with varieties of other species and genera, the variegated and oddly colored forms are inclined to be less vigorous than the originals, probably due to the simple fact that they have comparatively less chlorophyll.

Pycnanthemum. Comprised of about twenty-one North American natives, all of which can substitute for true mints, *Pycnanthemum* (mountain mint) is used to flavor soups, stews, and meats. The buds, flowers, and leaves were traditionally made into teas by Native Americans and used to treat minor internal ailments such as colds, fevers, and upset stomachs. These herbs prefer rich, well-draining soil in sun to partial shade and grow wild in dry woods and meadows. Some gardeners grow mountain mints in their gardens, while others gather them from the wild. The plants may spread by runners but do not tend toward invasiveness. *Pycnanthemum muticum* grows into a 28- to 40-inch (70- to 100-cm) bush with a minty fragrance and fuzzy gray-green leaves. *Pycnanthemum virginianum* (prairie hyssop) is another mountain mint often seen in the wild as well as in gardens.

Pogostemon. The best-known herb of more than five dozen species in the genus *Pogostemon* is *P. cablin* (patchouli). The leaves of this and other closely related species are used to make the distilled volatile oil called patchouli, the substance with the distinctive minty sandalwood odor that used to mark and distinguish fabrics made in India. Though distasteful to some, patchouli was popular in the 1860s as a fragrance for perfumes and other cosmetic products. A resurgence in popularity during the 1960s was probably linked to patchouli's association with India, known for religious sects such as Zen Buddhism that were popular among young people of that decade.

Rosmarinus. Unlike *Mentha* and *Origanum, Rosmarinus* includes just one species of major economic and horticultural importance: *R. officinalis* (rosemary). This one species has been bred and selected into a number of excellent varieties. Native to Mediterranean regions where it grew and continues to grow on rocky hillsides, rosemary has a long history as a culinary, medicinal, and strewing herb. Known and praised as the herb of remembrance and friendship, rosemary even developed a reputation as a protective herb, one that prevented evil and witchcraft. The name is from the Latin *ros marinus,* meaning "dew of the sea."

Rosemary is one of the most flavorful and aromatic herbs of the mint family. Rub the foliage lightly to feel the resinous oils that carry its wonderful fragrance. The needlelike leaves and woody stems contain volatile oils and other substances that have proven to be both antiseptic and healing, qualities that have made rosemary an unusually valuable medicinal herb. It has been taken internally to treat nervous exhaustion, headaches, digestive problems, and poor circulation and used externally for arthritis, muscular injuries, and dandruff.

Grow rosemary from stem or root cuttings for the best results since seeds are very slow to germinate. Gardeners may also ground-layer long stems to get new plants by simply pinning the stems to the soil until roots have formed, cutting off the new plant, and putting it in a pot or bed. *Rosmarinus officinalis* also contains a group of prostrate rosemary plants that make good choices for pseudo-bonsai projects, containers, and hanging baskets. Well-draining, light soil and a sheltered sunny location suit rosemary very well. Many gardeners in colder climates keep rosemary plants in containers all year long, putting them outdoors during warm months and bringing them inside for the winter.

The hardiest cultivar is 'Arp', which was discovered in Arp, Texas, in 1972. Other popular varieties include the white-flowered *Rosmarinus officinalis* var. *albiflorus,* the variegated 'Aureus', the prostrate 'McConnell's Blue' with broad leaves and sky blue flowers, the pink-flowered 'Pinkie' with shorter leaves than the species, the pink-flowered 'Roseus', and 'Sissinghurst Blue', a free-flowering and quite hardy form.

Salvia. Many wonderful herbal sages, most of which are aromatic and either tender or half hardy, belong to the genus *Salvia.* The old herbalists considered sage the immortality herb, an herb that could cure many diseases. It was prescribed internally for such conditions as anxiety, digestive problems, night sweats, and menopause and externally for skin infections, insect bites, and vaginal discharges. According to early Hungarian gypsies, sage was even said to attract good and destroy evil. The herb remains popular, though now more for its taste and fragrance. It is used in foods such as sausages and dressings, and as garnish on mixed dishes and salads. It also makes great herbal teas.

Salvia is a marvelous genus and the largest of all the mint genera, made up of fully 16 percent of all mint family species. Because it is so large, I will only skim the surface here, describing the major salvias useful for their herbal properties.

Cleveland sage (*Salvia clevelandii*) is a tender perennial that grows in the dry environments of chaparral and coastal scrub plant communities of southern and Baja California. The dry summers and winter rains of the region are keys to growing this herb successfully. This is why Cleveland sage is not especially well known to gardeners outside California, even though it has been in cultivation since the 1940s. The plant has a strong fragrance and bears elegant, long, upright spikes of sweet-scented lilac, blue, or white flowers for up to a month in May or June. Slender gray-green leaves have a pebbly, wrinkled surface. This salvia goes well with Mediterranean herbs such as lavender, rosemary, and the various forms of sage (*S. officinalis*). Cleveland sage is a good container plant, but beware of overwatering, and be sure to plant it in the sun in well-draining soil. Pinch young plants to promote bushiness. Leaves can be used in cooking or potpourris. Fresh flower stalks are also lovely in arrangements, and once the flowers drop, the stalk remains attractive for use in dried arrangements.

Fruit-scented sage (*Salvia dorisiana*) is a tender perennial described and introduced in 1950. In warm climates it is evergreen. Since fruit-scented sage must have a warm environment all year long, it thrives in a heated greenhouse and might well be a good choice for the home atriums or garden rooms that have become so popular. It adapts well to container growing and can be moved outdoors during warm weather. Plants prefer full sun and average soil that is well draining. When touched or brushed, the aromatic and velvety leaves of this bushy herb give off a characteristic fragrance that reminds one of pineapple and citrus fruits. The entire plant is covered with hairs that carry the scent. Large rose-pink to magenta flowers appear on spikes in early to late winter and are accented by large lime-green calyces. Leaves are tasty either fresh or dried in teas. Dried leaves are good additions to potpourris.

Pineapple sage (*Salvia elegans,* Plate 25) is native to mountainous regions of central Mexico at elevations between 6000 and 9000 feet (1800 and 2700 m), where it is a shrubby plant growing at the edges of woodlands. It is grown as an annual farther north. The leaves of pineapple sage may be used fresh or dried in teas and dried in potpourris. In Mexico it is taken to settle an upset stomach. Plants have young shoots and fruit-scented leaves covered with fine hairs. Though known primarily for its sweet, fruity pineapple flavor and aroma, pineapple sage also displays eye-catching red flowers that are a favorite among hummingbirds. Easy to grow in well-draining organic soil of average fertility, this sage is yet another mint that grows well from seeds, stem cuttings, or root cuttings. Take cuttings in late summer to early fall, and grow the plant indoors in a sunny location, garden room, or greenhouse.

The very aromatic *Salvia officinalis* (sage, Plate 26) is a star among mint family plants. It is widely used in herb gardens and perfumes and is a favorite of cooks everywhere (see chapter 2). It has also long been an important medicinal herb. Early herbalists prescribed it for ailments such as nervousness, indigestion, and sore throats. Modern studies have also indicated that sage does indeed have therapeutic qualities.

This shrubby, hardy perennial herb has a woody base and velvety gray-green leaves with a pebbly finish resembling a lizard's skin. It is evergreen where winters are mild but dies back to the ground in severe cold. The variegated forms are less hardy. Sage thrives in sunny sites with well-draining soil and is a good choice for raised beds because of its fussiness about good drainage. Grow from seeds, root cuttings, or stem cuttings.

A number of attractive varieties exist as well. *Salvia officinalis* 'Nana' (Plate 27), a 12-inch (30-cm) vigorous dwarf form, is well-suited for low borders and containers and is as hardy and tasty as the original species. Another popular form is the blue-green 'Berggarten' (Plate 28), notable for its large oval leaves, which are quite unlike those of *S. officinalis*. Other popular cultivars include the golden-leafed 'Aurea', 'Icterina' (Plate 29) with variegated green and gold foliage, 'Purpurescens' (Plate 30) with purple-green foliage and stems, and 'Tricolor' (Plate 31) with leaves of green, white, and purple. 'Icterina' and 'Tricolor' are tender, hardy only to about Zone 7. Pinching regularly will cause the taller sages to grow more bushy.

Clary (*Salvia sclarea*) is a hardy biennial or perennial salvia also known as cleareye and muscatel sage because of its earlier uses as a treatment for eye irritations and an ingredient in wine. It has also been used to treat digestive and renal disorders and has been made as a tea said to soothe upset stomachs. Now clary is mostly used to scent soaps and perfumes. During its first year of growth clary forms a rosette of large gray-green leaves. In its second year it sends up tall flower stalks bearing creamy white or lavender flowers with attractive bracts of white to pink or mauve. Clary will tolerate heavy soils better than most herbs but cannot take high humidity combined with heat. It prefers full sun in a well-draining soil that is average to low in nutrients. Both flowers and foliage have a strong fragrance, especially right after a rain. Clary is a favorite for old-fashioned borders. As a perennial, it is short-lived but easy to grow from seeds.

Satureja. The name of the genus *Satureja* (savory) derives from the Latin word for *satyr,* the mythical half-man, half-goat creature that symbolized lust—probably in reference to the savories' early reputation as an aphrodisiac. The genus includes two major herbs, summer savory (*S. hortensis*) and winter savory (*S. montana*), which have been used as culinary herbs and medicinals for more than two thousand years. Though both savories have nearly the same wonderful fragrance and taste, reminiscent of marjoram and thyme, they have different habits of growth. Summer savory is a bit milder and winter savory more peppery. Both blend well with other herbs. Savory teas are reputed to soothe sore throats and calm digestive ailments. The savories have also earned a reputation as antiflatulents.

Summer savory is an annual with smooth, narrow gray-green leaves and sparse, small white to purple flowers that appear from midsummer to frost. The leaves and stems carry the taste and fragrance. The texture of the foliage is softer than that of winter savory. Winter savory is a small shrubby perennial that is somewhat evergreen and woody at its base. The flowers appear from July through mid-September, bearing purple spots on their lower lips. Leaves are glossy, lanceolate, and pointed.

Yerba buena (*Satureja douglasii*) is a tender creeping perennial valued for its minty fragrance and taste. The leaves, whether fresh or dried, are good in teas. Yerba buena is a good container plant and grows well indoors.

Grow the plants of this genus in full sun in well-draining, neutral to slightly alkaline soil with average fertility. Because the seeds are slow to germinate, members of *Satureja* may be grown more easily from stem or root cuttings. When provided with five or more hours of sunlight, or the equivalent, they will grow well indoors.

Teucrium. Although in ancient times it was the recommended treatment for gout as well as fevers, asthma, and coughs, *T. chamaedrys* (wall germander, Plate 32) now serves primarily as a ground cover or small hedging. A hardy perennial, wall germander responds well to clipping, and clipped hedges of it make handsome edgings for herb gardens as well as ornamental beds and borders (Plate 33). These plants are good prospects as dividing borders within herb gardens and, of course, are an asset in formal knot gardens for gardeners willing to take on high-maintenance projects. Wall germander is also a good, small evergreen shrub to hold steep hillsides or to plant in niches in stone walls. It is an excellent bee attractor. The leaves, when rubbed, have an odor like garlic and are bitter and pungent to taste. Apparently the herb also has some qualities similar to *Marrubium vulgare* (horehound) since, when taken with honey, it is said to relieve coughs and asthma.

Wall germander has bright green leaves that are wrinkled, glossy, oval, and serrate. The species was named *chamaedrys,* meaning "ground oak," because the leaves look somewhat like oak leaves. Leaves toward the top of the plant have smooth edges. Purple to purple-pink or rose-colored flowers appear in midsummer to fall in terminal spikes and in the axils of leaf bracts. Wall germander spreads by rhizomes and has a woody base. Cut it back after flowering to promote bushiness and mulch with straw or evergreen branches in the winter to reduce damage from extreme cold and wind.

Teucrium marum (cat thyme) is a tender herb with oval leaves that are hairy underneath and have smooth edges. Its leaves and young stems are bitter to taste and, when rubbed, emit a volatile odor that causes sneezing. Purplish to purple-pink flowers grow on one-sided spikes.

Thymus. The genus *Thymus* (thyme, Plate 34) has been cultivated for more than five thousand years. It was grown in Sumeria three millennia before the time of Christ and had its place in Aristotle's garden. An important genus for herbs, thyme comes in many forms and flavors. Thymes may be dwarf or standard sizes of about 6 inches (15 cm), prostrate or erect, plain or variegated, hairy or smooth. Although some thymes lack significant taste, the best-loved varieties are full of flavor. In taste and fragrance thymes range from the traditional slightly peppery thyme to lemon to lavender to coconut. Several species are culinary favorites of good cooks everywhere.

Thymes also have a long history of use as medicinal herbs and were once thought to be of great benefit to those afflicted with melancholy and epilepsy as well as other diseases and conditions. The antiseptic qualities of thyme were used to combat plagues in Europe. Medical personnel in World War I used oil of thyme as an antiseptic. It was also once considered a love herb with great powers that enabled men to safely reproduce without danger of sexually transmitted diseases and, according to the herbalist Nicholas Culpeper, allowed women to avoid "the travails of childbirth."

Thymes have leaves that are oval to rounded and entire, without any notching or scalloping. They are easy to grow in full sun with a well-draining soil that has a pH of 5.5 to 7. Raised beds may help prevent problems caused by poor drainage. Some thymes are hard to grow in climates with high humidity such as regions along the Gulf Coast. Because they tend to get woody as they age it is a good idea to restart thymes every three to four years. Propagation is easy by divisions, cuttings, or ground layering, the latter of which is accomplished by pinning a long stem to the soil until it grows roots. The nonhybrid thymes can be grown from seeds, although germination may be slow. Thyme flavors are at their peak just before the plants flower.

Classification of thyme is confusing, a condition not uncommon with other genera of the mint family that are extremely variable in form and crossbreed enthusiastically. Garden thyme (*Thymus vulgaris*) may also be called English thyme or French thyme, and there are several forms within the genus called lemon thyme (*T.* ×*citriodorus*) that truly do not look much alike. The best thing to do, therefore, is to pick favorite thymes and maintain them through divisions, cuttings, or layering.

Lemon thyme (*Thymus* ×*citriodorus*), an extremely variable hybrid of broad-leafed thyme (*T. pulegioides*) and garden thyme (*T. vulgaris*), is one of the many varieties often found in nurseries and catalogs. Noted for its strong, delightful lemony flavor and aroma, lemon thyme is popular with gardeners everywhere. It has been bred and selected into a number of varieties including the gold-leafed 'Aureus', 'Golden King' with gold-edged leaves, and 'Silver Queen' (Plate 35) with white-edged green leaves. These have a tendency to revert to green foliage. Though not reliably hardy north of Zone 7, 'Silver Queen' is worth growing because of its unusual coloring and attractive texture.

Caraway thyme (*Thymus herba-barona,* Plate 36) is a creeping plant with bright pink flowers that appear in spring. It has flat, shiny, narrow dark green leaves that may carry a fragrance of caraway, lemon, or nutmeg when crushed.

Creeping thyme (*Thymus praecox,* Plate 37) is a somewhat woody herb that forms matlike growth. It has obovate to roundish leaves that are leathery. The flowers are purple to mauve, sometimes white. Creeping thyme makes a good low ground cover and is a great attractor of bees. *Thymus praecox* subsp. *arcticus* is hairy and has been bred and selected into white-flowered and dark green forms.

Woolly thyme (*Thymus pseudolanuginosus,* Plate 38) is a hardy thyme that is very prostrate and, as the name suggests, very woolly. The rosy purple flowers appear in late spring to summer. This plant is fussy, requiring perfect drainage if it is to thrive. Use the woolly thymes in rock gardens, stone wall niches, flagstone paths, and raised beds. 'Hall's Variety' has greener leaves than woolly thyme, which has gray-green foliage.

Mother of thyme (*Thymus serpyllum,* Plate 39) is a creeping, mat-forming herb that bears fragrant pink or purple flowers in late spring. Intensely aromatic, this herb is well known to gardeners and cooks alike. It roots at the nodes and is woody at the base. Among the varieties of this thyme are the white-flowered 'Albus', 'Annie

Hall' with pink flowers and pale green leaves, 'Coccineus' with red flowers and foliage that turns bronze in the fall, and 'Elfin', a dwarf thyme only 2 inches (5 cm) tall.

Garden thyme (*Thymus vulgaris*) has lilac, white, or pale purple flowers that grow in dense terminal whorls in summer. This is the thyme most commonly used as a culinary herb. It is essential in the French bouquet garni and very important in many dishes such as soups, stews, and vegetable dishes. Some cultivars include 'Erectus', which has a camphorlike scent and looks like a small pine tree, 'Lavender' with a creeping habit and lavender scent, 'Narrow-Leaf French', a common culinary thyme with several variations, and 'Orange Balsam', a 12-inch (30-cm) plant with a spicy orange scent and flavor.

CHAPTER 4

Ornamental Mints

Bee balms (*Monarda*), dead nettles (*Lamium*), hyssops (*Hyssopus*), Mexican hyssops (*Agastache*), obedient plants (*Physostegia*), Russian sages (*Perovskia*), sages (*Salvia*), and skullcaps (*Scutellaria*) are among the better-known ornamentals of the Lamiaceae. Some have a history of medicinal and herbal use, while others have always been favored strictly for their beauty. The members of *Hyssopus,* for example, were once most valued as medicinal, strewing, and culinary herbs but are now prized primarily for their ornamental value.

Although it may seem that all of the good ornamental plants have already been discovered and brought into cultivation, new plants are in fact introduced every year. One year I saw a brand new ornamental mint at the Missouri Botanical Garden. It was not in any of the botanical resources that I could find. With the help of horticulturists at the garden I discovered that it was *Orthosiphon stamineus* (Plate 40), commonly known as cat's whiskers because of the way its stamens protrude from the flower. Cat's whiskers is one of about a hundred species in a genus native to the tropics from Africa to Australia. It is a beautiful plant with fascinating flowers that appear from summer until frost. Strangely enough, it has only been introduced to gardens of the United States within the past few years.

Botanists, horticulturists, and everyday gardeners may find species and varieties of plants that offer special merit because of their color, form, flowering habit, or other features. After testing the plants, growers propagate them and introduce them to the marketplace. Sometimes plants that have been classed as weeds end up as prized garden specimens. Sometimes a tropical or subtropical plant is introduced to temperate gardens where it is from then on grown as an annual, as is the case with cat's whiskers.

Ornamental mints include annuals, perennials, and a number of ground covers, most of which thrive in sun with fertile, well-draining soil. Some ornamental mints grow in clumps that can be divided, while others are prostrate and can be multiplied by root cuttings, stem cuttings, or layering. Although most of these plants can be grown from seeds, hybrids may be sterile. If fertile, they will not always grow true from seeds.

The following list includes some major ornamental mints growing in American gardens. With the help of experts, catalogs, and botanical and horticultural resources, I have gathered as many details on specific cultivars as possible. Unfortunately, information about some newer or less well-known varieties may be slightly skimpy.

Agastache. Now valued primarily as ornamentals, the upright perennials that comprise *Agastache* (Mexican hyssop) were originally used in teas and food seasonings. White, orange, rose, violet, or blue flowers appear in summer. These plants are not good choices for hot, humid regions.

Anise hyssop (*Agastache foeniculum,* Plate 41) is the best-known garden plant of the genus, noted for its beautiful late-summer blue to purple flower stalks and licorice-scented foliage. This perennial has a bushy, erect habit of growth and reaches a height of about 30 inches (75 cm). It is twice as tall as it is wide and grows well in full sun and moist, moderately rich, well-draining soil. Anise hyssop is a good bee and honey plant, and also attracts hummingbirds and butterflies. Propagation is by seeds or by divisions in spring or fall.

Another plant known as anise hyssop, though better known as wrinkled great hyssop, is *Agastache rugosa,* which grows 24 to 30 inches (60 to 75 cm) tall and has rosy violet flowers with white teeth. This species produces good flowers for cutting.

Agastache barberi is suited for patio pots as well as ornamental beds. Plants flower all summer and into fall. The foliage is very fragrant and the flowers attract hummingbirds.

Ajuga. The reliable and hardy low-growing ground covers that make up the genus *Ajuga* (bugleweed) will grow in just about any soil providing it drains well. These creeping perennials are good shade plants that also tolerate quite a lot of sun. They are excellent plants to grow under trees, shrubs, and tall perennials. They make great edgings for beds and borders. Plants form rosettes of glossy foliage. Although ajugas are grown primarily for this foliage, the spring flower spikes are also attractive and usually of an intense blue to violet-blue. Some cultivars have pink or white flowers. Three species are popular garden subjects, all hardy from Zones 3 to 9. Ajugas divide and transplant easily, especially in the spring but also in the fall. Small new plants that appear at the ends of the runners can be easily cut off and transplanted. These mints spread by means of runners, often covering the ground so thickly that weeds will not grow. Avoid planting ajugas in areas such as rock gardens where small plants might be overrun by these often fast-spreading ground covers.

The best-known and most commonly found ajuga is *Ajuga reptans* (carpet bugleweed, Plate 42), a stoloniferous plant that grows into low mats that can spread faster and farther than desired if placed in a congenial setting. Because of its vigor this species is considered rampant and weedy where the environment is hospitable. A good cultivar is 'Purple Torch', which has 8-inch (20-cm) spikes of lavender-pink blooms atop abundant, shiny oval leaves. 'Atropurpurea' has oblong to spoon-shaped leaves colored an unusual dark bronzy purple. The small two-lipped flowers are usually blue but occasionally white or pink. This cultivar grows up to 6 inches (15 cm) high and spreads up to 36 inches (90 cm) wide. 'Multicolor' has spoon-shaped leaves that are dark green splashed with pink and cream. The flowers are similar to 'Atropurpurea'. It grows up to 5 inches (12.5 cm) tall with a spread of about 18 inches (45 cm). Some varieties have been selected for their flowers as is the case with the white-flowered 'Alba', pink-flowered 'Pink Spire', and rose-flowered 'Rosea'. Other varieties have been selected for their unusual foliage including 'Atropurpurea', 'Burgundy Glow' with variegated leaves touched with pink, rose, white, and green, and 'Gray Lady' with gray-green leaves and blue flowers. Other cultivars include 'Bronze Beauty' with brilliant bronze leaves, 'Catlin's Giant' with large bronze leaves, 'Jungle Beauty' with large dark green leaves and blue flowers, 'Pink Elf', a small variety with pink flowers, 'Purple Brocade' (Plate 43), a good if sometimes rampant ground cover, 'Silver Carpet' with silver-green foliage, and 'Variegata' with gray-green leaves edged in pale cream.

The other two ajugas commonly grown are not stoloniferous and therefore do not spread as rapidly. *Ajuga genevensis* (blue bugle) has dark green leaves and tolerates more sun than carpet bugleweed (*A. reptans*). *Ajuga pyramidalis* (upright bugleweed) forms upright plants without the rampant habit of carpet bugleweed. Both species have been selected into cultivars with white flowers.

Calamintha. The herbs included in *Calamintha* (calamint) were important pharmaceutically in medieval times but are more often used ornamentally today. The genus name derives from the ancient Greek word for "beautiful mint." Humidity does not agree with calamints, which are plants for cool, dry regions. The best-known garden plant of the genus is lesser calamint (*C. nepeta,* Plate 44). It has small leaves that are aromatically minty and less than 1 inch (2.5 cm) in length. Like many mints it requires well-draining soil and grows in full sun to partial shade. When its lilac to white flowers are at their peak, lesser calamint attracts hordes of bees. The 8- to 30-inch (20- to 75-cm) plant becomes thick, often woody at the base, and may benefit from hard pruning when it becomes lanky or overgrown. Large-flowered calamint (*C. grandiflora*) is about 18 inches (45 cm) in height and bears pink flowers.

Hyssopus. Valued today primarily as an ornamental, *H. officinalis* (hyssop) used to be valued more for its herbal properties (see chapter 3). Hyssop grows successfully in partial shade to full sun as long as the soil drains well. It will tolerate droughty conditions once established. Spikes of flowers are blue or violet, occasionally red, pink, or white, and appear in late spring to summer. Propagation is by seeds, cuttings, or divisions. Hyssop grows into an 18- to 24-inch (45- to 60-cm) round plant that is compact and responds well to clipping or pruning. Cut back old flower heads to encourage rebloom. There are several cultivars.

Lamium. Some great ground covers belong to the genus *Lamium,* called dead nettles because the leaves resemble the stinging nettle without bearing any tiny stinging hairs. These low-growing plants spread by stolons and are very easy to propagate by cuttings or divisions. Plants prefer shade to partial shade in soil that is moist and fairly organic. They are hardy from Zones 3 or 4 to Zones 8 or 9. *Lamium* also includes a number of invasive weeds (see chapter 5).

Yellow archangel (*Lamium galeobdolon,* Plate 45) is a handsome ground cover that grows low to the ground and spreads well. The cordate, serrate, pointed leaves have silver variegations except on the edges. This plant grows up to 12 inches (30 cm) tall and performs well in dense shade where little else will grow. If yellow archangel gets sparse, prune it back to promote bushiness. Yellow flowers appear in late spring to summer. 'Herman's Pride' has handsome variegation and is more restrained in its growth habit than the species.

Despite its ugly common name, spotted dead nettle (*Lamium maculatum*) is a handsome plant with a number of elegant cultivars that are increasingly popular as ground covers. Plants grow up to about 12 inches (30 cm) high and spread quickly by stolons and creeping stems. Purple to white flowers appear in late spring to midsummer growing in terminal whorls. 'Beacon Silver' is a cultivar noted for its pink flowers and silver leaves edged in green. 'Pink Pewter' has silver leaves and rich pink flowers. 'White Nancy' (Plate 46), my favorite, is one of the most elegant ground covers for shady to sunny sites as long as the soil is organic and regularly watered. It has white flowers and silver leaves edged with green. A number of other cultivars include variations on the flowers, leaf form, or coloration, but the varieties listed above appear to be among the best in many respects. *Lamium maculatum* is sometimes considered a weedy plant (see chapter 5).

Moluccella. The best-known ornamental of the genus *Moluccella, M. laevis* (bells of Ireland) doesn't look much like it belongs to the mint family. The 2-inch (5-cm) scalloped leaves that are equal and opposite do suggest the Lamiaceae; however, the plant is made more exotic in appearance by the pale green shell-like calyces, each up to 0.5 inch (1.25 cm) in diameter, which surround the small and unassuming white to pale lilac flowers. This 24-inch (60-cm) annual is grown for these ornamental calyces. Flower arrangers like to use the stems with their calyces dried because they are so unusual. The stems should be cut before the seeds have ripened; otherwise they will get brittle. Plants prefer cool nights and low humidity.

Monarda. Some sensational, tall perennial ornamentals can be found in the genus *Monarda* (bee balm). Plants grow up to 24 to 48 inches (60 to 120 cm) in height. Flowers appearing in summer grow densely in single or double circles and attract bees and hummingbirds. Deadhead spent flowers to encourage reblooming. Monardas are hardy in Zones 3 to 10. *Monarda didyma* and *M. fistulosa* are two commonly grown species.

Monarda didyma (bee balm) is a sun-loving plant that requires moist soil. It blooms over a period of many weeks if the soil is moist and if the faded flowers are removed regularly. Oddly, these plants often spread faster when grown in shady sites. Although bee balm is generally thought of as an ornamental more than an herb, the leaves do make a tasty tea, as discovered by the early settlers of New York who gave it the common name of Oswego tea. Some varieties are greatly prone to powdery mildew while others are noted for their resistance. 'Cambridge Scarlet' is a cultivar from the early twentieth century that remains very popular. Mildew-resistant cultivars include the pink-flowered 'Marshall's Delight' (Plate 47), the purple-flowered 'Scorpio', and 'Violet Queen'. Many other cultivars have been selected or bred for their white, pink, salmon, red, violet, and purple flowers.

Monarda fistulosa (wild bergamot) has pink, lavender, or lilac flowers that are smaller and less showy than those of *M. didyma.* The assets of this plant include its ability to tolerate dry conditions and its high resistance to powdery mildew. For the latter reason wild bergamot has been used in breeding programs that aim for better disease resistance. Use this hardy perennial in wildflower gardens or in mixed beds and borders that feature other pastel-flowering plants.

Nepeta. Aromatic and spreading, members of *Nepeta* (catmint) are often used as tall ground covers. The gray-green foliage of these plants is soothing in garden designs. Flowers bloom in spring to early summer and are typically lavender, blue, or white. If cut back right after the flush of bloom, they are likely to rebloom. The catmints require well-draining soil, full sun, and are hardy in Zones 3 to 9. They are easily grown by divisions, cuttings, or seeds with the exception of *N.* ×*faassenii*, which is sterile.

The most popular and most commonly known member of the genus is *Nepeta* ×*faassenii* (catmint, Plate 48), a good ornamental for borders, massed plantings, and for use as a tall ground cover. It grows up to 18 inches (45 cm) tall. In late spring and early summer this hybrid bears a multitude of lavender to blue flowers that grow in whorls at intervals on the stems, making a heavenly display against the gray-green foliage. Catmint may rebloom if cut back by one half after the first flowers fade. Good cultivars include 'Blue Wonder' with dark blue flowers, the large 'Six Hills Giant', 'Snowflake' with creamy white flowers, 'Souvenir d'André Chaudron' (synonym 'Blue Beauty') with blue flowers, and 'Superba' with lavender-blue flowers.

Perilla. The one cultivated species of the genus is *P. frutescens* (beefsteak plant, Plate 49). This tender perennial must be grown as an annual in most of the northern United States. Looking somewhat like a purple-leafed basil or purple coleus, beefsteak plant can be used in the same ways: as annual hedging, as back-of-the-border plants, or behind contrasting ornamentals such as chrysanthemums or asters to create excitement in the garden design. The plants grow 24 to 36 inches (60 to 90 cm) tall and have purplish green or bronzy green leaves that are deeply cut, ovate, and up to 5 inches (12.5 cm) or more in length. Plants tolerate poor soil but thrive in a sunny location with soil that is fertile and moist with good structure. They respond well to periodic pruning throughout the season by becoming bushier and more branched. Beefsteak plant is a longtime favorite of southern gardeners. Propagation is by seeds or cuttings. Once planted, this mint may well reseed every year. 'Fancy Fringe' is a cultivar with deeply cut, fringed leaves that are an especially attractive bronzy green color.

Although beefsteak plant (*Perilla frutescens*) is thought of as an ornamental in the United States, it is grown as food where it is native. The leaves are used in salads or as a vegetable, and the flower buds are sautéed or fried in a batter. The taste is reportedly something like a combination of mint and cinnamon. It also makes a good salad vinegar.

Perovskia. The single species of *Perovskia* widely grown as an ornamental perennial is *P. atriplicifolia* (Russian sage, Plate 7). It grows about 48 inches (120 cm) tall by some 36 inches (90 cm) wide. The woody base has many erect whitish gray stems bearing 1.5-inch (3.75-cm) leaves that are aromatic, coarsely toothed, pale silver-green above, and more silvery underneath. Spikes of soft lavender-blue flowers appear in summer months. Cutting off spent flowers will encourage reblooming.

The light airy appearance and soft coloration of Russian sage (*Perovskia atriplicifolia*) make it an asset in mixed beds and borders (Plate 50). Full sun and well-draining soil are the main requirements. Note that this mint is inclined to flop and get scraggly in regions with high summer heat and humidity. In spring, just as new growth begins to show, cut the plant almost to the ground to encourage bushiness. Periodic pruning every few weeks during spring months will also promote bushiness. Propagation is recommended by shoot cuttings taken in summer. Cultivars include 'Blue Haze' with pale blue flowers and leaves that are almost entire and 'Blue Spire' with deep violet flowers and finely dissected leaves. Some experts believe these cultivars resulted from the hybridization of Russian sage with *P. abrotanoides* (Caspian perovskia), a rare Asian species that is more thickly branched, with blue to pink flowers, and more finely dissected leaves.

Physostegia. The common name of *P. virginiana* (obedience plant, Plate 51), the species of *Physostegia* most widely grown as an ornamental, refers to the way individual flowers stay in place if bent one way or another. Rose, purple, pink, or white flowers with purple spots or streaks appear in late summer to fall on bushy plants that are 24 to 48 inches (60 to 120 cm) or more in height and about 36 inches (90 cm) in width. Plants prefer full sun to partial shade. Adaptable to most soils, they thrive almost too well in soils that are moist and highly fertile with a pH of 6.5 to 7. Cultivars include the white-flowered 'Alba', 'Nana', a smaller version only 12 to 18 inches (30 to 45 cm) tall with pink flowers, the pink-flowered 'Rose Pink', the pink-flowered 'Variegata' with green and white foliage, and the compact pink-flowered 'Vivid' (Plate 8).

Salvia. Many sensational ornamentals included in the genus *Salvia* (sage) are enjoying increased popularity because they are not only beautiful but also quite pest- and disease-free. They also make excellent cut flowers. Five dozen or more species are known in the nursery trade, plus dozens more selected and bred varieties. I have included just a few of the better-known species and varieties of this huge genus.

Salvia argentea (silver sage) is a handsome if short-lived perennial, sometimes grown as a biennial or annual. It is valued for its woolly silver foliage. Handsome basal rosettes have long furry leaves. Bell-shaped white flowers tinged with yellow or pink and often flecked with pink to violet grow in 4- to 8-inch (10- to 20-cm) spikes on

36-inch (90-cm) stems, but the plant is used primarily for the ornamental foliage of its low main growth. Silver sage thrives in full sun and well-draining soil. It is a good choice for drier, less humid climates. Propagation is recommended by seeds or by lateral offshoots that appear in spring.

Salvia azurea (blue sage) is a tall perennial with smooth, narrow grayish green leaves. In late summer to fall it bears 1-inch (2.5-cm) flowers of true blue or white at the ends of a dense mass of hairy stems. This plant is extremely tolerant of both humidity and heat. Propagation is by seeds, cuttings, or divisions. Although *S. azurea* var. *grandiflorum* enjoys quite a bit of popularity, some gardeners believe it no better than the species.

Salvia coccinea (tropical sage, Plate 52) is found wild in tropical South America and so must be treated as an annual in all but the warmest of American regions. The hairy leaves are large and primarily triangular in shape. The flowers that appear from mid to late summer are typically scarlet but may also be white, pink, salmon, orange, and bicolors. Full sun, regular moisture, and a well-draining soil are the main requirements for tropical sage. Regular pruning of faded flowers encourages more blooms. In warm climates where it is perennial a hard spring pruning will promote bushiness. There seems to be some confusion between this species and *S. greggii,* some authors referring to *S. coccinea* as Texas sage, a common name for *S. greggii.* Propagation is by seeds or cuttings.

Salvia farinacea (mealy sage) is far more attractive than its common name would suggest. Mealy sage is covered with short white hairs that give it a whitish floury look, hence the common name and species name, which comes from the Latin word for flour. Blue to blue-violet to white flowers appear in terminal spikes during a long bloom period from midsummer to frost. The flower stalks themselves sometimes have a bluish cast. Full sun, well-draining and moderately fertile soil, and moisture are all this plant needs to thrive. It tolerates high heat very well. Mealy sage makes great cut flowers and is well suited for annual and mixed beds and borders. Propagation is by seeds or cuttings. A number of attractive cultivars can be found in the marketplace including 'Argent' with white flowers, 'Blue Bedder' with compact blue flowers, 'Cirrus' (Plate 53) with white flowers, and 'Victoria' (Plate 54), a 19-inch (47.5-cm) plant with violet-blue flowers. Tender salvias such as 'Victoria' bloom all season long and mix well with many perennials and annuals in beds and borders.

Salvia greggii (autumn sage) is a variable plant that may grow in an erect pattern or form mounds. Medium green leaves are smooth and glossy. Flowers up to 1 inch (2.5 cm) long appear in smallish whorls from June until frost and are mostly crimson but may also be white, yellow, peach, pink, lavender, or rose. Tolerant of low humidity, plants thrive in full sun to partial shade with loamy soil that is well-draining and moist. They are bushier and more floriferous if regularly deadheaded and periodically pruned back. Some good cultivars include 'Cherry Red', which tolerates high humidity, 'Furman's Red' with its dark red autumn flowers, and 'Purple Pastel' with its heavy repeat blooms in the fall. Plants are variable, so propagation of plants true to parent plants must be done by cuttings.

Salvia nemorosa (violet sage) is a narrow, erect plant with narrow, rough leaves. Thin terminal spikes of violet-blue flowers grow above the foliage from summer through fall. Sun and a well-draining, moist, moderately fertile soil will result in vigorous plants. To produce plants true to parents, propagate by cuttings. The best-known cultivar is the popular 'East Friesland' (Plate 55) with its violet-purple flower spikes on 18-inch (45-cm) plants. This cultivar combines well with a variety of plants and remains in bloom for many weeks. 'Rose Queen' is a smaller compact plant, only 12 inches (30 cm) tall and not as vigorous as 'East Friesland', with spikes of bright pink flowers. Some horticultural taxonomists place these two cultivars within the hybrid group *Salvia ×superba*.

Salvia pratensis (meadow clary) is a perennial with large coarse clumps of basal leaves. Flowers up to 1 inch (2.5 cm) in length grow in terminal spikes on branching stems for up to three or four weeks in the spring. In northern areas the flowering season may come as late as June or even July. Flowers are violet-blue but may also be white, pink, and bluish white. Cut back fading flower spikes to encourage reblooming later in the growing season. Plants prefer full sun, well-draining loamy soil, and occasional water. Propagation is by seeds or cuttings.

Salvia splendens (scarlet sage) was a great favorite for Victorian bedding gardens, those bright geometrically designed beds and borders so popular at the turn of the twentieth century. It is a stocky, rather coarse plant that bears brilliant red flowers from June until frost. In recent years this sage has been bred into a number of equally strident forms with flowers of varying shades including purple, salmon, white, and lilac.

Salvia ×*superba* is probably a hybrid of *S. sylvestris* and *S. villicaulis*. It includes a number of popular varieties that are well loved in perennial gardens for their beauty and toughness. Plants are hardy from Zones 5 through 9 and grow in roundish shapes up to 24 inches (60 cm) tall by 24 inches wide. Long spikes of violet-blue flowers appear throughout summer months. *Salvia* ×*superba* tolerates drought but thrives in moist, well-draining soil that is reasonably fertile. Propagation is by divisions or stem cuttings.

Salvia viridis (bluebeard), which is low in fragrance and taste, is primarily an ornamental. Showy colorful bracts of pink, bluish purple, or white with green veins overshadow the tiny whitish flowers. These bracts are what make bluebeard so popular with floral arrangers, who generally use the stalks after the flowers drop. This salvia prefers a sunny site with good drainage, moderate moisture, and friable soil. Among the many cultivars, all chosen for the color of their showy bracts, are 'Alba', 'Bluebeard', 'Pink Sunday', and 'Rose Bouquet'.

Solenostemon. Although there are as many as sixty species in the genus *Solenostemon*, only *S. scutellarioides* (coleus, Plate 56) seems to have proven itself a valuable member of temperate gardens. Coleus is an ornamental foliage plant that usually grows about 12 to 18 inches (30 to 45 cm) tall and makes bright splashes in the garden. It is a favorite annual and house plant and a good subject for beds, window boxes, hanging baskets, and tubs. Plants grow in almost any soil as long as it is well draining but thrive in a rich fertile soil of good structure. While coleus can be grown easily from cuttings it is usually grown from seeds. Plant outside only when all danger of frost is past. Pinch off insignificant flower spikes as they appear, and lightly prune young plants to encourage bushiness.

There appear to be literally hundreds of distinct coleus cultivars in existence, and every year more varieties of these highly variable plants appear in the marketplace. While coleus used to be considered a plant for shady sites, many new cultivars are top choices for sunny gardens as well. Among the varieties bred for good performance in sunny sites are 'Burgundy Sun' with oval to cordate leaves of a rich deep burgundy color and 'Super Sun Plum Parfait' with ruffled lanceolate leaves of a purplish plum color. 'Yellow in Sun' reaches its most intense coloration only in sunny sites. 'Alabama Sunset' and 'Copper Queen' are large-leafed cultivars that are also at their best with lots of sun. 'Rusty' (Plate 57) is a brightly variegated cultivar of this vigorous annual.

Many other coleus varieties grow well in shady or sunny sites. 'India Frills' is a tiny-leafed coleus with deeply cut leaves and a habit of trailing over the ground. Other favorites include 'Inky Fingers' with small, green-edged, hand-shaped purple leaves, 'Japanese Brocade', a giant 48-inch (120-cm) coleus with leaves of rich greens and burgundies, 'Kiwi Fern' with heavily scalloped leaves in patterns of green, red, purple, and cream, and 'Max Levering', noted for chartreuse foliage flecked with red.

Stachys. The mints that comprise *Stachys* (betony) flourish in just about any soil as long as the drainage is excellent. The leaves are typically rough or hairy. Plants should be divided and replanted when the centers begin to die out, as they do after a time. Propagation is by seeds or divisions.

Stachys byzantina (lamb's ear, Plate 58) is the best-known species of the genus. It has ornamental, furry, tongue-shaped leaves and spreads by runners to form mats of woolly foliage. Lamb's ear is grown primarily for its foliage. Plants grow 12 to 15 inches (30 to 37.5 cm) tall with an 18-inch (45-cm) spread. Many gardeners remove the furry stalks of purple flowers that appear in summer, believing them to distract from the silvery foliage. Perfect drainage is the key to success with this plant. Lamb's ear may dwindle in high heat and humidity or during extended rainy spells. It is a good ground cover for sites with afternoon shade or high open shade. Among the better-known cultivars are 'Cotton Ball' (synonym 'Sheila McQueen'), a compact 12-inch (30-cm) plant with cottony flowers, 'Primrose Heron' with spring foliage of yellow-green that turns to the typical gray-green as the season moves toward summer, and 'Silver Carpet', considered the best because it spreads easily and produces no flowers.

Stachys macrantha (big betony, Plate 59) grows up to 24 inches (60 cm) in height with a width of 12 inches (30 cm). In late spring to early summer showy purple-pink flowers appear on tall spikes held above the foliage. The leaves that grow in 12-inch (30-cm) clumps or rosettes are scalloped, rough, hairy, and wrinkled. If grown in rich, moist soil with excellent drainage the plants spread and form a tall matlike growth. Big betony grows well in full sun although the flowers tend to last longer if the plant is grown in light shade or sheltered from afternoon sun. Cultivars include the white-flowered 'Alba', rich rosy pink-flowered 'Robusta', and purple-flowered 'Violacea'.

Stachys officinalis (common betony) is very similar to *S. macrantha,* the main difference being the slightly larger size.

CHAPTER 5

Weedy Mints

The best way to define a weed is as a plant growing where it is not wanted. Thus, as one saying goes, a rose in a wheat field is a weed. Sometimes weeds move in and take over space allotted to crops or ornamentals. At other times they are poisonous and therefore undesirable in living areas, as is the case with poison ivy (*Toxicodendron radicans,* Anacardiaceae). Some weeds grow in infrastructure sites where they may eventually break up the material—clover (*Trifolium,* Leguminosae) and knotweed (*Polygonum,* Polygonaceae) growing in sidewalk cracks are good examples. Sometimes gardeners just don't like a particular plant. Native and adventive plants that are too commonly seen, such as goldenrod (*Solidago,* Compositae) and creeping Charlie (*Glechoma hederacea*), have a hard time earning a place in gardens even though they may be beautiful. Whatever the reasoning behind the designation of plants as weeds, once they are so designated, a war may be declared, and the very sight of the plant in a garden may be enough to send gardeners into a frenzy of spraying and weeding.

With its overall reputation for adaptability, toughness, and ease of growing, it is not surprising that the mint family includes plants that most gardeners consider weeds. Although some people would class creeping Charlie as a garden thug, a weed to be eradicated at all costs, I find this small creeper at least as attractive as some of the ground covers gardeners buy and nurture. The small round leaves are undeniably attractive, and the vining, spreading habit of the plant is swift to cover the ground. I first got to know creeping

Charlie when it grew thickly under a large apple tree where I was living. Although grass would not grow in that spot, I marveled at the way this plant covered the ground. The children and dogs played right over it, and it was at least as attractive as the periwinkle (*Catharanthus,* Apocynaceae) and pachysandra (*Pachysandra,* Buxaceae) ground covers more usually admired by gardeners. To appreciate a ground cover of creeping Charlie, a gardener must be unprejudiced and prepared to defend the choice—for as sure as it rains in April, more conventional gardeners will remark on the "weeds" and suggest they be removed.

Henbit (*Lamium amplexicaule*) is another weedy mint that most gardeners detest. It has a more delicate texture than creeping Charlie, and I confess that I like this one too. I like its small spring flowers and small-leafed deep green foliage. I also like the way it covers shady spots with poor compacted soil.

Both creeping Charlie and henbit are good at covering the ground swiftly, and both have earned a number of common names—including a few rude and not so acceptable versions. They are considered the two most prominent weedy mints, but there are a few other species worth mentioning. Garden mints that may become weedy but that are not covered in the list below include catnip (*Nepeta cataria*), horehound (*Marrubium vulgare*), oregano (*Origanum vulgare*), peppermint (*Mentha* ×*piperita*), and spearmint (*Mentha spicata*).

Glechoma. Although the species originated in Europe and Asia, *G. hederacea* (creeping Charlie, Plate 60) has naturalized so widely and so well as to become a regular in any resource on common American weeds. It has become particularly prevalent in the northern United States and southern Canada. Plants bloom from April to June, depending on the specific climate, with small blue or violet flowers that grow in small clusters in the axils of leaves. Creeping Charlie is a perennial that spreads by both seeds and creeping stems that grow 15 to 30 inches (37.5 to 75 cm) long. The long prostrate stems root at the leaf nodes so that the plant is able to gather nutrients and moisture at many sites. In the spring there are many fairly short and erect flowering stems, yet the overall height of the plant remains at about 3 inches (7.5 cm). The bright green leaves, which are smooth to slightly hairy, have long stems and are nearly round or kidney-shaped with scalloped edges. 'Rosea' is a vigorous form with large pink flowers. 'Variegata' has green leaves with edges and zones of silver-gray and white. These attractive cultivars can sometimes be found in garden centers and nurseries.

As previously mentioned, I personally like the look of creeping Charlie (*Glechoma hederacea*). Its texture is even and the color is an attractive shade of green. The spring flowers give it an added dimension. Creeping Charlie also tolerates foot traffic fairly well. It responds well to mowing due at least in part to the fact that new plants grow from pieces of stem or stolon so that mowing increases the thickness of the low mat of growth. Creeping Charlie grows well in lawns, orchards, and disturbed places, especially if these areas are shady and have moist, rich soil. Planting it may well solve the problem of an area where nothing else will grow. To keep creeping Charlie where it is wanted, edge the chosen ground cover area with a boundary barrier of bricks or some other hard material. Keep a close eye on the growth and clip it back if it jumps the barrier. The plants are very shallow-rooted. Control and removal can be as simple as repeatedly hard raking an area where creeping Charlie is not wanted.

Lamium. The least popular member of its genus, *L. amplexicaule* (henbit) is as commonly found in references on American weeds as creeping Charlie (*Glechoma hederacea*). Especially prevalent in eastern North America and along the Pacific Coast, henbit is a winter annual or biennial with pink to purplish pink flowers spotted with red. Flowers appear from April to June, depending on the region, and sometimes in fall, growing in small tight clusters in the axils of upper leaves. The leaves are scalloped or coarsely toothed. Upper leaves clasp the stems, while lower leaves have long stems.

Henbit (*Lamium amplexicaule*) thrives in gardens, thin lawns, roadsides, and cultivated fields, especially where the soil is rich in nutrients. It reproduces by seeds, rooting stems, or stolons. The stems, mostly low to the ground or prostrate with ascending tips, take root where they touch the soil. Seeds usually germinate in the fall. The plants grow slowly throughout the winter and become extremely visible during their spring bloom season when the flowers may paint the landscape with swaths of pink and purplish pink.

Although henbit belongs to the same genus as several favorite garden ground covers, including *Lamium maculatum* 'Beacon Silver' and *L. maculatum* 'White Nancy', this is generally not a good plant for gardens. Not only is it less attractive than these other lamiums, it also dies out in hot weather. Henbit makes a pretty splash along roadsides and in fields when it blooms in the spring, but that is about its only benefit.

Since it is very shallow-rooted, henbit is easy to weed out of places where it is not wanted. Repeatedly use an iron rake to get rid of unwanted plants in problem areas. To keep henbit from taking hold in the yard, make sure that lawns are kept vigorous and thick by mowing tall and often. Mulch in garden areas to prevent henbit seeds in the soil from germinating. Those that do grow are easy to pull, especially after a rain.

Though best known for its ornamental ground covers, *Lamium maculatum* (spotted dead nettle) is also a common weed in the northern United States. It is perennial and usually found in places where the soil is rich and moist: in old gardens, along roadsides, and where the soil has been disturbed. Spotted dead nettle has decumbent stems and spring flowers that are purple to white. Leaves are scalloped, oval to cordate, and pubescent.

Lamium purpureum (red dead nettle, Plate 61) is, like henbit (*L. amplexicaule*), a winter annual or biennial. Most prevalent in the eastern United States and Canada, where it grows in the rich soil of gardens and cultivated fields, red dead nettle remains uncommon in western North America. Purple whorls of flowers appear in the spring above prostrate stems and scalloped leaves.

Prunella. Also thought of as a weedy perennial, *P. vulgaris* (selfheal) has deep blue, purple, or occasionally white flowers and grows in thick spikes that appear in late spring through summer. The stems of this plant can be erect or prostrate, usually prostrate in lawns and pastures where they are regularly mowed or grazed. The long-stemmed, pubescent to glabrous leaves are either entire or irregularly toothed and oval to oblong. Self-heal reproduces by seeds or rootstocks.

CHAPTER 6

Pests and Diseases

Most mints are rugged, adaptable, and highly resistant to pests and diseases. They are also notoriously easy to grow, which adds to their value as herbs and ornamentals. One needs only follow the requirements for soil and exposure to end up with a thriving plant. When problems do arise, however, following a general program should help solve them.

A horticultural philosophy and practice that is gaining in popularity is called, simply, Plant Health Care (PHC). The concept, first articulated in the 1980s by Roger Funk of the Davey Tree Expert Company, calls for addressing the entire garden and maintaining this overview while learning to grow healthy plants. The fact is that healthy plants have few problems with pests and diseases. It is when plants are stressed by the wrong soil structure and pH, improper nutrients, too much or too little water, extremes of heat and cold, or other environmental factors that they become more susceptible to these problems.

To practice PHC, begin by choosing plants that have proven successful in the region. Determine what they will require. See that the garden soil is of the structure required by the plants, and conduct soil tests to find what might be lacking. Regularly inspect the plants to check for cultural problems, pests, or diseases. Finally, if a problem does develop, diagnose it at home or take a sample to an expert for diagnosis. Use conservative measures to control the problem.

Integrated Pest Management (IPM) is a conservative method for pest control that originated in agriculture and has been adopted by forward-thinking gardeners. It consists of several steps. First, identify the pest and use knowledge of its biology and natural enemies to control it. Monitor pest populations through observation or traps, observing the extent of injury to plants. Establish a tolerable threshold of injury. Control unacceptable pest populations using cultural, biological, and mechanical methods. Selectively use the least toxic pesticides only as a last resort. Finally, evaluate the effects of each control strategy used.

The techniques of IPM are simple and conservative in their approach. Handpick or squash pests as soon as they are noticed, or knock insects off plants with a hard spray of cold water from the hose. Use natural predators that consume pests, parasitic insects that kill destructive pests by living on or in them, or microbial organisms that make pests sick. Choose disease- and pest-resistant varieties and rotate crops. Keep a clean and tidy garden, removing and destroying any diseased plants. Maintain healthy, fertile soil with abundant microbial life.

Increasing numbers of gardeners are learning to use conservative measures in controlling plant pests and adopting horticultural philosophies like PHC and IPM that will result in healthier plants. It is important to realize that there are more beneficial organisms in the garden than destructive ones and that using strong, lasting pesticides often kills off more of these beneficial creatures than the unwanted pests. Understanding this is a fundamental step toward safe gardening and conservative pest control.

GARDEN PESTS

The majority of plant pests are insects, which have six legs, segmented bodies, antennae, and, in the adult stage, usually wings. Insects undergo four life stages: egg, larva, pupa, and imago. While in the pupal stage insects go through extraordinary structural changes. Moths and butterflies are examples of this, but the less spectacular insects also go through miraculous bodily transformations.

Among arthropod pests are mites, which have eight legs and no wings. Mites hatch from the egg stage into miniature adults. As they grow they periodically shed their exoskeletons until they reach adult size. Another group of invertebrate plant pests are the destructive nematodes (as opposed to the beneficial nematodes mentioned later), microscopic round worms that live in the soil and feed on or around plant roots. Snails and slugs are also invertebrate pests that can ravage a garden.

Because pests generally avoid plants with strong scents and tastes, few tend to attack mints. In fact strongly aromatic mints such as the true mints and pennyroyal are often used as insect repellents. That said, mints do at times experience pest problems. Insect species belonging to the same genus often feed on the same kinds of plants and can be controlled in similar ways. This is true of the many kinds of aphids, for instance.

Aphids, mint flea beetles, mealybugs, spider mites, spittle bugs, webworms, and whiteflies can often be controlled with the simple application of a fine, hard spray of cold water. Knock them off plants regularly and most will not return. If the problem persists, however, apply insecticidal soap and/or ultrafine horticultural oil, spraying the foliage to cover the tops and bottoms of the leaves. The same remedy can be administered to rosemary (*Rosmarinus officinalis*), which often attracts mealybugs, aphids, and spider mites when grown indoors, although outdoor rosemary plants seldom experience these problems.

Scale insects are more difficult to control. If there are only a few, simply wipe them off the plants or, to kill them, swipe them with a cotton swab soaked in rubbing alcohol or vodka. In case of an epidemic of scale it may be wise to destroy the infected plants.

Pest predators can be useful for pest control. Lacewings (*Chrysopa rufilabris*), for example, are excellent predators that tend to stay where they are introduced in the garden. They prey on aphids, leafhoppers, mealybugs, plant lice, scales, spider mites, thrips, and whiteflies, some of which may infest certain mints—especially if the plants are grown under less than desirable conditions. For aphids, mealybugs, scale, and other pests, use mealybug destroyer (*Cryptolaemus montrouzieri*), an orange-headed black ladybug used in both larvae and adult form. Pests that spend a part of their lives as larvae in garden soil are vulnerable to another kind of pest predator, beneficial predator nematodes, which are proving successful in many gardens. They are easy to apply and will eat juvenile slugs, grubs, cutworms, and the larvae of other plant pests such as sod web worms, flea beetles, and others. Use Bt (*Bacillus thuringiensis*) to control the larvae of butterflies and moths that are often destructive to plant foliage. Remember, however, that beautiful butterflies and moths come from caterpillars. If a butterfly garden is the aim, learn to identify the larvae and be willing to tolerate their feeding habits.

Timing is important when using biological pest controls. Consult with an expert and follow directions carefully. The controls mentioned here are both nontoxic and effective. Other conservative controls that work include slug baits, slug traps, diatomaceous earth, sticky insect traps, neem oil, pirate bugs, spider mite predators, and whitefly predators.

Mammals such as deer, gophers, moles, rabbits, squirrels, voles, woodchucks, or even our own dogs and cats may create havoc in gardens. Unfortunately, all of these creatures can be difficult to keep out of these areas. Increasingly effective animal repellents, however, should help if used correctly. Properly constructed fences can also keep mammals out of the garden, and growing plants with strong scents and tastes can help prevent plant damage by deer, rabbits, and other nuisances.

In most cases these selective controls are more effective than strong, persistent chemical pesticides since they target the pests and not the beneficial organisms. Every year new, improved, natural, and safe controls for both weeds and animal pests appear in the marketplace. My primary pest experience has involved slugs decimating many of my garden favorites. Beneficial nematodes have thus far proven quite successful, more so than the usual slug-warfare combinations of copper barriers, slug bait, slug traps, and diatomaceous earth. I continue to use slug traps, however, as they are a good way to monitor slug populations. Whatever the pest problem, combinations of conservative pest control measures help gardeners to gain and keep the upper hand in pest control.

GARDEN DISEASES

Diseases may be fungal, bacterial, or viral, with fungal diseases by far the most common. It should be added, however, that mints are not especially prone toward contracting diseases.

Fungi cause such plant diseases as blight, blister, canker, damping off, leaf blotch, leaf curl, leaf spot, mildew, mold, root rot, rust, and smut. Diagnosis of fungal disease involves closely examining infected areas with a hand lens or microscope to look for the telltale signs of spores. It may only be possible to tell exactly which fungus is affecting a plant by researching books on plant diseases, consulting with an expert, or sending plant samples to a state university plant pathology lab.

There are a few general strategies for dealing with fungal diseases. It is helpful, for example, to begin with disease-resistant varieties. See that plants enjoy good air circulation, and avoid heavy spring fertilizer applications that are very high in nitrogen as this can cause development of lush, tender foliage. Also make sure to clean up and destroy affected leaves and other plant parts carrying the fungus.

Most mints thrive on average fertility. Mulch around the bases of plants. If the plants are susceptible to fungal diseases, water at the soil surface rather than at foliage level. In the case of particularly noxious fungal diseases such as crown rot, stem rot, damping off, or rhizome rot, the best solution may be to first remove and destroy the plant and second to remove and replace the soil within a couple of inches of the area of the plant's roots. Fungal diseases may be carried as spores through the air, through the soil, in water splashing up from the soil, and on tools.

Powdery mildew is a common fungal disease that may occur in mints such as bee balm (*Monarda didyma*), lemon balm (*Melissa offi-*

cinalis), and rosemary (*Rosmarinus officinalis*), especially when the latter is grown indoors. One of the most widespread fungal diseases, powdery mildew is easily recognized by the whitish to grayish powdery growth that usually appears on the top surfaces of leaves. Small black dots produce spores that are carried to other plants by the wind. Choosing plants known to be resistant to powdery mildew is the best defense. Apply powdered sulfur on a weekly basis to plants that are especially vulnerable.

Bacterial diseases include stem rot, root rot, leaf spot, leaf wilt, and stem canker. They may look like fungal diseases, but there will be no sign of spores or spore sacs. There may be a foul smell and plant tissue may look watery or rotten. Fortunately bacterial diseases are not common and it is rare to see these diseases affecting mints. If a plant does show signs of bacterial disease, however, remove and destroy affected foliage, stems, or other tissue. If it is heavily infected, remove and destroy the plant as cures are next to impossible and rarely practical. Prevention is the key with bacterial diseases that are carried from plant to plant by insects, splashing water, air currents, and garden tools. It is important to keep tools clean and examine plants closely on a regular basis. To clean tools, dip in a dilute solution of one part household bleach to nine parts water.

Viral diseases cannot be cured and their methods of transmission are not well understood, although it is known that they can be spread by garden tools. The often distinctive symptoms of viral diseases may include leaf curl that affects the entire plant, mottling or streaking of leaves and flowers, and stunted bushy growth over the entire plant. Since viral diseases are incurable the only solution is to remove and destroy affected plants. It is unlikely, however, that mints will contract viral diseases.

CHAPTER 7

Botany of Mints

The mint family includes about 221 genera and more than 3000 species. Its members grow over much of the earth but are especially prevalent in the Mediterranean region where they comprise a dominant portion of the landscape. Many mints are also native to the Orient and to mountains of subtropical regions. They are even occasionally found growing in arctic and alpine regions.

Many mints, such as catnip (*Nepeta cataria*) and bee balm (*Monarda didyma*), are herbaceous perennials. These plants periodically die back to the ground and resume growth from the root structure when conditions are once again right for them. Other mints, like sage (*Salvia officinalis*), may grow as woody shrubs, resuming their growth from persistent branches aboveground. Some mints are even annuals, as is the case with basil (*Ocimum*). Annuals complete their entire life cycle during a single growing season and then die.

BOTANICAL STRUCTURE

Mints share a number of physical characteristics, most of which are easy to see. The stems are typically square. The leaves, which are usually opposite but sometimes whorled, are equal in size and shape and lack stipules, which are the appendages at the base of the leaves. The edges of leaves may be smooth, toothed, scalloped, or so deeply and repeatedly divided as to appear tattered. Mints characteristically contain essential oils. The leaves, therefore, are more or less fragrant, giving off characteristic scents when crushed. They also carry the distinctive flavors of the particular species. Rosemary (*Rosmarinus officinalis*) is so loaded with essential oils that the leaves feel resinous.

The flowers of mints, which may be solitary or in clusters, may grow in the axils of leaves. This is true, for example, of horehounds (*Marrubium*). Flowers may also grow in groups, usually verticils formed by axillary pairs of cymes, or in terminal heads, whorls, spikes, or cymes. Such is the case with lavender (*Lavandula*), sage (*Salvia*), and self-heal (*Prunella*). When growing in spikes or whorls, terminal flowers may bloom first, as with obedient plants (*Physostegia*).

The individual flowers are usually perfect, meaning that each flower contains both male and female parts. The sepals of the calyx are fused, at least near the base, to form a tubular structure. Flowers are irregular in shape with corollas that are more or less two lipped. The stamens are usually four in number, two long and two short. They are either attached to the corolla in two unequal pairs or there may be only two stamens, the other pair (upper or lower) having aborted.

The petals and sepals form a tube with the stamens attached inside. The flower emerging from the tubular calyx may have a hooded appearance or be strongly lipped. Trumpetlike flowers have five, sometimes ten lobes. Use a hand lens to examine the individual flowers of bee balm (*Monarda didyma*), sage (*Salvia*), or other mints and discover the beauty of their flower structure.

The pistil has a superior four-parted, deeply lobed ovule. Four hard seedlike nutlets form, each containing a single seed. The nutlets are attached at their bases around the slender style, which appears like a stalk connecting the stigma to the ovule.

Some characteristics shared by mints are also found in unrelated plants of other families. The opposite leaves and square stem, for instance, which are considered to be strongly indicative of the mint family, may also apply to a figwort (*Scrophularia,* Scrophulariaceae) such as carpenter's square (*S. marilandica*), a North American native wildflower named for its rigidly geometrical square stem.

CLASSIFICATION

For our purposes the first important grouping of plants can be said to be the family. As demonstrated by the Lamiaceae, plants in a given family share similar characteristics. Genus is the taxonomic rank between family and species. It includes a group of one or more species that share distinctive characteristics. Species (abbreviated sp., plural spp.) is the lowest of the major taxonomic ranks, below the level of genus. Species may be divided into subspecies (subsp.), variety (var.), and form (f.). A cultivar is simply a cultivated variety. Cultivars may be selected from existing species or purposely bred by crossing varieties, species, and even genera if they are genetically compatible.

Classification of the mint family is often confusing, with experts disagreeing as to exactly which plants belong to which genera. Further, since many genera are extremely variable, meaning they are genetically inclined to develop new forms and colors, finding the right plant in a nursery or catalog is often a challenge. Some scientific names used by growers and nurseries are outdated or just plain incorrect, which is unfortunate because once an erroneous name gets into the nursery trade it tends to perpetuate itself.

It is not always easy to make sure a mint is what it seems to be. When grown from seeds mints are not always consistent. When propagated vegetatively there may be similar cultivars, and sometimes two or more are known by the same descriptive name. I have seen at least three quite different varieties grown as "lemon creeping thyme."

For these reasons, gardeners and plant collectors interested in mints need a certain degree of flexibility and tolerance as well as an awareness of the botanical pitfalls of cultivated plants. Lucky are those with botanical gardens or well-labeled public gardens where they can observe and study plants at all stages of development. For most of us the selection of one plant over another depends on its performance and physical qualities.

Knowing the botanical or scientific name of a plant rather than just its common name is the first step in searching for plants to study or grow. This is important because different plants may have identical common names, but scientific names are the same all over the world. When seeking a special variation of a species, the variety or cultivar name is also important.

The basic unit of naming is the binomial. The genus name is italicized and capitalized to make up the first part of the binomial. The species name, italicized and lower cased, is the second part of the binomial. Cultivars, if applicable, are capitalized, set in roman type, and listed within single quotes. This system originated with Carl Linnaeus, the eighteenth-century Swedish botanist who perfected the binomial scientific naming system and in doing so united biologists throughout the world. Linnaeus based his system upon the characteristics of the sexual organs of plants. Proof of his genius lies in the fact that much of his work is still considered valid.

A scientific name may also provide meaningful clues to a plant's identity and relationship to other plants. The genus name represents the race of the plants belonging to it. It may be an ancient or native name, it may be descriptive, or it may be made in honor or memory of an individual. The species name is usually more descriptive, depicting the plant or its origins, though it may also be made in honor of someone. Variety and cultivar names are selected by the plant breeder or grower.

To illustrate, *Monarda didyma* 'Cambridge Scarlet' belongs to the genus *Monarda,* named to commemorate N. Monardez, a physician in Seville. The species name *didyma,* from the Latin word for "twin," may refer to the way monarda sometimes carries double flower heads, one above the other on a single stem. 'Cambridge Scarlet' describes the origin of the cultivar and the flower color.

CHAPTER 8

Catalog of Mints

Plant breeders and other horticulturists introduce new varieties of mints every year. During this process certain older forms become rare or even disappear while others remain favorites. Some lesser-known genera and species also gain popularity to become new choice varieties. Cat's whiskers (*Orthosiphon stamineus*), as previously mentioned, is a marvelous tender perennial that has begun to appear in gardens only in very recent years, even as the genus itself is missing from some botanical and horticultural references.

Many old favorites as well as a number of lesser-known mints are worthy of consideration. I have grown many myself and have discovered that the genera of this family have much in common including cultural requirements. I have made special note of any unusual environmental requirements in earlier chapters.

The following catalog includes many of the better-known garden mints. Some 65 of the estimated 221 genera that make up the mint family consist of plants more commonly found in the wild or grown commercially and in home gardens. I have included most of these genera, though some are so obscure that references to them are rare even in the best of resources. For information on some of the rarities, I have relied on expert advice and other resources. The plants listed display the major physical characteristics of the family including the typically square stems, equal and opposite leaves, and two-lipped flowers. Other significant botanical characteristics are provided for the different genera and species when I have been able to find them. Some are obvious, others more subtle.

Each entry includes information about such topics as habit, origin, and hardiness zones. Some varieties and cultivars are treated at greater length in earlier chapters. The catalog is organized alphabetically by genera. Species are also listed alphabetically within the genera, as are the cultivars within the species.

Acinos

Acinos includes ten annuals and woody, evergreen perennials native to temperate regions of Europe and Asia, but the genus is insignificant in today's herb gardens. The plants, closely related to the calamints (*Calamintha*), are small and bushy or prostrate and spreading. Leaves are elliptical and small. The small two-lipped flowers, usually lavender marked with white, appear to whorl around the stem. Plants prefer dry, sunny places. They are not very well known, probably because they are weak in flavor and fragrance, thereby making other herbs a better choice.

Acinos alpinus (alpine calamint) is a prostrate, pubescent perennial found in the mountains of central and southern Europe. Alpine calamint grows most often in rocky, arid pastures. The small flowers are violet with white markings on the lower lip. Zone 5.

Acinos arvensis (basil thyme, mother of thyme; synonym *A. thymoides*) is a pubescent annual or short-lived perennial with small ovate leaves. It is native to the Mediterranean region, Eurasia, and northern Europe. Plants grow to 12 inches (30 cm). Whorl-like clusters of small violet flowers with white markings on the lower lips appear in summer to fall. Although old herbals recommended it as a substitute for thyme, basil thyme is only faintly aromatic and its comparatively little fragrance would make a pale imitation. Herbals also recommended the plant and its oils be used as a diuretic and stimulant for improving digestion and as a pain reliever to alleviate soreness caused by bruises and other injuries. Zone 4.

Agastache

Agastache (giant hyssop, Mexican hyssop) is comprised of twenty to thirty aromatic species native to North America and eastern Asia. Tall, robust, and coarse in texture, they have serrate leaves and flower spikes that are interrupted along the stems. Each floret has four stamens that usually extend beyond the upper lip. Grow plants of this genus in full to partial sun in ordinary but well-draining soil. They are good choices for prairie gardens. Easy to grow from seeds, they may also be propagated by dividing large clumps in the spring. The most common species is anise hyssop (*A. foeniculum*), a handsome addition to herb or mixed gardens.

Agastache barberi is a tender native of Arizona and New Mexico. 'Firebird' is the best-known cultivar. It grows about 12 inches (30 cm) in height and has spikes of bright copper-orange flowers. 'Tutti-frutti' has flowers of pinkish raspberry purple. Other cultivars display flowers of different hues. Zones 6–10.

Agastache foeniculum (anise hyssop, anise mint, fragrant giant hyssop, lavender hyssop; Plate 41) is a perennial North American native known for its anise-scented foliage as well as for its spikes of summer flowers that are often blue with lavender bracts and calyces. Plants grow to about 30 inches (75 cm) tall with oval, coarsely toothed leaves about 3 inches (7.5 cm) in length. The foliage on these erect, bushy plants is gray-green to green. The double-lobed flowers each have two pairs of protruding stamens that make them resemble the true hyssop. American Indians made medicinal teas by brewing the leaves of anise hyssop and used them to treat fevers. Zones 6–10.

Agastache rugosa (anise hyssop, Korean mint, wrinkled great hyssop) is native to eastern Asia. This plant grows 36 to 48 inches (90 to 120 cm) in height and has ovate leaves 2 to 4 inches (5 to 10 cm) long. Flower spikes grow 2 to 6 inches (5 to 15 cm) long and feature rosy violet flowers with white teeth. Zone 7–11.

Agastache rugosa (wrinkled great hyssop). From Flora of China 1998.

Ajuga

Ajuga (bugle, bugleweed) includes forty annual or perennial species native to temperate regions of Europe, Asia, Australia, and Africa. Ajugas bloom in the spring and early summer, displaying attractive flowers and foliage that may be smooth or hairy. They grow 6 inches (15 cm) or less in height and may spread up to 36 inches (90 cm). The plants spread most freely in moist, fertile, well-draining soil, although they are not good choices for the Deep South with its hot nights and often high humidity. Ajugas are tolerant of most soils, however, as long as the moisture is constant. These perennials can be grown from seeds but the results will be quite variable. Propagation is recommended by divisions or cuttings. *Ajuga genevensis, A. pyramidalis,* and *A. reptans* hybridize easily and are the species most commonly known to home gardeners.

Ajuga genevensis (blue bugle, Geneva bugleweed, upright bugle) is a hardy herbaceous perennial. It has flower spikes up to 6 inches (15 cm) long and forms clumps of handsome foliage. The leaves have comparatively long stems. Some varieties have variegated foliage. 'Pink Beauty' bears light pink flowers above lustrous green foliage. The leaf color of this cultivar is at its best when the plant is grown in a site with more sun than shade. Other cultivars include 'Alba' with white flowers, 'Robusta', which is larger than the species, 'Rosea' with pink flowers, 'Tottenham' with dense spikes of lilac-pink flowers, and 'Variegata' with leaves of mottled green and creamy white. Zones 3–9.

Ajuga genevensis (blue bugle). From Fiori et al. 1895–1904.

Ajuga pyramidalis (upright bugleweed) is well represented by its best-known cultivar, 'Metallica Crispa', noted for its crinkled metallic green leaves. The flowers of 'Metallica Crispa' are pale violet-blue, sometimes pink or white. The basal leaves are hairy and slightly toothed. It grows to a maximum of about 6 inches (15 cm) in height. Zones 3–9.

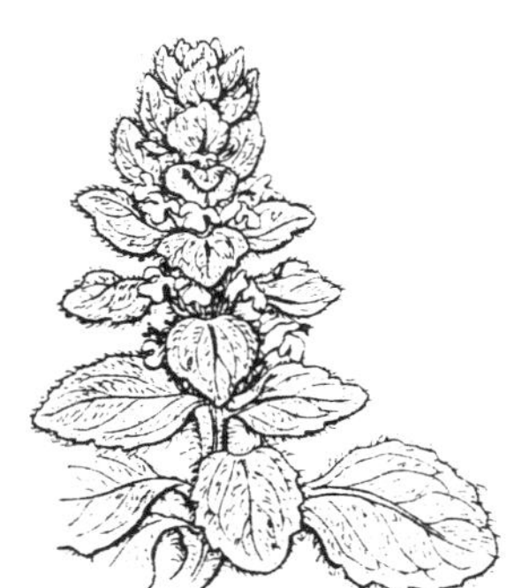

Ajuga pyramidalis (upright bugleweed). From Heukels 1909–1911.

Ajuga reptans (carpet bugleweed, common bugleweed; Plate 42) is an enthusiastic, often invasive ground cover. Unlike *A. genevensis* and *A. pyramidalis,* this is a stoloniferous species. This is a major reason why this species is such a good ground cover, although it can become weedy, spreading into lawns and gardens if not confined. Among the cultivars are 'Alba', 'Atropurpurea', 'Bronze Beauty', 'Burgundy Glow', 'Catlin's Giant', 'Gray Lady', 'Jungle Beauty', 'Multicolor' (synonym 'Tricolor'), 'Pink Elf', 'Pink Spire', 'Purple Brocade' (Plate 43), 'Purple Torch', 'Rosea', 'Silver Carpet', and 'Variegata'. Zones 3–9.

Amethysteya

Amethysteya caerulea is the single species of the genus. It is native to temperate Asia from Turkey through Japan and grows to a height of about 30 inches (75 cm). As the binomial suggests, the flowers are blue. Zone 7.

Ajuga reptans (carpet bugleweed). From Goebel and Balfour 1900–1905.

Ballota

Ballota includes some thirty-five subshrubs and perennial plants native to the Mediterranean region, Europe, and western Asia. The leaves are toothed to scalloped and the tubular flowers appear in whorl-like clusters. Zone 8.

Ballota nigra (black horehound) is the only species of horticultural significance in the genus. Common in Europe, North Africa, and western Asia, it has also naturalized in the northeastern United States where it is commonly found growing along roadsides and in waste places. The plant grows to a height of 36 inches (90 cm) or more and has somewhat hairy leaves

Ballota nigra (black horehound). From Heukels 1909–1911.

and stems. The leaves are ovate to lanceolate. Purplish to reddish purple or white flowers appear in abundance in midsummer growing in whorl-like clusters. Zones 4–9.

Blephilia

Blephilia is a North American genus of perennial herbs.

Blephilia hirsuta (hairy wood mint, wood mint) grows in moist woods from Vermont to Minnesota and south throughout much of the eastern United States. It grows from 3 to 6 feet (0.9 to 1.8 m) or more with hairy stems and summer flower heads or whorls of light purple flowers spotted with darker purple. The sharply toothed leaves are egg-shaped. Zone 3.

Calamintha

Calamintha (calamint) includes seven species of aromatic perennial herbs, most of which are native to western Europe and central Asia. Like sage, they may become woody in time. The leaves are ovate to oblong.

Calamintha grandiflora (large-flowered calamint) is native to southern Europe. This bushy plant grows to 18 inches (45 cm). Its roots are rhizomatous, thin, branched, and creeping. Pink flowers appear in summer. There is also a variegated form. Zones 4–7.

Calamintha nepeta (basil thyme, lesser calamint, mountain mint; Plate 44) is native to southern Europe and the Mediterranean region and is very aromatic. This rhizomatous plant is very bushy and grows about 8 to 30 inches (20 to 75 cm) in height with hairy gray-green foliage. The lilac to white flowers appear in summer. Zones 5–10.

Calamintha sylvatica (common calamint) has a mintlike fragrance and in summer to early autumn it bears purple flowers spotted with pink. The slightly pubescent leaves are green and may be smooth to coarsely toothed. *Calamintha sylvatica* grows up to about 24 inches (60 cm) in height. Zones 5–10.

Cedronella

Cedronella canariensis (balm of Gilead, canary balm) is the single species of the genus. This woody perennial subshrub is native to the Canary Islands. It has a cedarlike scent and, when grown for garden use, is propagated by either seeds or cuttings. Zone 9.

Clinopodium

Clinopodium includes four to ten species of aromatic perennials native to temperate Europe, eastern Asia, and the southeastern United States. Zone 7.

Clinopodium chinense is native to eastern Asia and grows to about 30 inches (75 cm). Pale rose-purple flowers appear in late summer. The abundant straight white hairs on the leaves and stems give it a silvery appearance.

Clinopodium georgianum is native to the southeastern United States. This herbaceous perennial grows to about 24 inches (60 cm) and has slightly hairy leaves. Pink flowers appear in summer.

Clinopodium vulgare (cushion calamint, dog mint, wild basil) is a 30-inch (75-cm) Eurasian native with rose-purple flowers that appear in summer to early fall.

Colebrookea

Colebrookea oppositifolia is the single species of the genus. It is a low-growing, aromatic evergreen subshrub native to western India. The leaves are covered with thick woolly hairs. Small off-white flowers grow in spikes. Zone 9.

Collinsonia

Collinsonia (horse balm, horseweed) includes about five very aromatic perennials native to eastern North America.

Clinopodium chinense. From Flora of China 1998.

Collinsonia canadensis (citronella, richweed, stoneroot) is the best-known species of the genus. It grows 12 to 48 inches (30 to 120 cm) tall and has smooth, hairless foliage. The coarsely toothed leaves smell strongly of lemon when crushed. Zones 3–9.

Colquhounia

Colquhounia is comprised of about a half dozen evergreen shrubs native to the eastern Himalayas through southwestern China. Plants have red flowers.

Colquhounia coccinea, the most commonly known species of the group, is a sprawling shrub that reaches 4 to 10 feet (1.2 to 3 m) in height. The leaves, which are covered with dense white hairs, look almost felted. Pink to scarlet flowers appear in late summer. Zones 8–9.

Conradina

The four to seven low shrubs in *Conradina* are native to the southeastern United States. The flowers may be white, pink, lavender, or purple.

Conradina canescens, a bushy shrub that grows 12 to 36 inches (30 to 90 cm) tall, is found in sandy coastal pinelands. The flowers are pale purple. Zones 5–9.

Conradina grandiflora is a shrub that grows to about 36 inches (90 cm) in height and has blue to pink flowers. Zones 5–9.

Conradina verticillata is a prostrate or low, trailing shrub with lavender flowers spotted with purple. Zone 7.

Cunila

Cunila (dittany) is a genus of fifteen aromatic perennial herbs native to North and South America. The leaves may be smooth edged or toothed and are sometimes spotted.

Cunila origanoides (American dittany, stone mint, sweet horsemint) is native to eastern North America. The plant grows 8 to 16 inches (20 to 40 cm) tall and has pink-purple to purple to white flowers. The leaves are smooth and gland-dotted. Zone 6.

Dracocephalum

Dracocephalum (dragonhead) includes forty-five species—annuals and perennials, sometimes subshrubs—mostly native to Eurasia although some are found in northern Africa and the northern United States. Plants thrive in moist, shady locations.

Dracocephalum argunense is a perennial native to northeastern Asia that grows up to 30 inches (75 cm) tall and has toothed leaves. Blue or white flowers are about 1 inch (2.5 cm) in length. Zone 7.

Dracocephalum austriacum is native to southeastern France through the Caucasus Mountains. It is a perennial herb or dwarf shrub that grows up to 24 inches (60 cm) tall. The blue-violet flowers are up to 2 inches (5 cm) in length and grow in dense spikes. Zone 4.

Dracocephalum botryoides is a prostrate evergreen with a woody base and shaggy, ovate leaves that are woolly underneath. It bears dense spikes of lavender-pink flowers in summer. Though native to the Caucasus Mountains, the plant is sometimes found in culture in the northeastern United States where it is hardy to Zone 5.

Dracocephalum calophyllum is a loosely branched perennial that grows to 20 inches (50 cm) in height. It is native to southwestern China through southeastern Tibet. The foliage is covered with short, minute hairs. Plants bear blue-violet spikes of flowers. Zone 7.

Dracocephalum moldavicum is a fragrant, branching, annual, herbaceous native of Europe, central Asia, and Siberia. This erect species grows 6 to 10 inches (15 to 25 cm) tall with sparsely hairy, lanceolate, toothed leaves. It bears whorls of white or violet flowers. The cultivar 'Album' has naturalized in central Europe and eastern North America. Zone 7.

Dracocephalum argunense.
From Flora of China 1998.

Dracocephalum nutans is a 12- to 28-inch (30- to 70-cm) biennial or perennial with rhizomatous roots and ovate, coarsely toothed leaves. It bears bright blue flowers in early summer. The species is native to eastern Russia through Siberia. Zone 3.

Dracocephalum parvifolium is native to the northeastern United States through New Mexico and Arizona. The species is 36 inches (90 cm) tall and has lanceolate, toothed leaves that are 1 to 3 inches (2.5 to 7.5 cm) long. It bears pale blue to violet flower spikes. Zone 7.

Dracocephalum peregrinum is a perennial native of central Asia that grows from prostrate stems up to 30 inches (75 cm) tall. The large-toothed leaves are lanceolate and slightly hairy. Showy flowers appear in whorls and range in color from white to red-purple, blue-purple, dark blue-gray, or rose red. Zone 7.

Dracocephalum purdomii is a small, erect perennial native to northwestern China. It grows to only 6 to 8 inches (15 to 20 cm) tall with lightly hairy leaves. The summer flowers are blue-violet with purple markings on the lower lip. Zone 7.

Dracocephalum renatii is a small perennial that grows to only 10 inches (25 cm) tall. It is covered with white hairs that give it a silvery gray appearance. Florets that appear in spikes are white with a flush of red inside the flower tube. Zone 7.

Dracocephalum rupestre is a small perennial herb native to western China. It forms dense clumps and grows up to 24 inches (60 cm) tall with ovate leaves covered with sparse hairs. A reddish calyx caps the blue-violet florets of the short dense flower spikes. Zone 5.

Dracocephalum ruyschianum is a perennial that grows erect or ascending from low stems. It reaches a height of 24 inches (60 cm) and has slightly hairy, entire, lanceolate leaves. The florets of the flower whorls are blue to violet or occasionally white to pink. Zone 3.

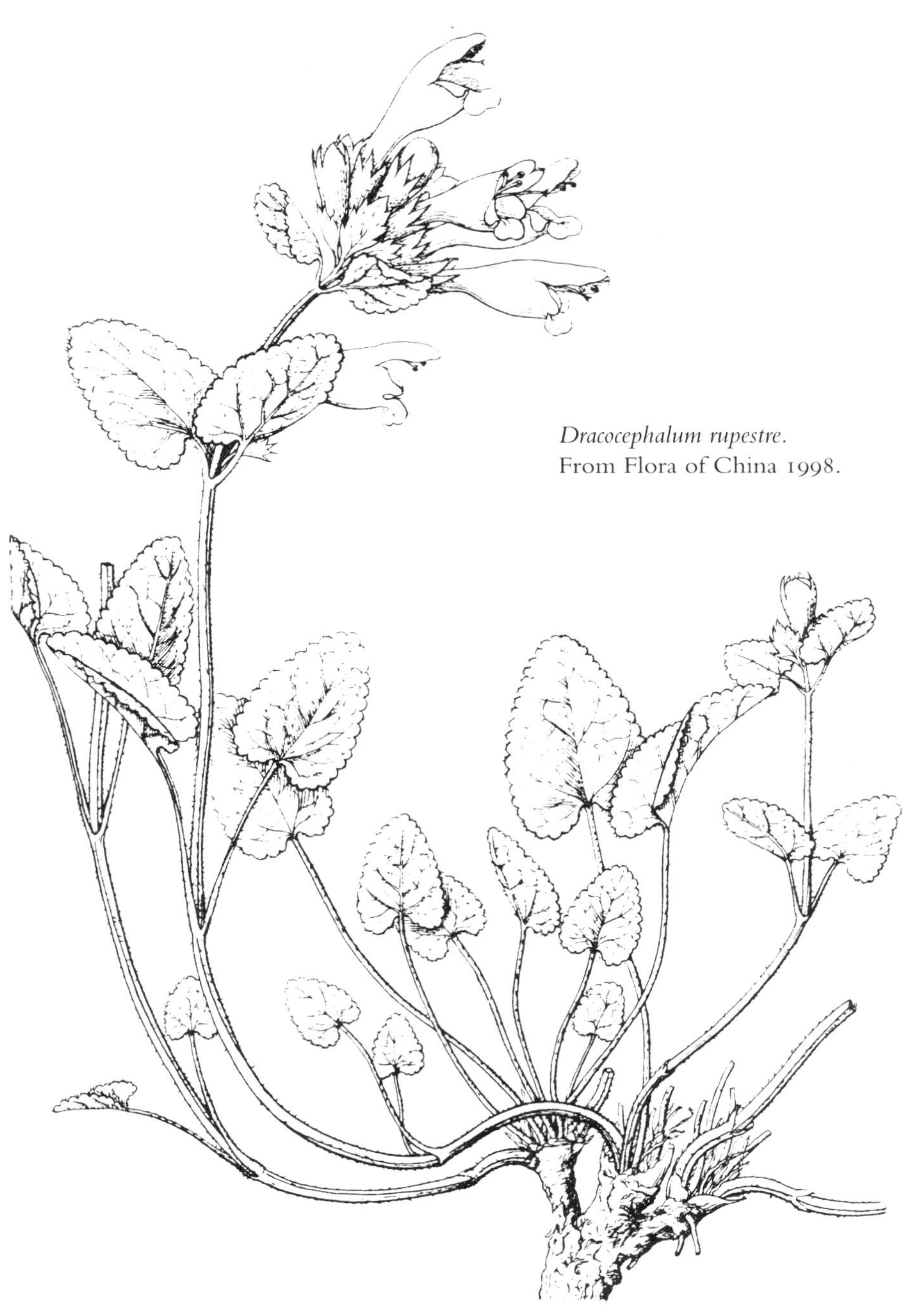

Dracocephalum rupestre.
From Flora of China 1998.

Elsholtzia

Elsholtzia includes thirty to thirty-eight annual or perennial herbs or subshrubs native to Europe, central and eastern Asia, and northeastern Africa. Most species are aromatic. The opposite leaves are toothed and the genus is noted for its attractive flowers that bloom late in the growing season.

Elsholtzia ciliata is an erect 5-foot (1.5-m) herbaceous annual native to central and eastern Asia, and naturalized in Europe and the eastern United States. The leaves, which are 2 to 4 inches (5 to 10 cm) long and 1 inch (2.5 cm) wide, are scalloped and have a light covering of soft hairs. Purple to pale rose or lilac flowers appear in late summer. Zone 5.

Elsholtzia stauntonii (mint shrub) is a subshrub native to China. It grows 3 to 5 feet (0.9 to 1.5 m) tall and has foliage covered with fine hairs. The leaves are ovate to elliptical and coarsely toothed. The species displays spikes of dark pink flowers. 'Alba' is a white-flowered cultivar. Zone 4.

Eremostachys

Depending on which authority is read, *Eremostachys* includes about sixty species or just five. These extremely variable species of tuberous perennial herbs are native to western and central Asia. Yellow flowers are borne on long spikes. Plants require well-draining sandy soils.

Eremostachys laciniata is native to the mountains of western through central Asia. It is a hairy perennial that grows more than 36 inches (90 cm) tall with fleshy roots. The toothed, pinnate leaves grow 6 to 12 inches (15 to 30 cm) in length. The yellow to creamy yellow flowers appear in early summer. Zone 8.

Eremostachys superba is a native of the western Himalayan Mountains. This plant grows to more or less 36 inches (90 cm) in height. The pinnate leaves are up to 10 inches (25 cm) long and 5.5 inches

(13.75 cm) wide. The primrose yellow flowers appear in summer. Zone 8.

Galeopsis

Galeopsis (hemp nettle) consists of about ten species of erect herbaceous annuals with dense whorls of florets. Native to temperate Europe, these weedy plants are often found in waste places and on disturbed land.

Galeopsis pubescens may grow to 20 inches (50 cm) in height. The stems are very hairy and the leaves are ovate and toothed. The flowers of this European species are of a bright pinkish red, usually with yellow blotches.

Galeopsis pubescens. From Heukels 1909–1911.

Galeopsis segetum is native to western Europe. The 12- to 18-inch (30- to 45-cm) stems are silky with soft white hairs. The leaves are ovate, coarsely toothed, and up to 2 inches (5 cm) in length. Flowers are usually pale yellow but sometimes lilac or pink with purple blotches.

Galeopsis speciosa is a large annual that grows up to 36 inches (90 cm) or more with lanceolate, toothed leaves up to 3 to 4 inches (7.5 to 10 cm) long. The yellow flowers grow in whorls, each with a large purple blotch on its lower lip.

Glechoma

Glechoma includes ten to twelve species of low, creeping, perennial herbaceous plants native to Europe and Asia. They have naturalized widely throughout North America. The stemmed leaves are almost round and the flowers appear in the axils of foliage leaves.

Glechoma hederacea (alehoof, cat's foot, creeping Charlie, field balm, gill-over-the-ground, ground ivy, runaway robin; synonym *Nepeta hederacea;* Plate 60) is a rhizomatous, creeping Eurasian native usually grown in moist soil. It is smooth to slightly hairy. The flowers may be blue or violet. 'Rosea' and 'Variegata' are attractive cultivars. Although it makes a handsome ground cover, this plant can also become a serious weed in lawns and gardens. Zones 4–9.

Hedeoma

Hedeoma is comprised of more than two dozen annual or perennial herbs native to North and South America.

Hedeoma pulegioides (American pennyroyal) grows up to 18 inches (45 cm) in height. The leaves grow on long stalks and are rounded at their bases. Very small bluish flowers appear in summer and fall growing in small clusters in the axils of leaves. This herb prefers dry open areas. Its strong scent is very much like that of *Mentha pulegum.* In fact these two plants share a similar chemistry. American pennyroyal was well known to Native Americans, who drank it as an herbal tea to sooth the digestive system. It was also prescribed for headaches, colds, menstrual cramps, and even used in abortion practices. Zone 4.

Horminum

Horminum pyrenaicum (dragon mouth) is the single species of the genus *Horminum* (dragon mouth, Pyrenean dead-nettle). This rhizomatous perennial grows to a height of about 18 inches (45 cm). The leaves, which are 1 to 3 inches (2.5 to 7.5 cm) long, are mostly in basal rosettes. Bluish white flowers are showy, with corollas more than 0.5 inch (1.25 cm) long. Among the cultivars are the white-flowered 'Album', large-flowered 'Grandiflorum', and pinkish purple-flowered 'Roseum'. Zones 6–8.

Hyssopus

Hyssopus (hyssop) consists of five to ten species of aromatic perennial herbs or subshrubs native to southern Europe and the Mediterranean region through central Asia. The genus differs from *Origanum* in not having a bearded calyx. The leaves are entire and linear to lanceolate. Plants are grown both as sweet herbs and ornamentals. Propagation is easy by seeds, divisions, or cuttings.

Hyssopus officinalis (hyssop) is an aromatic subshrub native to southern and eastern Europe that has naturalized widely in Europe and the United States. It has a persistent woody base and soft stems that die back in winter. It is an erect plant that grows to 18 to 24 inches (45 to 60 cm) tall. In its several forms hyssop ranges from hairless to very hairy and the leaves range from elliptical-linear to linear-lanceolate. The flower spikes are slender and the flowers are blue or violet, occasionally red, pink, or white. A variable species, it is available in several cultivars including the white-flowered 'Alba', the large-flowered 'Grandiflora', the rose-flowered 'Rosea', the red-flowered 'Rubra', and the compact dwarf 'Sissinghurst'. Zones 3–9.

Hyssopus officinalis (hyssop). From Heukels 1909–1911.

Lallemantia

About five species of small annual, biennial, or short-lived perennials make up *Lallemantia,* all native to southwestern and central Asia. The foliage ranges from smooth to pubescent and is gray-green in color.

Lallemantia canescens is native to southwestern Asia. This short-lived perennial grows to about 18 inches (45 cm) in height with pubescent foliage. Blue to bluish lavender flowers appear in late summer. Gardeners usually treat this plant as an annual or biennial. Zone 7.

Lallemantia iberica is native to the Caucasian Mountains but has naturalized elsewhere. It grows to 16 inches (40 cm) tall. The leaves are under 1 inch (2.5 cm) in length and are generally oval with scalloped, crenate edges. The flowers appear in late summer and are lavender to blue or occasionally white. Zone 7.

Lallemantia peltata, a native of southwestern and central Asia, grows to a height of about 20 inches (50 cm). The leaves are just under 2 inches (5 cm) in length and the flowers are usually violet but sometimes white. Zone 7.

Lallemantia royleana is a small 8-inch (20-cm) plant with pubescent leaves slightly more than 1 inch (2.5 cm) in length. It is native to southwestern Asia and China. Flowers are blue. Zone 7.

Lamium

Lamium (dead nettle) includes forty to fifty annual or perennial species, some of which are well known to gardeners both as prized garden specimens and as weeds. Plants are native to Europe, northern Africa, and Asia. They are decumbent, making good ground covers. The leaves are mostly toothed with long stems. The flower stalks appear in the axils of upper leaves.

Lamium album (archangel, dumb nettle, snow flake, white dead nettle) is a creeping perennial with stoloniferous stems 30 to 36 inches

Lallemantia royleana.
From Flora of China 1998.

(75 to 90 cm) in length. Native to Europe and Asia, this species has naturalized in eastern North America. The ovate leaves, which may be sparsely to densely hairy, grow to 3 inches (7.5 cm) in length. White summer flowers grow in verticillasters of eight to ten florets. Among the many garden cultivars are the greatly variegated 'Friday', 'Goldflake' with gold-striped green leaves, and 'Pale Peril' with young golden shoots. Zones 3–9.

Lamium amplexicaule (bee nettle, blind nettle, dead nettle, henbit) is a weedy winter annual or biennial. Growing only about 10 inches (25 cm) in height, henbit reproduces by seeds and rooting stems. Although it originated in Europe and Asia, it is also common throughout eastern North America and along the Pacific Coast, where its flowers paint pink to purplish pink swathes in the rich soils of roadsides, gardens, cultivated fields, and disturbed lands. The flowers appear in spring growing in small whorls in leaf axils. Its nearly glabrous leaves are deeply scalloped or bluntly toothed. Zones 3–9.

Lamium galeobdolon (yellow archangel; synonym *Lamiastrum galeobdolon;* Plate 45) is a vigorous, creeping perennial that spreads rapidly by means of its stoloniferous rooting habit. It grows up to 12 inches (30 cm) tall. The leaves are somewhat to very hairy, ovate to orbicular, and usually coarsely toothed. Yellow flowers flecked with brown appear from spring to summer. One of the best-known cultivars is 'Herman's Pride' with its narrow, toothed, silver-streaked leaves. This variable species is known for a number of other attractive cultivars including the prostrate, fast-growing 'Silver Angel', the silver-leafed 'Silver Carpet', and 'Variegatum', which has smaller, midgreen leaves marked with silver-white. Zones 3–9.

Lamium garganicum is a perennial that may form mats or have growth from the prostrate stems as tall as 18 inches (45 cm). The notched leaves may be ovate to deltoid and are about 2.5 by 2 inches (6.25 by 5 cm). The flowers are pink to purple, occasionally white. The best-known cultivar is 'Golden Carpet', which has pink-and-white-striped flowers and gold variegated leaves. Zones 3–9.

Lamium album (white dead nettle). From Constantin and Brehm 1894–1896.

Lamium amplexicaule (henbit). From Flora of China 1998.

Lamium maculatum (spotted dead nettle) is a perennial native to Europe and Asia that has naturalized in North America. It grows to about 12 inches (30 cm) tall. The foliage is pubescent and mottled with white or silver-white. The stoloniferous plants are ascending to trailing with ovate leaves that are toothed to scalloped. Purple to white flowers appear from spring to summer. Among the many handsome cultivars are the popular 'Beacon Silver', 'Pink Pewter', and 'White Nancy' (Plate 46). Zones 3–9.

Lamium purpureum (dead nettle, red dead nettle; Plate 61) is a winter annual or biennial that was introduced many years ago from Eurasia and has naturalized widely throughout much of eastern North America. Stems are decumbent and numerous. The whorled flowers are many and grow in the axils of upper leaves. Plants thrive in gardens, cultivated fields, and other disturbed ground, especially where the soil is moist and rich. Zones 3–9.

Lamium purpureum (red dead nettle). From Blytt and Dahl 1906.

Lavandula

One of the mint family's better-known genera, *Lavandula* (lavender) includes twenty to twenty-eight species of extremely aromatic herbs or shrubs native to the Mediterranean region through the Atlantic islands, northern Africa, western Asia, and India. The leaves are simple and entire or dentate to dissected to pinnate. Blue, lavender, purple, pink, or white flowers appear in whorled spikes on terminal growth. Plants thrive in sunny locations with well-draining soil and are subject to root rot in even slightly soggy soils. Propagation is recommended by cuttings taken in spring or fall, but lavender may also be propagated by seeds or divisions.

Lavandula angustifolia (English lavender) is a very aromatic perennial shrub native to Italy, France, northeastern Spain, and the eastern Pyrenees. It grows 24 to 36 inches (60 to 90 cm) tall or more and is tomentose. The leaves are entire and lanceolate, oblong, or linear. Flowers are usually purple. Among the many cultivars are 'Alba' with white flowers, 'Hidcote' (Plate 14) with purple flowers, 'Jean Davis' (Plate 15) with pale lavender flowers, 'Munstead' (Plate 16) with lavender-blue flowers, the dwarf form 'Nana', 'Rosea' with rose flowers, and the robust 'Vera' with lavender flowers. Zones 6–9.

Lavandula dentata (French lavender, saw-toothed lavender; Plate 17) is an aromatic perennial shrub native to North Africa and Spain. It grows 12 to 36 inches (30 to 90 cm) tall and has gray, tomentose, linear, toothed leaves. Whorled clusters include six to ten purple to powder blue flowers. With its abundance of soft white hairs, most parts of this plant appear silvery. Zones 8–9.

Lavandula multifida is a gray-green, tomentose subshrub native to the western Mediterranean region. It grows 12 to 36 inches (30 to 90 cm) tall and has blue-violet flowers. Zones 8–9.

Lavandula pinnata is a 36-inch (90-cm) silvery shrub native to the Canary Islands. Plants are densely covered with short gray hairs. The flowers are lavender to blue-purple. Zones 9–10.

Lavandula stoechas (French lavender, Spanish lavender) grows to 36 inches (90 cm) in height with flowers that are usually purple. Known both for its ornamental value and for its use in perfumery, this shrub has been developed into several cultivars including the white-flowered 'Alba' and the bright purple-flowered 'Papillon'. Zones 8–9.

Lavandula angustifolia (English lavender). From Flora of China 1998.

Leonotis

Leonotis (lion's ear) includes some thirty species of annual and perennial herbaceous plants and shrubs native to southern Africa. Leaves are usually toothed. White, yellow, orange, or scarlet flowers appear in large and showy whorls. Propagation is by seeds or cuttings taken in the spring. Plants should be pinched back to encourage branching.

Leonotis leonurus is a tender, pubescent shrub from southern Africa. It grows 6 to 7 feet (1.8 to 2.1 m) and has leaves that are ovate-lanceolate and toothed to scalloped. The leaves grow up to 3 inches (7.5 cm) long by 1.5 inches (3.75 cm) wide. Large orange-red to scarlet flowers up to 2.5 inches (6.25 cm) long appear in late fall. Zones 9–10.

Leonotis nepetifolia, which is thought to have originated in India, has naturalized in the United States. It is a pubescent annual herb that grows 1 to 5 feet (0.3 to 1.5 m) tall. Crenate, ovate leaves grow 2 to 5 inches (5 to 12.5 cm) in length. Orange-yellow to scarlet flowers appearing in winter are up to 1 inch (2.5 cm) long and showy. Zone 8.

Leonotis ocymifolia is a subshrub native to southern Africa. Growing to about 24 inches (60 cm) in height, the species is hirsute with ovate-cordate, toothed leaves up to 3 inches (7.5 cm) long. The orange flowers may be up to 1.5 inches (3.75 cm) long. Zone 9.

Leonurus

Leonurus (motherwort) includes four to nine perennial herbs native to temperate Europe and Asia. The foliage is often pubescent and the leaves are lobed or toothed, sometimes palmate in shape. Many flowers appear in verticillasters.

Leonurus cardiaca (motherwort), the best-known species of the genus, is native to Scandinavia through Italy and Greece and has naturalized in Great Britain. It grows up to 5 feet (1.5 m) in height.

The lower leaves are up to 3 inches (7.5 cm) long and palmate with three to seven deep lobes. The upper leaves are shallowly tri-lobed. Flowers appearing in summer are white to pale pink, usually with purple spots. Zone 3.

Leonurus cardiaca (motherwort). From Heukels 1909–1911.

Lepechinia

Lepechinia includes thirty-five to forty species of shrubs or perennial herbs native to the Americas from California and Hawaii to Argentina. The leaves may be toothed to nearly entire. The flowers appear singly or in groups in the leaf axils. Propagation is by seeds or cuttings. Zone 8.

Lepechinia calycina (pitcher sage) is a pubescent shrub that grows up to 48 inches (120 cm) or more and is a native of California. The ovate to oblong-lanceolate leaves grow to 3.5 inches (8.75 cm) long and may be nearly entire to serrate. The bell-shaped, single flowers are lavender to pink or white, sometimes with purplish blotches. Zone 8.

Lycopus

Lycopus is comprised of four to fourteen species of perennial, stoloniferous herbs of the North Temperate Zone and Australia. Bell-shaped flowers appear in dense whorls. Plants prefer wet sites and do well in wild flower gardens.

Lycopus americanus (water horehound) is a North American plant that grows 12 to 36 inches (30 to 90 cm) in height. Leaves are ovate-lanceolate, up to 3 inches (7.5 cm) in length, and bluntly toothed to pinnate with long, slender segments. Dense whorls of small pink flowers appear in summer. Zone 4.

Lycopus europaeus (gypsywort) is a perennial native to Europe and Asia and naturalized in North America. It grows up to 36 inches (90 cm) tall and is sparsely to densely hairy. The leaves are ovate-lanceolate, pinnately lobed, and up to 4 inches (10 cm) long. White flowers with dottings of purple on the lower lip appear in summer. Zone 5.

Lycopus europaeus (gypsywort). From Blytt and Dahl 1906.

Lycopus virginicus (bugleweed) is a tuberous, erect plant native to the eastern United States. It grows 8 to 30 inches (20 to 75 cm) or more in height and is covered with tiny, soft hairs. The ovate to elliptical leaves are coarsely toothed and grow 1 to 6 inches (2.5 to 15 cm) long. Flowers are white. Zones 5–9.

Macbridea

Macbridea includes two perennial herbaceous species native to the southeastern United States. The leaves are slightly hairy. Clusters of bell-like flowers appear in late summer.

Macbridea alba is like *M. pulchra* but with white flowers. Zone 9.

Macbridea pulchra grows to a height of 12 to 24 inches (30 to 60 cm). It is characterized by its toothed, elliptical to linear elliptical leaves and rose-purple flowers striped with white and purple. Zone 9.

Marrubium

Marrubium (horehound) is made up of thirty to forty aromatic herb species. The whitish, very woolly plants are native to the Mediterranean region, Europe, and Asia, and are naturalized in North America. The flowers are small and crowded, appearing in axillary clusters. Propagation is by seeds or divisions.

Marrubium incanum is a white, woolly species native to Italy and the western Balkans. It grows 15 to 24 inches (37.5 to 60 cm) tall and has oval leaves that are scalloped to toothed. Whitish flowers appear in late summer. Zone 7.

Marrubium leonuroides, a native of the Crimean and Caucasian regions, is a hairy plant that grows to just 18 inches (45 cm) tall with coarsely toothed leaves. Pink to lilac flowers grow in axillary clusters. Zone 6.

Marrubium vulgare (common horehound, horehound, marvel, white horehound) is a whitish hairy plant with round to oval, scalloped leaves almost 2 inches (5 cm) long. It grows 18 to 24 inches (45 to 60 cm) tall and displays small white flowers in summer. Native to waste places in Europe, northern Africa, and Asia, it has naturalized in North America. Zones 3–8.

Meehania

Meehania (Japanese dead nettle, Meehan's mint) includes about a half dozen creeping perennial herbs native to temperate eastern Asia and North America. Sparse clusters of bell-shaped, showy purplish flowers grow in short, erect spikes. These plants are easy to grow and thrive in rich mountain woods.

Marrubium vulgare (horehound). From Flora of China 1998.

Meehania fargesii. From Flora of China 1998.

Meehania cordata (creeping mint, Meehan's mint) is native to the eastern United States. It is a low, slightly hairy plant with slender stolons. It grows only 4 to 8 inches (10 to 20 cm) tall and has 1- to 2-inch (2.5- to 5-cm) scalloped leaves. Bright lavender to lilac flowers appear in clusters of three to six in early summer. This plant makes a good ground cover for shady sites. Zone 4.

Meehania fargesii is covered with fine hairs and grows 6 to 16 inches (15 to 40 cm) tall with triangular to cordate, irregularly toothed leaves. The species is native to western China. The flowers, two to six per cluster, are blue streaked with purple and have white lobes. Zone 7.

Meehania urticifolia is a hairy herb native to Japan, northeastern China, and Korea. It grows 6 to 12 inches (15 to 30 cm) tall with leaves 1 to 2 inches (2.5 to 5 cm) long. The coarsely toothed leaves are triangular to cordate. The one-sided terminal flower spikes each have three to twelve bluish purple flowers with lower lips spotted with purple. Zones 5–9.

Melissa

Melissa (balm) is made up of three deciduous, perennial herbaceous plants. Native to Mediterranean Europe through central Asia and Iran, they have naturalized in northern Europe and North America. The leaves are ovate. The bell-shaped, lipped, usually white flowers appear in clusters.

Melissa officinalis (bee balm, lemon balm, sweet balm; Plate 18) is native to southern Europe and has naturalized elsewhere in Europe and also in the eastern United States. This upright, pubescent perennial grows 12 to 30 inches (30 to 75 cm) tall. It has broad, oval leaves that grow 1 to 3 inches (2.5 to 7.5 cm) long and are scalloped to toothed and rugose in appearance. Clusters of four to twelve white to pale yellow flowers appear in summer. Variegated varieties are also available. Zones 4–9.

Melittis

Melittis melissophyllum is the single species of the genus *Melittis* (bastard balm). It is a perennial herbaceous plant native to southern Europe through the Ukraine. This erect, hairy plant grows to 20 inches (50 cm) tall with oval, scalloped leaves up to about 3 inches (7.5 cm) long or more. Each summer up to six white to pink to purple flowers appear in whorls, each with a large purple blotch on its lower lip. Zones 6–9.

Mentha

Mentha (mint) is comprised of the true mints, undoubtedly the best-known of the many species in the family Lamiaceae. The true mints include some twenty-five aromatic annuals or perennials, most of which are native to temperate regions of Eurasia and Africa. They may be erect or decumbent in their growing habit. Terminal spikes include many flowers, usually white to lavender in color. A number of the true mints are commercially cultivated for their essential oils. They remain major ingredients in household products, teas, gums, and candies. Many are grown ornamentally and for use in the kitchen. The best way to propagate true mints is by cuttings rather than by seeds. Propagation is also easy by divisions, stolons, or runners. Some true mints spread rapidly and tend to be weedy. Because the species hybridize so readily, there are as many as six hundred cultivars in existence. Experts believe all of these cultivars can be lumped in with the estimated twenty-five well-defined species.

Mentha aquatica (bergamot, orange mint, water mint; synonyms *M. hirsuta, M. ×piperita* var. *citrata*) is a

Mentha aquatica (water mint). From Heukels 1909–1911.

strong-scented native of Eurasia. It grows to 36 inches (90 cm) in height and may be nearly smooth to quite hairy. The toothed leaves are about 1 by 2 inches (2.5 by 5 cm) and ovate to ovate-lanceolate. The terminal flowers consist of two to three whorls of small purple flowers that appear in summer. Zones 6–11.

Mentha arvensis (corn mint, European corn mint, field mint; synonyms *M. austriaca, M. canadensis, M. gentilis*) is a strongly scented native of Europe and Asia that grows up to 24 inches (60 cm) tall. The toothed leaves are hairy, ovate to elliptical, and may grow to nearly 3 inches (7.5 cm) long. The lilac, pink, or sometimes white flowers grow in terminal whorls, appearing in summer. Zones 6–9.

Mentha cervina (pennyroyal) is a fairly smooth procumbent perennial native to southwestern Europe. It grows 4 to 17 inches (10 to 42.5 cm) tall and has a scent that is strongly similar to *M. pulegium*. The smooth leaves are up to 1 inch (2.5 cm) in length and may be slightly dentate. Lilac or white flowers appear in whorls. Zone 7.

Mentha longifolia (horsemint; synonyms *M. incana, M. sylvestris*) is native to Europe through western Asia and to Ethiopia through South Africa. This strong-scented, creeping perennial has stems up to 48 inches (120 cm) long. It is whitish to grayish green because of the thick hairs on the foliage. The leaves are smooth to serrate and linear-lanceolate to elliptical. Dense whorls of lilac or white flowers appear in summer. Zones 6–9.

Mentha ×*piperita* (peppermint; synonyms *M.* ×*piperita* var. *citrata, M.* ×*piperita* var. *crispa*) is a hybrid between water mint (*M. aquatica*) and spearmint (*M. spicata*). It grows 18 to 36 inches (45 to 90 cm) tall and about 24 inches (60 cm) wide and has a tendency to creep. Peppermint has somewhat elongated, pointed leaves and summer spikes of pink to lavender flowers. Because it is a hybrid, this plant does not set viable seeds. Zones 4–9.

Mentha pulegium (pennyroyal) is a strongly scented species native to western Asia, Europe, and Great Britain. It is almost smooth to

Mentha arvensis (corn mint). From Flora of China 1998.

Mentha ×piperita (peppermint). From Constantin and Brehm 1894–1896.

hairy, creeping to erect, and grows to 12 inches (30 cm) or more in height. The leaves, 0.5 to 1.5 inch (1.25 to 3.75 cm) long, are ovate to almost orbicular and may be smooth or toothed. Lilac flowers appear in summer on dense verticillasters. Zones 6–9.

Mentha requienii (Corsican mint, crème-de-menthe plant, menthella) is native to Corsica and Sardinia and has naturalized in western Europe. Smooth to partially hairy, it is a creeping herb that forms mats with its thin stems. Tiny oval to round 0.25-inch (0.6-cm) leaves may be entire or shallowly scalloped. Zones 7–9.

Mentha spicata (spearmint; Plate 12) is undoubtedly the best-known plant of the entire mint family. Although its true origin is not known, spearmint is thought to come from Europe and can be

Mentha pulegium (pennyroyal). From Constantin and Brehm 1894–1896.

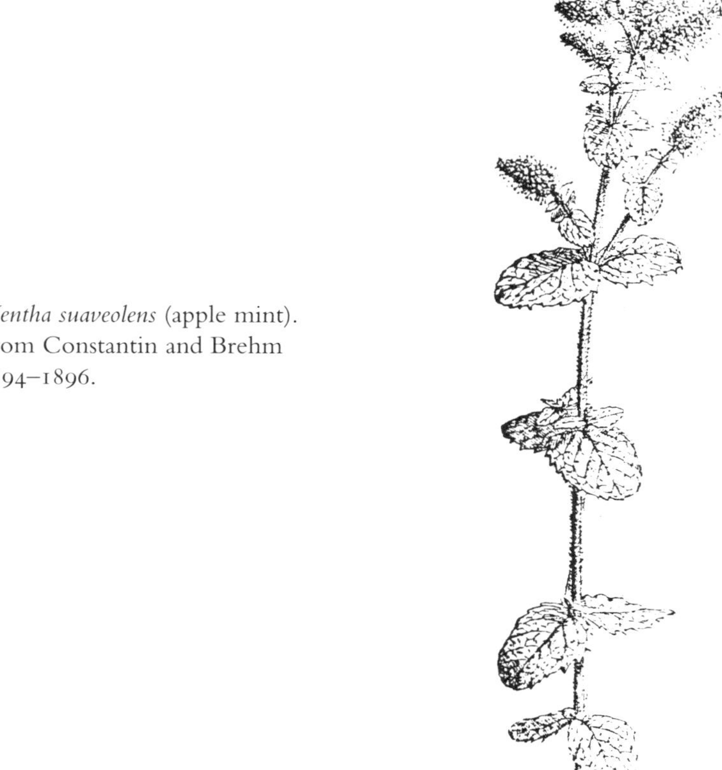

Mentha suaveolens (apple mint). From Constantin and Brehm 1894–1896.

found throughout the continent. It is a rambling perennial that may grow more than 36 inches (90 cm) in height. The toothed, lanceolate, normally smooth leaves grow up to 2 inches (5 cm) long and have a very strong characteristic scent. The summer flowers appear in cylindrical spikes up to about 2.5 inches (6.25 cm) long and may be white, pink, or violet. Zones 4–9.

Mentha suaveolens (apple mint, woolly mint; synonyms *M. insularis, M. macrostachya, M. rotundifolia*) is a sweet-scented perennial native to southern and western Europe. It grows up to 36 inches (90 cm) tall. The foliage is covered with silvery hairs and the toothed leaves are nearly oval in form. White to pink flowers appear in summer in dense whorls. The cultivar 'Variegata' (Plate 13) is known as pineapple mint. Zones 5–9.

Micromeria

Micromeria includes about seventy aromatic annual or perennial herbs or shrubs native to North America, the Mediterranean region, the Caucasian Mountains, and southwestern China. The flowers appear in whorls. These plants are easy to propagate by seeds, divisions, or cuttings.

Micromeria chamissonis (yerba buena) is a trailing perennial herb that has stems up to 24 inches (60 cm) or more in length. Solitary white or purple flowers appear in axils in spring and fall. Zone 7.

Micromeria croatica is a dense-haired native of the Balkans. It grows to only 8 inches (20 cm) tall with leaves that are ovate and entire. The purple flowers grow in whorls of up to fifteen flowers each. Zone 7.

Micromeria dalmatica is native to the Balkan Peninsula. This plant is an erect pubescent perennial that grows to a height of 20 inches (50 cm). It has slightly dentate, ovate leaves and whorls of up to sixty white or pale lilac flowers. Zone 6.

Micromeria graeca is a dwarf shrub that grows up to 15 inches (37.5 cm) tall. It is native to the Mediterranean region and central to southern Portugal. The small leaves are ovate toward the bottom of the plant and lanceolate to linear at the top. Six to eighteen purple flowers appear in loose whorls. Zone 7.

Micromeria juliana (savory) is a dwarf, pubescent shrub that grows to 12 inches (30 cm) in height. It is native to the Mediterranean region, southeastern France, and central Portugal. The leaves are ovate to linear-lanceolate and grow up to 0.5 inch (1.25 cm) long and 0.13 inch (0.3 cm) wide. Four to twenty purplish flowers grow in verticillasters. Zones 7–9.

Micromeria thymifolia is native to the Balkans, southern Italy, and Hungary. It is a smooth to very slightly hairy, shrubby perennial with a woody base. It grows to about 20 inches (50 cm) tall. The ovate to oblong leaves grow to 0.5 inch (1.25 cm) long. Up to thirty white flowers grow in whorls. Zone 6.

Moluccella

Moluccella is comprised of four tall annuals or short-lived perennials native to the Mediterranean region through northwestern India. Plants are hairless and have scalloped leaves. Axillary flower whorls have many large, bell-like flowers. Propagation is by seeds.

Moluccella laevis (bells of Ireland, lady-in-the-bath, molucca balm, shellflower) is an annual that grows about 24 inches (60 cm) tall. The leaves are ovate-triangular, up to 2 inches (5 cm) long, and deeply scalloped. White to pale lilac flowers with green, shell-like calyces appear in late summer. Zone 7.

Monarda

Monarda (bee balm, horsemint, wild bergamot) includes some of the most beautiful and most ornamental plants in the mint family. The genus is comprised of twelve to sixteen species of aromatic annuals or perennials native to North America. The leaves are simple and usually toothed. The flowers appear densely in glomerules that are either terminal and solitary or in interrupted spikes. While they are often rather coarse-looking plants, monardas make bright, handsome impressions when planted in masses in beds and borders. They have been bred and selected into a wide variety of garden plants favored by many gardeners. Propagation is easy by divisions in spring. Monardas may also be propagated by seeds or cuttings.

Monarda citriodora (lemon mint) can be found in sweet soil from Florida and South Carolina to Missouri, Texas, and Mexico. This pubescent annual or biennial grows to a height of 24 inches (60 cm) and has narrow, lanceolate to oblong leaves up to 2 inches (5 cm)

Monarda fistulosa (wild bergamot). From Flora of China 1998.

long that are very slightly serrate. Flowers appearing in spring and summer grow in headlike clusters up to 1.5 inches (3.75 cm) across and may be superimposed, one above another on the stems. The flowers are white to pink with purple spots. Zone 5.

Monarda clinopodia is a smooth to slightly hairy perennial native to eastern North America. It may grow to a height of 48 inches (120 cm). The ovate, toothed leaves grow up to 5 inches (12.5 cm) in length. The flowers are pink to white with purple spots and appear in glomerules up to more than 1 inch (2.5 cm) across. Zone 5.

Monarda didyma (bee balm, bergamot, Oswego tea; synonym *M. coccinea*) is a perennial herbaceous plant familiar to many gardeners in temperate zones. This native monarda thrives in woodsy rich soil from New England to Tennessee and Georgia. It is smooth to slightly hairy and grows up to 48 inches (120 cm) tall. The serrate leaves are ovate-acuminate and up to 4 inches (10 cm) long. Flower glomerules that appear at the top of stems grow up to 1.75 inch (4.4 cm) across. Summer flowers are red. Among the cultivars are 'Cambridge Scarlet', 'Marshall's Delight' (Plate 47), 'Scorpio', and 'Violet Queen'. Zones 4–10.

Monarda fistulosa (wild bergamot) is similar to *M. didyma* but with fewer flowers and pink-tinted bracts. Pink, lavender, or lilac flowers appear in summer. Zones 3–9.

Monarda pectinata (plains lemon monarda) is a pubescent annual that grows up to 12 inches (30 cm) tall. It is native to dry-soil country from Nebraska and Colorado to Arizona and Texas. The serrate to nearly entire leaves are slightly hairy and up to 2 inches (5 cm) long. Pink to whitish summer flowers appear in two or more superposed flower clusters up to 1 inch (2.5 cm) across. Zone 7.

Monarda punctata (dotted mint, horsemint), native to the United States, is an annual, biennial, or perennial plant usually under 36 inches (90 cm) tall. The pubescent leaves are lanceolate to oblong, up to 3.5 inches (8.75 cm) long, and serrate to almost entire. The summer flowers are yellow or white with purple spots and grow in two or more superposed, headlike verticillasters, one above the other on the flower stem. Zone 6.

Monardella

Monardella is comprised of nineteen or twenty species of aromatic annuals or perennials native to western North America. The leaves are small and either entire or serrate. Flowers are usually rose-purple and, like monardas, grow in headlike verticillasters. These are erect or creeping plants. The shorter, creeping types are good candidates for rock gardens. Propagation is by seeds or divisions.

Monardella lanceolata is an erect annual that grows to 20 inches (50 cm) tall. It is native to California, Nevada, and Arizona. Lanceolate, entire leaves are up to 1.5 inches (3.75 cm) long. Glomerules of rose-purple flowers appear in summer growing to a diameter of 1 inch (2.5 cm). Zone 9.

Monardella linoides is also native to California, Nevada, and Arizona. It is a prostrate, woody shrub and grows 12 to 15 inches (30 to 37.5 cm) tall. The foliage is pubescent and silvery. The leaves are up to 1.5 inches (3.75 cm) long, entire, and narrowly oblong to lanceolate. The flowers are white to rose to purple and bloom in summer in flower heads up to 1 inch (2.5 cm) in diameter. Zone 8.

Monardella macrantha is a rhizomatous perennial or subshrub that grows up to 12 inches (30 cm) in height. The leathery leaves of this somewhat prostrate plant are lanceolate to ovate, entire to slightly scalloped, smooth to hairy, and up to 1.5 inches (3.75 cm) in length. Summer flowers of scarlet to yellow appear in flower heads up to 1.5 inches (3.75 cm) in diameter. Zone 9.

Monardella odoratissima (mountain mint) is native to Washington through New Mexico. It is a silvery, prostrate subshrub and grows to 18 inches (45 cm) tall. The pubescent leaves are oblong-lanceolate to ovate-lanceolate and entire to slightly toothed. Rose-purple flower heads up to 2 inches (5 cm) in diameter appear in summer. Zone 8.

Monardella villosa (coyote mint) is a subshrub that grows up to 24 inches (60 cm) tall. It has a somewhat prostrate habit of growth. The orbicular to lanceolate leaves grow to 1.25 inches (3.1 cm) in length and are entire to toothed. The rose-purple flowers grow in flower heads up to 1.5 inches (3.75 cm) in diameter and appear in summer. Zone 8.

Nepeta

Nepeta (catmint) is a large genus of about 250 often aromatic species of perennial and sometimes annual plants native to Eurasia, northern Africa, and the mountains of tropical Africa. Flowers appear during summer in dense spikes or heads. Catmints may be useful as ground covers, in rock gardens, as borders, and for medicinal purposes. Propagation of these easy-to-grow plants is by seeds, divisions, or cuttings. Considerable taxonomic confusion exists regarding the exact species and varieties in the genus *Nepeta*.

Nepeta camphorata, a native of southern Greece, grows up to 18 inches (45 cm) tall. Hairy, ovate, viscid leaves grow up to 0.75 inch (1.9 cm) long and give off a camphorlike scent when crushed. Flowers appearing in terminal clusters are purple with white spots. Zone 8.

Nepeta cataria (catnip, catmint) is native to Eurasia and has naturalized widely elsewhere. It is a hairy gray-green perennial herb that grows to 36 inches (90 cm) or more in height with ovate leaves about 2 to 3 inches (5 to 7.5 cm) long. The leaves are toothed to scalloped. Spikes of white flowers spotted with pale purple appear in summer to mid fall. Zones 4–9.

Nepeta ×faassenii (catmint; synonym *N. mussinii;* Plate 48) is a garden favorite considered to be a cross between *N. racemosa* and *N. nepetella.* Some experts consider *N. racemosa* a synonym for *N. ×faassenii.* Catmint is native to the Caucasus and Iran. It grows up to 18

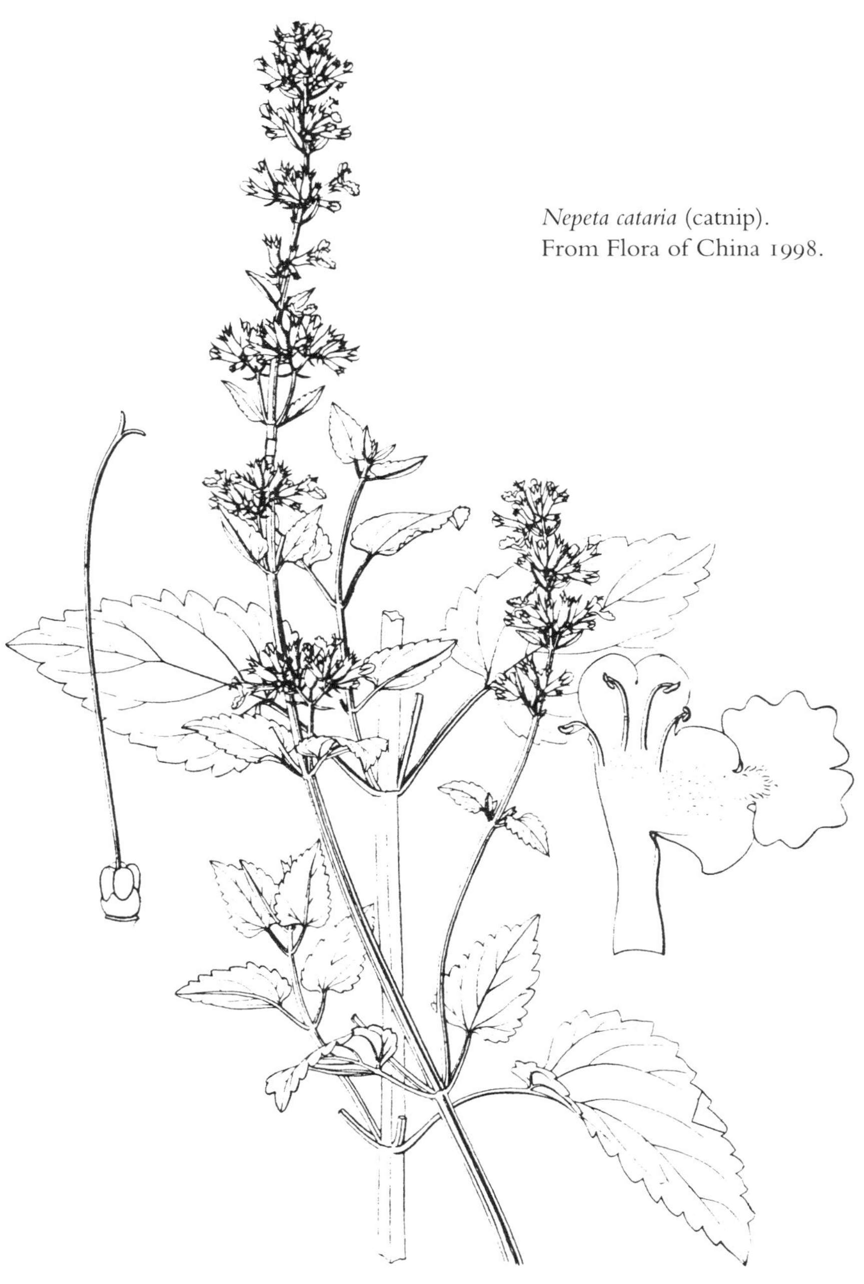

Nepeta cataria (catnip).
From Flora of China 1998.

inches (45 cm) tall and has ovate-cordate, scalloped leaves only about 1 inch (2.5 cm) in length. Lavender to blue flowers appear in loose terminal racemes. Catmint has been bred and selected into a number of handsome varieties often found in gardens, including 'Blue Wonder', 'Six Hills Giant', 'Snowflake', 'Souvenir d'André Chaudron' (synonym 'Blue Beauty'), and 'Superba'. Zones 3–8.

Nepeta grandiflora is a smooth to slightly hairy plant native to the Caucasus and naturalized in eastern Europe. It grows 18 to 36 inches (45 to 90 cm) tall and is smooth to very slightly hairy. The ovate leaves are cordate and scalloped. Spikes of blue to lavender-blue flowers appear in summer. Zones 4–8.

Nepeta melissifolia grows to a height of 8 to 15 inches (20 to 37.5 cm). It is a hairy to shaggy plant native to Greece and the southern Aegean region. The ovate leaves grow to nearly 1.5 inches (3.75 cm) long and are coarsely scalloped. The racemose flowers are blue with red dots. Zone 8.

Nepeta nepetella is a large plant that grows up to 48 inches (120 cm) tall. The species is native to the Iberian Peninsula and northern Africa. Lanceolate leaves are about 1 inch (2.5 cm) long and toothed to scalloped. Whorled spikes of flowers are white, pink, or blue. Zone 8.

Nepeta nervosa is a 24-inch (60-cm) nearly hairless plant native to Kashmir. It has narrow, lanceolate leaves up to 4 inches (10 cm) long and entire to slightly toothed. Dense cylindrical spikes of blue to yellowish flowers appear in summer. Zones 5–7.

Nepeta nuda is native to southern Europe and Asia. This nearly hairless plant grows up to 48 inches (120 cm) tall and has ovate to oblong-ovate leaves up to 2 inches (5 cm) long. Whorls or spikes of white to pale violet flowers appear in summer. Zone 6.

Nepeta racemosa is an aromatic plant native to the Caucasus and north and northwestern Iran. It grows to a height of 12 inches (30 cm) and may be erect to decumbent, nearly prostrate. Ovate leaves grow to about 1 inch (2.5 cm) in length and have prominent veins. Flowers of lilac to deep violet appear in dense verticillasters. Zone 4.

Nepeta raphanorhiza, native to the western Himalayan Mountains, is nearly hairless and grows to 18 inches (45 cm) in height. Its leaves grow to only about 0.5 inch (1.25 cm) in length. It bears purplish blue flowers in dense oval racemes. Zone 5.

Nepeta sibirica is a smooth to very slightly hairy Siberian species that grows to about 36 inches (90 cm) tall. It has lanceolate to ovate-lanceolate leaves that are toothed and grow up to 3.5 inches (8.75 cm) in length. Racemes of violet-blue flowers appear in summer. Zone 3.

Nepeta tuberosa is a tuberous plant native to the Iberian Peninsula and Sicily. It grows 30 inches (75 cm) tall and is pubescent to woolly. The ovate to ovate-lanceolate leaves grow 2 to nearly 4 inches (5 to nearly 10 cm) long. It bears simple spikes of violet to reddish purple flowers. Zone 8.

Nepeta ucranica is an erect, bushy, very slightly hairy 24-inch (60-cm) plant with crenate leaves that grow up to 1.75 inches (4.4 cm) long. It is native to Bulgaria, Romania, and Asia, and bears loose clusters, each with three to five violet-blue flowers. Zone 9.

Ocimum

Ocimum (basil) includes about thirty-five aromatic herbs or shrubs primarily native to warm-temperate or tropical regions of the Old World, especially Africa. Plants are erect with somewhat toothed leaves and bear small flowers in dense to slack terminal spikes. Easily propagated from seeds, basils are often grown for their fragrant foliage and use as sweet herbs. The harvested leaves can be used fresh or dried. Many cultivars are available to gardeners.

Ocimum americanum (hoary basil; synonyms *O. canum, O. micranthum*) is an annual to short-lived perennial native to tropical and southern Africa, China, and India. It is somewhat hairy, woody at

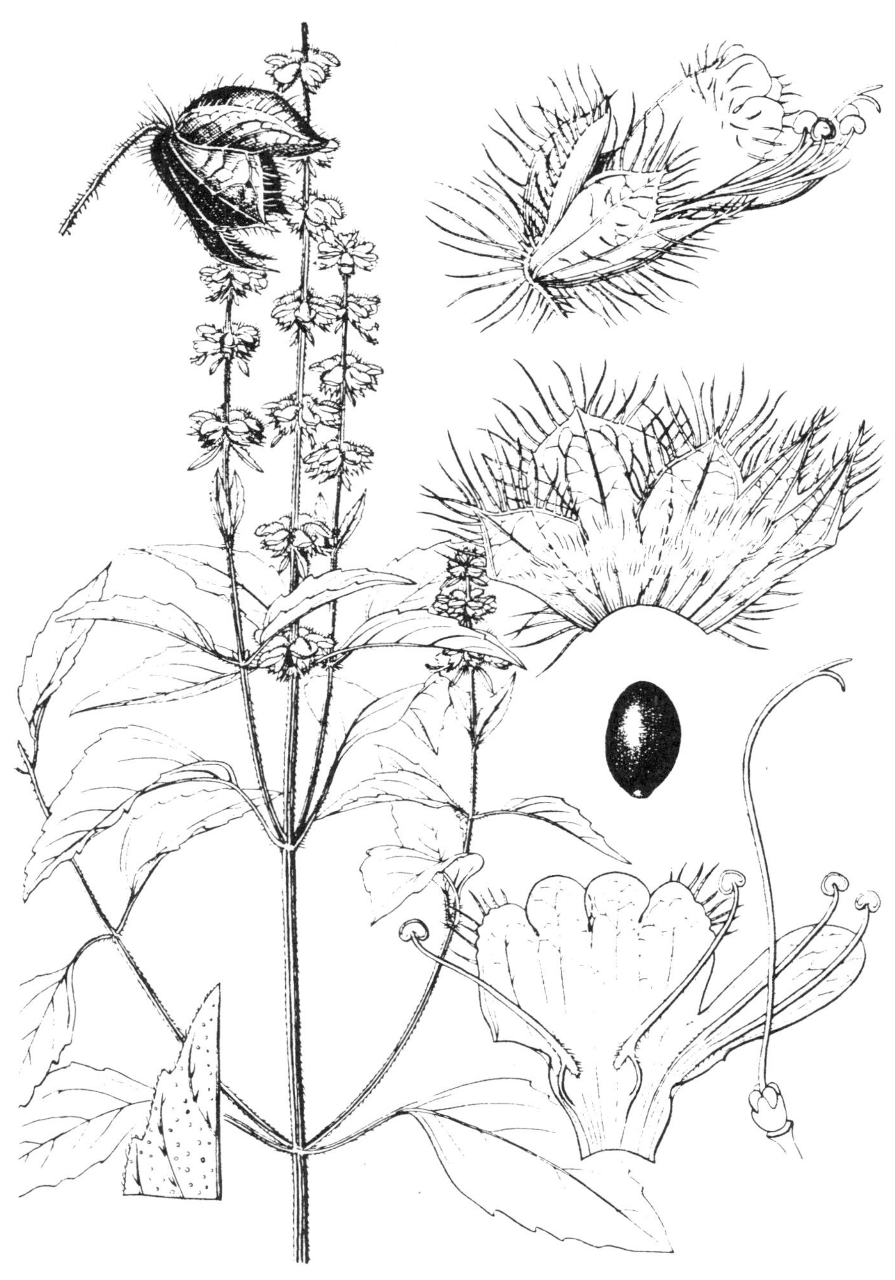

Ocimum basilicum (sweet basil). From Flora of China 1998.

its base, and grows 5 to 28 inches (12.5 to 70 cm) tall. The narrow-ovate to elliptic leaves grow up to about 3 inches (7.5 cm) or more in length and are either entire or shallowly toothed. The plant bears whorls of white to pale mauve flowers. Zone 10.

Ocimum basilicum (common basil, sweet basil) is a smooth to slightly hairy annual that grows to about 24 inches (60 cm) tall and has ovate to ovate-elliptic leaves up to 5 inches (12.5 cm) long. Summer spikes bear white, purplish, pink, or creamy yellow flowers. Among the many cultivars, which are often named for their appearance, taste, or origin, are the more popular forms 'Anise', 'Cinnamon' (Plate 20), 'Genovese', 'Purple Ruffles' (Plate 22), 'Sweet Thai', and 'True Thai' (synonym 'Siam Queen'; Plate 23). Zone 10.

Ocimum gratissimum is a shrubby perennial native to India and Africa. This herb grows 2 to 6 feet (0.6 to 1.8 m) tall and is woody at its base. It may be smooth or hairy and has leaves that are elliptical to ovate and serrate. The white to green or dull yellow flowers are borne in dense or loose racemes. Zone 10.

Ocimum tenuiflorum (holy basil; synonym *O. sanctum*) is an aromatic, somewhat woody herb that grows 18 to 24 inches (45 to 60 cm) tall with broad, elliptical, toothed leaves covered with short hairs. It bears loose clusters of pink or white flowers. Zone 10.

Origanum

Oregano and marjoram are the best-known members of *Origanum,* which includes fifteen to twenty species of aromatic subshrubs, annuals, biennials, or perennials native to dry places in the Mediterranean region from Europe to Asia. Most species belonging to the genus grow well in warm garden soils. Several are grown as potherbs. The leaves are harvested just before the plant flowers. The flowers, which may be tubular or bell-shaped, grow in whorls of spikelets that may each have a few to many flowers. Propagation is by seeds or cuttings. The perennial species may also be propagated by divisions in either spring or fall.

Origanum dictamnus (dittany of Crete, hop marjoram; Plate 24) is a whitish, woolly dwarf shrub native to the mountains of Greece and Crete. It grows to 12 inches (30 cm) tall with ovate to orbicular, prominently veined leaves up to 1 inch (2.5 cm) long. Pink to rosy purple flowers appear midsummer to fall and grow in compact spikelets arranged in loose panicles. Propagation is by cuttings taken in summer. This species grows well in containers, window boxes, and hanging baskets. Zones 8–9.

Origanum majorana (annual marjoram, knotted marjoram, sweet marjoram; synonym *Majorana hortensis*) is a smooth to slightly hairy, tender perennial that grows up to 24 inches (60 cm) in height. Native to the Mediterranean region, northern Africa, and southwestern Asia, this widely used culinary herb has naturalized widely in southern Europe. The ovate, entire leaves grow to only 1 inch (2.5 cm) in length. White, pink, or purplish flowers grow in dense terminal panicles or racemes. Zones 9–10.

Origanum ×*majoricum* (hardy marjoram, Italian oregano) grows into upright mounds 12 to 18 inches (30 to 45 cm) tall and reaches about 24 inches (60 cm) in height. The 1-inch (2.5-cm) ovate leaves are grayish green. Though it looks much like *O. majorana,* Italian oregano is a bit hardier, tolerating temperatures down to 23°F (−5°C). Zone 8.

Origanum maru (Egyptian marjoram, Syrian marjoram) is a sweet-scented, pungent herb. Though now horticulturally rare, this herb of the eastern Mediterranean region, commonly known in biblical times, grew in tough environments such as wall niches and rocky soils. The thick leaves are gray-green due to the moisture-preserving covering of thick whitish hairs. Many tiny yellowish flowers appear in spring to summer. Zone 9.

Origanum onites (Cretan oregano, Greek oregano, pot marjoram; synonym *Majorana onites*) is a tender perennial herb native to southeastern Europe, Turkey, and Syria. This hairy, shrubby plant forms mounds up to 24 inches (60 cm) tall. The oval leaves are aromatic, slightly toothed, and grow to less than 1 inch (2.5 cm) in length. Pale mauve or white flowers appear in late summer growing in clumps of spikelets. This aromatic herb is not often cultivated. Zones 8–10.

Origanum sipyleum is a subshrub that grows about 24 inches (60 cm) tall. This plant is slightly hairy at its base but smooth elsewhere. It has flexible wandlike stems and leaves that are entire, elliptical or cordate, and grow to about 1 inch (2.5 cm) in length. It bears pink flowers. Zone 8.

Origanum vulgare (oregano, organy, pot marjoram, wild marjoram) is a woody perennial herb that grows up to 30 inches (75 cm) tall and is rhizomatous and aromatic. The round to oval leaves are entire to slightly toothed, slightly hairy, and up to 1.5 inches (3.75 cm) in length. Whitish to purplish flowers appear in loose panicles or corymbs in late summer. Zones 5–9.

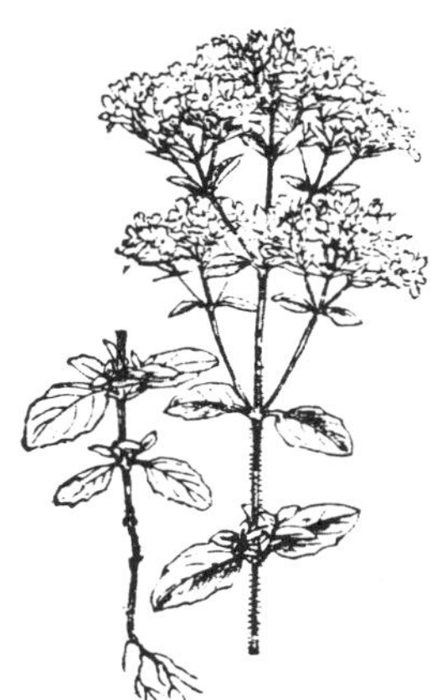

Origanum vulgare (oregano). From Blytt and Dahl 1906.

Orthosiphon

Orthosiphon is comprised of one hundred or more annual or perennial plants, sometimes subshrubs, all of which are native to the tropics from Africa to Australia. Each whorl of flowers contains two to six florets and sometimes has colored bracts at the top. The leaves are ovate and opposite although, unlike the majority of the mints, they are sometimes whorled. Leaves and stems may or may not be hairy. The significant botanical feature of this genus is that the stamens are very long, extending well beyond the corolla tube. Because of this feature, the flowers give the distinct impression of cat's whiskers, which is also the common name for the best-known species, *O. stamineus*. With the exception of this species, the group is little known in cultivation.

Orthosiphon stamineus (cat's whiskers; synonym *O. aristatus;* Plate 40) features flowers with unusually long stamens that strongly resemble a cat's whiskers. The dark green leaves and sprays of flowers are striking and attractive. Flowers are white or sometimes pale lilac or purple and about 1 inch (2.5 cm) long. This short and somewhat woody plant grows to a height of 12 to 24 inches (30 to 60 cm). Until recently this species, one of the few of the genus commonly cultivated, was known only in greenhouse cultivation. Now it is propagated by stem cuttings and grown as an annual in temperate zone gardens. Cat's whiskers are equally effective in pots or mixed borders. Remove faded flowers to encourage rebloom. To make the plants bushier and more compact, give them a pruning or two in the spring while the plants are still small. They will respond by branching. Zones 9–11.

Perilla

Perilla consists of about six species of annual plants native to southeastern Asia from India to Japan. The leaves are often colored or variegated. The flowers grow in loose or dense terminal racemes. These plants are commonly used in summer plantings for sunny to half-sunny sites and are easily propagated by seeds.

Perilla frutescens (beefsteak plant; Plate 49) is an erect, densely branched, hairy, aromatic annual that grows 24 to 36 inches (60 to 90 cm) tall. It is native to the Himalayan Mountains and eastern Asia and has leaves that are broadly ovate, toothed, and 5 inches (12.5 cm) or more in length. The leaves may be solid or variegated

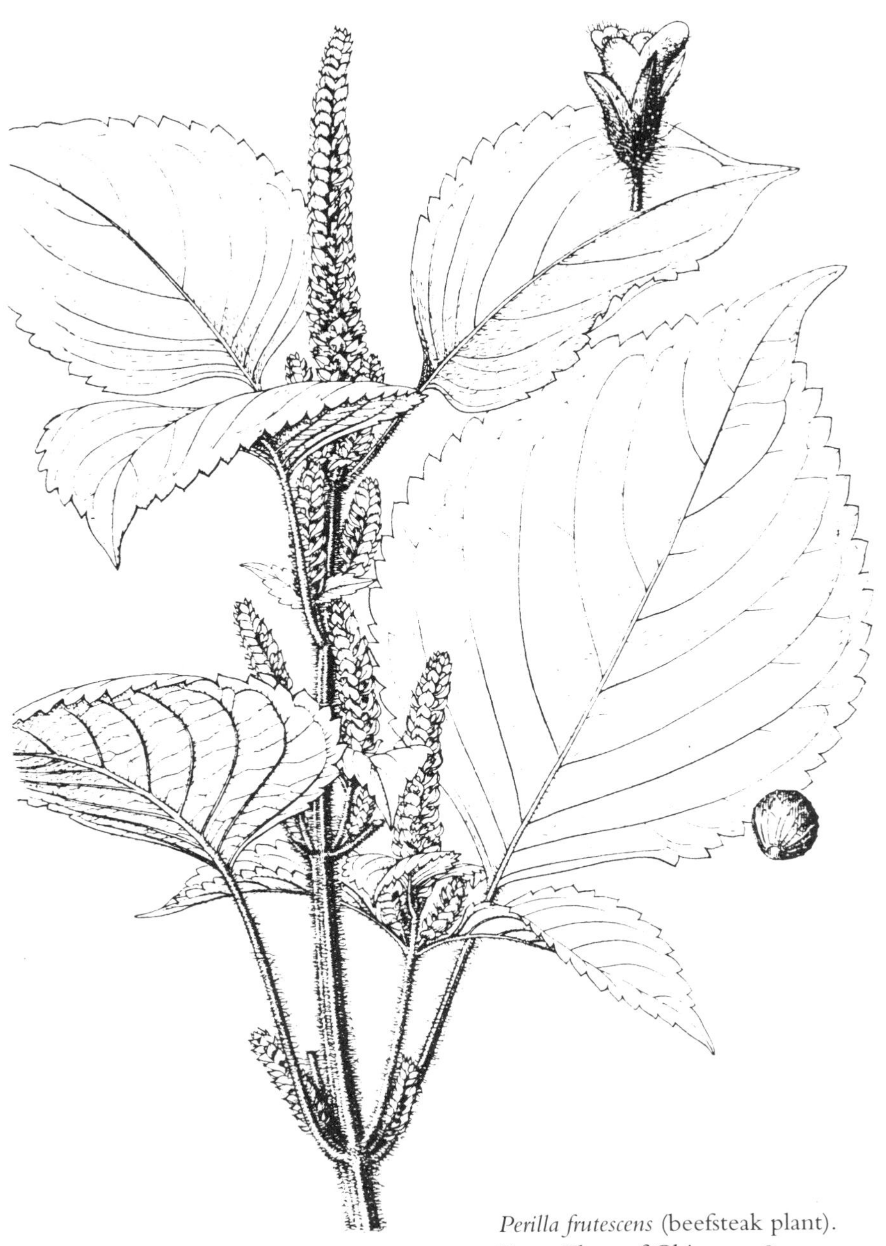

Perilla frutescens (beefsteak plant).
From Flora of China 1998.

with shades of purple, bronze, green, or pink. Leaf margins may be crisp and wrinkled or fringed. The species is cultivated in eastern Asia and Japan for its oily seeds. Zone 8.

Perovskia

Perovskia (Russian sage) includes about seven perennial subshrubs native to Asia Minor and central Asia from eastern Iran to northwestern India. The deeply toothed leaves are aromatic and so hairy as to appear gray and felted. Flower clusters grow in terminal racemes or panicles. These plants are easy to grow in average soil in full sun. They are tough, hardy, and easily propagated by seeds or under glass or mist by cuttings of young wood.

Perovskia abrotanoides (Caspian perovskia), a native of Afghanistan through the western Himalayas, grows to 36 inches (90 cm) in height and has oval to oblong, pinnately cut leaves up to 2 inches (5 cm) in length. Blue to pink flowers appear in late summer growing in narrow spikes. Zone 5.

Perovskia artemesioides is native to southeast Iran through western Pakistan. This 36-inch (90-cm) species has ovate to oblong, pinnate leaves up to 1.25 inches (3.1 cm) long. Blue-purple flowers appear in late summer. Zone 6.

Perovskia atriplicifolia (Russian sage; Plate 7) grows up to 48 inches (120 cm) tall with ovate to oblong leaves that are silver-green and scalloped to coarsely toothed. Native to Afghanistan through western Pakistan, the species has soft blue to lavender-blue flowers that grow in narrow spikes. Zones 5–9.

Phlomis

Phlomis includes about one hundred hairy to woolly herbaceous plants or subshrubs native to the Mediterranean region and Asia. The leaves are usually large. Yellow to white to purple flowers grow in long terminal spikes. These coarse-looking plants are best suited for wild gardens and the back areas of perennial borders.

Propagation is by seeds, cuttings, or divisions. *Phlomis tuberosa* can also be propagated by its tubers.

Phlomis alpina is native to the Altai Mountains and Mongolia. This 18-inch (45-cm) plant is hairy enough to appear whitish. The ovate-lanceolate leaves grow up to 8 inches (20 cm) long. Twenty to thirty purplish flowers grow in whorled spikes. Zone 8.

Phlomis cashmeriana is a robust, woolly plant that grows to 36 inches (90 cm) in height with ovate-lanceolate leaves up to 7 inches (17.5 cm) in length. Many-flowered verticillasters bear large lavender flowers, each more than 1 inch (2.5 cm) long. Zones 8–10.

Phlomis fruticosa (Jerusalem sage) is a sturdy subshrub that grows up to 48 inches (120 cm) tall. This handsome tender perennial is native to the Mediterranean region. It is tomentose and appears whitish green. As many as thirty-six bright yellow flowers grow on terminal spikes that appear in late spring and continue through summer. Zones 4–8.

Phlomis herba-venti is a pubescent perennial native to the Mediterranean region and the Balkans through southwest and central Asia. It grows up to 18 inches (45 cm) in height and has lanceolate leaves that are scalloped to toothed and up to 6 inches (15 cm) in length. Pink or purple flowers grow in whorled spikes that appear in summer. Zone 7.

Phlomis russeliana is a native of Asia Minor. This shrubby, hairy species grows to about 36 inches (90 cm) or more in height with ovate, scalloped leaves that appear gray-green because they are covered with dense hairs. The yellow flowers grow in spikes that appear in summer. Zones 5–9.

Phlomis samia is a perennial species native to north Africa and the Balkans through Greece. It grows to a height of 36 inches (90 cm) and has crenate to serrate, hairy leaves. Twelve to twenty purple flowers grow on whorled flower spikes that appear in spring to summer. Zone 7.

Phlomis tuberosa is a tall pubescent perennial that may reach a height of 6 feet (1.8 m). This plant is native to central and southeastern Europe through central Asia. The roots have small tubers, an unusual feature in the mint family. The ovate to cordate leaves are scalloped and grow to a length of about 10 inches (25 cm). Fourteen to forty summer flowers grow in flower spikes 12 inches (30 cm) or more in length. The flowers are purple or pink. Zone 6.

Physostegia

Physostegia (false dragonhead, lion's heart, obedience, obedient plant) includes twelve to fifteen species of smooth to very slightly hairy plants. The word *obedient* is applied to these rhizomatous perennials, all native to North America, because of the curious way in which the flowers stay in position when bent. The leaves are often toothed and the showy summer flowers grow in dense, erect spikes. Flowers are white, pink, purple, or red. These plants are handsome choices for wild flower gardens as well as perennial beds and borders. Propagation is easy by seeds or divisions.

Physostegia digitalis is a sturdy, tall annual native to sandy soils from eastern Texas through Louisiana and Arkansas. It grows to a height of 5 feet (1.5 m) or more and has oblong-lanceolate to elliptical leaves up to 3 inches (7.5 cm) wide and nearly entire to slightly toothed. Midsummer flowers of white to lavender, often with purple spots, grow in dense spikes. Zone 8.

Physostegia parviflora is a perennial native to Missouri through Colorado, Oregon, and British Columbia. It grows to a height of about 24 inches (60 cm) or more with elliptical to lanceolate leaves that are toothed to nearly entire and up to nearly 5 inches (12.5 cm) long. Tightly packed flowers grow in spikes that appear in mid to late summer. The flowers are reddish violet to lavender and spotted or streaked inside with purple. Zone 2.

Physostegia virginiana (obedience plant, stay-in-place; Plate 51) gets its common name from the way the flowers stay where they are bent. It is native to New Brunswick through Minnesota, Missouri, South Carolina, and southeastern Mexico. This handsome stoloniferous perennial grows 24 to 48 inches (60 to 120 cm) or more in height and has entire to sharply toothed leaves up to 5 inches (12.5 cm) long. Rose, purple, pink, or white flowers with purple spots or streaks grow in whorled spikes. A number of garden cultivars offer great returns in beauty and robustness for a small investment in care. Zones 2–9.

Plectranthus

Plectranthus (prostrate coleus, spur flower, Swedish begonia, Swedish ivy) includes 250 to 350 species of herbaceus annual and frost-tender perennial plants and shrubs native to the Old World tropics of Africa, Asia, and Australia. The leaves are often toothed and may be succulent or partially succulent. Flowers may grow in whorls or cymes. These plants may be grown indoors or in greenhouses in colder climates. Propagation is by seeds or cuttings.

Plectranthus amboinicus (country borage, French thyme, Indian mint, Mexican mint, soup mint, Spanish thyme) is an aromatic plant native to the tropics through South Africa. It grows to a height of 5 feet (1.5 m) and has decumbent, ovate leaves that are hairy and scalloped. Mauve, lilac, or white flowers grow in dense clusters. Zone 10.

Plectranthus fruticosa is a slightly hairy, erect shrub that grows up to 6 feet (1.8 m) tall with leaves that are broad, coarsely toothed, and up to 4 inches (10 cm) long. The blue to pale blue, mauve, blue-mauve, or pink flowers grow in whorled clusters. Zone 10.

Plectranthus madagascariensis is a native of southern Africa and Madagascar that grows up to about 36 inches (90 cm) in height. It is a decumbent to procumbent shrub that may be more or less hairy. The leaves are up to about 1.75 inches (4.4 cm) long and somewhat succulent. Six to sixteen flowers grow in whorled spikes. The flowers may be white, mauve, or purple and are often spotted with red glands. Zone 10.

Plectranthus oertendahlii (Brazilian coleus, candle plant, prostrate coleus) is a pubescent, decumbent perennial that grows up to about 36 inches (90 cm) in height. The semisucculent, pubescent leaves are ovate, scalloped to toothed, whitish on top, and purplish underneath. Whitish, mauve, or lavender flowers grow in whorls. These plants are good prospects for hanging baskets. Zone 10.

Plectranthus thyrsoideus (flowering bush coleus) is a shrubby perennial native to central Africa that grows to about 36 inches (90 cm) tall. Leaves are up to 3 inches (7.5 cm) long and crenately toothed. Blue to indigo flowers grow on long-stemmed whorls. Zone 10.

Plectranthus verticillatus is a procumbent perennial native to southeastern Africa. This smooth to slightly hairy plant grows more than 36 inches (90 cm) in height. The ovate to round leaves are succulent and crenate-dentate. White to mauve flowers spotted with purple grow in small, flat clusters on whorled spikes. Zone 10.

Pogostemon

Pogostemon consists of more than five dozen species of subshrubs and shrubs native to India and Malayasia. The plants are aromatic and hairy with ovate to triangular leaves.

Pogostemon cablin (patchouli) is an aromatic, hairy herb that grows up to 36 inches (90 cm) in height with ovate to triangular leaves up to 5 inches (12.5 cm) in length. White flowers are marked with violet and have violet filaments. The flowers grow both in terminal spikes and as spikes in leaf axils. Zone 10.

Prostanthera

Prostanthera (Australian mint bush, mintbush) includes fifty species of very aromatic evergreen shrubs to small trees native to southeastern Australia and Tasmania. Leaves are simple, and solitary flowers grow in axils or in terminal clusters.

Prostanthera lasianthos (Victoria dogwood, Victorian Christmas bush) is a shrub to small tree native to southeastern Australia and Tasmania. It grows up to 20 feet (6 m) tall with toothed, lanceolate leaves up to 3.5 inches (8.75 cm) long. Summer flowers growing in panicles are cream or white, sometimes pale blue, lavender, or pink and have throats that are tinged or spotted with yellow or brown. Zone 9.

Prostanthera melissifolia (balm mint bush) is a very aromatic, slender bush from southeastern Australia. It grows up to 6 feet (1.8 m) or more in height. The oval to elliptical leaves are 1 inch (2.5 cm) in length and toothed. Flowers of pink, mauve, or purple grow in terminal whorls. Zone 9.

Prostanthera nivea (snowy mint) is a shrub that grows 3 to 6 feet (0.9 to 1.8 m) in height with 1.5-inch (3.75-cm) leaves that are quite linear and revolute. Flowers are usually white, sometimes tinted blue, and grow singly in the axils of upper leaves. Snowy mint is grown outdoors in warm climates and indoors in cold climates. Zone 9.

Prostanthera rotundifolia (mint bush, round-leaf mint) is a large shrub native to southern and southeastern Australia and Tasmania. It grows up to 12 feet (3.6 m) tall. The circular to oval leaves are slightly toothed or scalloped and only a bit more than 0.25 inch (0.6 cm) long and wide. Lilac flowers grow in short, loose clusters in spring. Zones 9–10.

Prostanthera sieberi is a spreading to erect, aromatic 6-foot (1.8-m) shrub native to New South Wales in southeastern Australia. The dentate 1-inch (2.5-cm) leaves are oblong to oval. Rose-violet to mauve to violet spring flowers grow in short, loose clusters. Zone 9.

Prunella

Prunella (heal-all, self-heal) includes about seven perennial herbs native to Asia, Europe, northern Africa, and North America. These spreading plants grow decumbently at first, then ascendingly. Dense terminal verticillasters each bear about a half dozen flowers. Prop-

Prunella vulgaris (self-heal). From Flora of China 1998.

agation is by seeds or divisions. Although they may tend to be weedy, these herbs can be useful garden plants in somewhat shady rock gardens or borders.

Prunella grandiflora is a slightly hairy European native that grows to a height of 24 inches (60 cm). The 4-inch (10-cm) leaves are oval to ovate-lanceolate and either entire or scalloped. Whitish flowers with violet lips are up to 1 inch (2.5 cm) or more in length and grow in spikes. Zones 5–7.

Prunella lancineata is a densely pubescent plant from southwestern to central Europe. It grows to 12 inches (30 cm) tall with lobed or pinnatifid leaves more than 2 inches (5 cm) long. The summer flowers grow in spikes and are yellowish white, sometimes pinkish or purplish. Zone 6.

Prunella vulgaris (heal-all, self-heal) is a smooth to slightly hairy, decumbent or creeping plant with stems up to 20 inches (50 cm) in length and oval leaves that may be entire or slightly scalloped. It is native to Europe and North America. Deep blue, purple, or sometimes white summer flowers grow in spikes. Zones 4–9.

Pycnanthemum

About twenty-one mint-scented perennial species native to eastern North America and California belong to *Pycnanthemum* (American mountain mint, mountain mint). The leaves may be entire or dentate. Flowers appearing in summer or fall grow in cymes and may be white or pink, often dotted with purple. Plants are easily propagated by seeds, divisions, or cuttings.

Pycnanthemum flexuosum is native to the eastern United States and grows to a height of 24 to 36 inches (60 to 90 cm) or more. Leaves are linear, entire, and 1 to 2 inches (2.5 to 5 cm) long. The flowers are white to pinkish. Zones 3–7.

Pycnanthemum muticum is a hairy herb from the eastern United States. Plants grow 28 to 40 inches (70 to 100 cm) with leaves that are usually serrate and narrowly oval to ovate-lanceolate. Small pinkish flowers grow in dense, roundish cymes in late summer to fall. Zones 3–7.

Pycnanthemum pilosum, another native of the eastern United States, is an upright perennial that grows up to 5 feet (1.5 m) in height. Leaves are nearly 3 inches (7.5 cm) long and either entire or shallowly toothed. Flowers are pink. Zones 3–7.

Pycnanthemum virginianum (prairie hyssop, Virginia mint, wild basil) is an upright perennial very much like *P. muticum* only with more branching. It grows up to 36 inches (90 cm) tall and displays lilac to white flowers in late summer to fall. Zones 5–10.

Pycnostachys

Pycnostachys consists of thirty-five to forty erect tropical perennials native to southern Africa and Madagascar. The leaves are pubescent and often toothed. Flowers grow in dense terminal spikes. These tender plants should be grown under glass or, in the Deep South, outdoors. Propagation is by seeds or cuttings.

Pycnostachys dawii is a stout plant that grows 4 to 6 feet (1.2 to 1.8 m) tall with toothed, lanceolate to linear-lanceolate leaves 5 to 12 inches (12.5 to 30 cm) long. It is native to tropical central Africa. Cobalt blue flowers up to 1 inch (2.5 cm) long appear in summer and grow in dense 5-inch (12.5-cm) spikes. Zone 9.

Pycnostachys stuhlmannii is a 48-inch (120-cm) native of Rhodesia. The minutely serrate leaves are 4 to 7 inches (10 to 17.5 cm) long and give off a skunky odor when crushed. Blue flowers grow in small, short spikes. Zone 9.

Pycnostachys urticifolia is native to tropical and southern Africa. The species grows 5 to 7 feet (1.5 to 2.1 m) tall with oval, densely hairy, deeply toothed leaves up to 4 inches (10 cm) long. Bright blue or occasionally white-tinted blue flowers grow in 3-inch (7.5-cm) spikes. Zone 9.

Rosmarinus

Rosmarinus includes two to three aromatic, tender, shrubby, evergreen plants native to southern Europe and northern Africa. Linear leaves may be entire or toothed. Pale blue, lavender, or occasionally pink or white flowers grow in whorled spikes. Rosemary plants are about as hardy as lavenders. Propagation is recommended by cuttings.

Rosmarinus officinalis (rosemary) is native to the Mediterranean region and prefers a mild climate. It generally grows to about 24 inches (60 cm) tall, although in ideal conditions it can reach up to 6 feet (1.8 m). Plants may be erect or procumbent and have leathery, linear leaves about 1 inch (2.5 cm) in length. Among the many cultivars are 'Arp', 'Aureus', 'McConnell's Blue', 'Pinkie', 'Roseus', and 'Sissinghurst Blue'. Zones 8–10.

Rosmarinus officinalis (rosemary). From Flora of China 1998.

Salazaria

Salazaria mexicana (bladder sage) is the single species of the genus. As its name suggests, this plant is native to Mexico. It is a broad, densely branched, spreading species with spine-tipped branchlets. Plants grow to a height of 36 inches (90 cm) and bear violet flowers in whorled spikes from winter to spring. Zone 9.

Salvia

Salvia (sage) is an enormous genus, consisting of 750 to 900 annual, perennial, or biennial herbs, subshrubs, and shrubs as well as many cultivars and hybrids. Native throughout much of the world, these handsome plants commonly grow in dry, stony sites. The leaves are entire and simple to pinnate to deeply pinnate. Flowers grow in terminal or axillary spikes that may have few or many flowers. Salvias are widely cultivated both as ornamentals and herbs. They grow most easily from stem cuttings but may also be grown from seeds, root cuttings, or by ground layering (pinning long branches to the soil until they form roots).

Salvia aethiopis (African sage) is a perennial or biennial herb native to central and southern Europe through western Asia. It grows to a height of 24 inches (60 cm) and has oval or elliptical to oblong leaves about 8 inches (20 cm) long. Whorls of white flowers, sometimes with yellow lips, grow in branched candelabralike forms. Zones 7–9.

Salvia apiana (California white sage, greasewood, bee sage), native to California, is a large subshrub that grows up to 10 feet (3 m) tall and has whitish, hairy leaves up to 3 to 4 inches (7.5 to 10 cm) long. White to pale lavender flowers grow in erect, much-branched whorls. Zones 8–10.

Salvia argentea (silver sage) is native to northern Africa and southern Europe through eastern Bulgaria. This erect, heavily branched shrub grows 24 to 48 inches (60 to 120 cm) tall. The leaves grow to

6 inches (15 cm) in length and are toothed to irregularly lobed and woolly when young. White flowers tinged with yellow or pink and often flecked with pink to violet appear in spring to summer growing in verticillasters of four to eight flowers each. Zones 6–8.

Salvia azurea (azure sage, blue sage, pitcher's salvia, prairie sage) is an erect perennial herb that grows up to 5 feet (1.5 m) tall with lower leaves that are lanceolate to oblong, toothed, and up to 3 inches (7.5 cm) in length. Upper leaves are more narrow. Blue sage is native to Minnesota and Nebraska through Arkansas and Texas and has naturalized in the eastern United States. Blue or occasionally white flowers appear in spikes from summer to fall. *Salvia azurea* var. *grandiflorum* (synonym *S. pitcheri*) is a popular form. Zones 5–9.

Salvia barrelieri (Spanish sage) is an erect 36-inch (90-cm) biennial or perennial native to southwestern Spain and northwestern Africa. The oval leaves are toothed to broadly lobed to pinnate. Loose whorls each contain four to six bluish violet flowers with white lower lips. Flowers bloom in summer. Zone 8.

Salvia bracteata is a well-branched subshrub native to the Middle East and Asia Minor. The species is very slightly hairy, has ovate to oblong leaves that are pinnatifid, and grows to a height of about 24 inches (60 cm). Purplish to pink flowers grow in whorled spikes. Zone 9.

Salvia brandegei is a well-branched Californian shrub that grows up to 36 inches (90 cm) or more. The pubescent linear-oblong leaves grow to a length of 2 inches (5 cm) or so. Lavender flowers grow in interrupted spikes. Zone 9.

Salvia broussonetii is a bushy 36-inch (90-cm) perennial herb to subshrub native to the Canary Islands. It has broad, oval leaves that grow 6 inches (15 cm) long and are scalloped, quite smooth on top, and whitely woolly underneath. White to pink flowers grow in panicles that appear from winter to summer. Zone 9.

Salvia canariensis is also native to the Canary Islands. This 3- to 6-foot (0.9- to 1.8-m) woolly shrub has lanceolate leaves. Racemes or panicles of purple to white flowers appear in winter to spring. Zone 9.

Salvia carduacea (thistle sage) is a thistlelike, hairy annual or perennial native to California. It grows up to 24 inches (60 cm) tall. Its oblong 3- to 6-inch (7.5- to 15-cm) leaves are toothed and spiny. Summer flowers of lavender grow in dense verticillasters. Zone 8.

Salvia clevelandii (blue sage, Cleveland sage, Jim sage) is an aromatic and hairy gray-green 36-inch (90-cm) shrub. It is a native of southern and Baja California. The oblong, elliptical leaves are scalloped and up to about 1.25 inches (3.1 cm) in length. Lilac, blue, or white 0.75-inch (1.9-cm) flowers grow in interrupted spikes up to 12 inches (30 cm) long. Zones 9–10.

Salvia coccinea (tropical sage; Plate 52) is an annual or perennial herb or subshrub. It varies in height from 24 to 48 inches (60 to 120 cm) and, being well-branched, spreads to a width of 30 inches (75 cm) or more. It is native to South Carolina through Florida, Texas, Mexico, and tropical South America. Oval to triangular, scalloped, crenate leaves grow 1 to 2 inches (2.5 to 5 cm) long. Flowers appear in summer on whorled spikes and are typically scarlet but may also be white, pink, salmon, orange, and bicolors. Zones 8–10.

Salvia columbariae (chia) is an annual or perennial herb native to the southwestern United States and Baja California. It grows 21 to 24 inches (52.5 to 60 cm) tall with pubescent to woolly, pinnate leaves up to 4 inches (10 cm) long. Blue flower heads appear in summer. Zone 7.

Salvia costaricensis is a 12- to 24-inch (30- to 60-cm) erect or ascending herb, probably perennial, native to Costa Rica. Leaves are broad and triangular, notched to toothed to scalloped, and grow up to 6 inches (15 cm) long. Lavender-blue to dark blue flower clusters grow in spikes or verticillasters. Zone 10.

Salvia divinorum is a semitropical perennial plant native to Mexico that can grow up to 48 inches (120 cm) or more in height under warm, humid conditions. Its emerald green leaves are large, up to 8 inches (20 cm) or more in length. The flowers are nondescript and off-white. Propagation is by cuttings.

Salvia dorisiana (fruit-scented sage, peach sage) is a shrubby perennial native to Honduras that grows 36 to 48 inches (90 to 120 cm) tall. The ovate leaves are thin and papery, toothed, lightly covered with hairs, and grow up to 7 inches (17.5 cm) long by 4 inches (10 cm) wide. Rose-pink to magenta flowers up to 2 inches (5 cm) long appear on 6-inch (15-cm) spikes in winter. Zones 10–11.

Salvia dorrii (desert sage, gray ball sage, purple sage) is a bushy, low 36-inch (90-cm) shrub native to the west coast of the United States. The pubescent, linear leaves are entire and about 0.5 inch (1.25 cm) in length. Pink to blue to violet flowers grow in dense or interrupted spikes. Zone 5.

Salvia elegans (pineapple sage, pineapple-scented sage; synonym *S. rutilans;* Plate 25) is a perennial or subshrub from Mexico that grows up to 48 inches (120 cm) tall. The ovate leaves are bright green, pointed, serrate, hairy, and about 3 inches (7.5 cm) long by 2 inches (5 cm) wide. Six to eight scarlet flowers appear on 8-inch (20-cm) spikes from late summer until frost. Zones 9–10.

Salvia eremostachya is a California native found in desert areas. This bushy shrub grows 24 to 36 inches (60 to 90 cm) tall and has lanceolate to oblong leaves that are hairy and about 1 inch (2.5 cm) in length. Pink, blue, or purple flowers grow on interrupted spikes. Zone 8.

Salvia farinacea (mealycup sage, mealy sage) is an erect, pubescent perennial herb that grows to a height of about 36 inches (90 cm) with a width of 24 inches (60 cm). This native of New Mexico and Texas has ovate to ovate-lanceolate leaves 1.5 to 3 inches (3.75 to 7.5 cm) long that are undulate to coarsely, irregularly serrate. Blue to blue-violet to white flowers appear in summer to fall on interrupted spikes. Good cultivars include 'Argent' and 'Cirrus' (Plate 53), both with white flowers, 'Blue Bedder', 'Victoria' (Plate 54), and 'Victoria Blue'. Zones 8–10.

Salvia fruticosa is native to the Canary Islands and northern Africa through the Middle East. This 36-inch (90-cm) shrub is whitish and tomentose with leaves that are simple, ovate to lanceolate, and up to 2 inches (5 cm) long. Spring to summer flowers of pink, mauve, lilac, or occasionally white grow in terminal spikes. Zones 8–9.

Salvia glutinosa (Jupiter's staff) is an erect 36-inch (90-cm) perennial herb native to Europe through western Asia. The oval to oblong leaves are simple, toothed to scalloped, and pubescent. Yellow flowers flecked with reddish brown appear in summer on terminal spikes. Zone 5.

Salvia greggii (autumn sage, Texas sage) is a perennial herb or subshrub native to the high-altitude regions of Texas and Mexico. It grows from 12 to 36 inches (30 to 90 cm) tall, less in width. Oblong to oval to elliptical leaves are up to 1 inch (2.5 cm) long, entire, and leathery. Showy flowers are mostly crimson but may also be white, yellow, peach, pink, lavender, or rose and grow in whorled spikes that appear in early summer to fall. Zones 7–10.

Salvia guaranitica is a perennial to subshrub often grown as an annual and native to South America from southeastern Brazil to eastern Paraguay and northern Argentina. It grows to a height of 5 feet (1.5 m). The oval leaves are 2 to 5 inches (5 to 12.5 cm) long, coarsely scalloped, and lightly covered with hairs. Dark blue to violet or occasionally bluish rose flowers up to 2 inches (5 cm) long grow in verticillasters. Zones 7–10.

Salvia hispanica is a 24-inch (60-cm) annual native to Mexico through Peru and naturalized in the West Indies. The 2- to 3-inch (5- to 7.5-cm) oval leaves are smooth with notched edges. Pale blue summer flowers grow densely in 2- to 4-inch (5- to 10-cm) racemes. Zone 9.

Salvia interrupta is a bushy 48-inch (120-cm) subshrub native to Morocco. The species is woolly and has broad, oval, pinnate leaves 6 to 10 inches (15 to 25 cm) long. The 1.5-inch (3.75-cm) spring to summer flowers are dark violet-purple to blue, flecked with pink, and have white throats. The flowers grow 2 to 3 inches (5 to 7.5 cm) apart in long verticillasters up to 24 inches (60 cm) long. Zones 8–10.

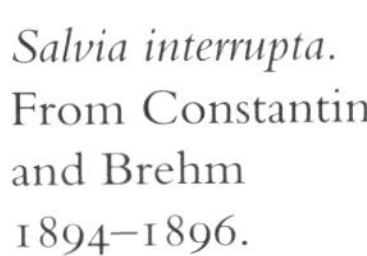

Salvia interrupta. From Constantin and Brehm 1894–1896.

Salvia involucrata (rosy leaf sage) is an erect, perennial native of Mexico and Central America. It grows to 48 inches (120 cm) with 4-inch (10-cm) ovate leaves that are entire to crenate and smooth to very slightly hairy. Flowers appearing late summer to autumn are red, rose, or pink, up to 2 inches (5 cm) long, and grow in dense spikes. Zones 8–10.

Salvia judaica (Judean sage) is an erect, bushy perennial 3.5 feet (1 m) in height and native to Palestine, Lebanon, and Israel. It has puckered leaves that are oblong-ovate and scalloped to irregularly toothed. Flower spikes are branched and bear maroon to violet flowers. Zone 9.

Salvia leucantha (Mexican bush sage) is a woolly, white 24-inch (60-cm) herb to subshrub. The linear, lanceolate, scalloped leaves of this Mexican native are 2 to 6 inches (5 to 15 cm) long. Winter flowers are lavender to purple and grow in 6- to 10-inch (15- to 25-cm) racemes. Zones 7–10.

Salvia leucophylla (chaparral sage, gray sage, purple sage, San Luis purple sage) is a 5-foot (1.5-m) bushy shrub native to southern California. It is hairy and whitish gray. Ovate or oblong to lanceolate leaves grow to 2.5 inches (6.25 cm) long and are scalloped to notched. Pink, blue, or purple spikes of interrupted flowers grow in whorled spikes. Zone 8.

Salvia lyrata (cancerweed, lyre-leafed sage) is an 8- to 24-inch (20- to 60-cm) perennial herb or subshrub from the United States. It forms rosettes and has leaves that are lyrate and toothed to erose. Violet to purple summer flowers grow interruptedly on simple or branched flower spikes. Zone 5.

Salvia mexicana is a pubescent shrub from Mexico that grows to 36 inches (90 cm) in height with oval to oblong, scalloped to toothed leaves up to 3 inches (7.5 cm) long. Blue, violet, or purple flowers appear in winter growing in loose spikes. Zone 8.

Salvia microphylla (baby sage) is a 36-inch (90-cm) shrub. The oval to elliptical leaves are small, only 0.5 to 0.75 inch (1.25 to 1.9 cm) long, and scalloped to toothed. Deep red, pink, magenta, or purple 1-inch (2.5-cm) flowers appearing in late summer to fall grow in long racemes. Zones 8–10.

Salvia munzii is native to southern and Baja California. This is a large shrub, up to 8 feet (2.4 m) tall with oval to oblong, notched leaves up to about 1.25 inches (3.1 cm) long. Spikes of clear blue flowers grow up to 6 inches (15 cm) in length. Zone 8.

Salvia nemorosa (violet sage) is a bushy 36-inch (90-cm) perennial herb native to Europe through central Asia. Oval to oblong-lanceolate leaves are notched and woolly. Dense spikes of violet-blue flowers appear from summer to fall. 'East Friesland' (Plate 55) is a handsome and well-known cultivar hardy in Zones 5 to 9. Some confusion exists between *S. nemorosa* and the naturally occurring hybrid *S.* ×*superba*. Zone 5.

Salvia officinalis (common sage, garden sage, sage; Plate 26) is an aromatic herbal favorite native to Spain through the western Balkan Peninsula and Asia Minor. Growing to about 24 inches (60 cm), it is grayish and rugose with leaves more or less 2 inches (5 cm) long. Flowers of white, pink, violet, or purple bloom in summer growing in simple spikes. Some well-known cultivars include 'Aurea', 'Berggarten' (Plate 28), 'Icterina' (Plate 29), 'Nana' (Plate 27), 'Purpurescens', and 'Tricolor' (Plate 31). The fancy-colored sages are tender, hardy only to Zone 7. The species is widely grown as a potherb. Zones 4–7.

Salvia pachyphylla (rose sage) is a decumbent, spreading 36-inch (90-cm) shrub with 1.25-inch (3.1-cm) leaves that are hairy, entire, and ovate to oblong. The species is native to California and bears flowers on interrupted spikes. Zone 8.

Salvia patens (gentian sage) is a pubescent perennial herb native to the mountains of Mexico. It grows 12 to 36 inches (30 to 90 cm) tall. Oval to oblong-ovate leaves are 2 to 6 inches (5 to 15 cm) long and notched to scalloped. In summer to fall flower spikes up to 15 inches (37. 5 cm) or more in length bear bright blue or occasionally white flowers nearly 3 inches (7.5 cm) long. Zones 8–10.

Salvia pratensis (meadow clary, meadow sage) is an aromatic woolly sage native to Morocco and Europe, including Great Britain. Plants grow 12 to 40 inches (30 to 100 cm) tall. Ovate to oblong leaves are 3 to 6 inches (7.5 to 15 cm) long and lobed or doubly crenate. Four to six 1-inch (2.5-cm) summer flowers grow in simple, loose, or branched spikes. Flowers are typically violet-blue but may also be white, pink, or bluish white. Zones 3–7.

Salvia pratensis (meadow clary). From Heukels 1909–1911.

Salvia purpurea (gentian sage) is a large 9-foot (2.7-m) woody subshrub native to Mexico and Central America. Broad, oval, smooth to slightly pubescent leaves grow up to 5 inches (12.5 cm) in length and are toothed to scalloped. Dense spikes of pink to purple flowers appear in summer. Zone 9.

Salvia reflexa is a 24-inch (60-cm) annual native to Wisconsin through Montana and south through Arkansas and Mexico. It has naturalized in the eastern United States. This species is erect and branched with 2-inch (5-cm) linear-lanceolate leaves that are entire to irregularly toothed. Summer flowers of lilac to blue grow in interrupted spikes. Zones 4–9.

Salvia ringens is an erect 24-inch (60-cm) subshrub native to the eastern Balkans through southeastern Romania. The woolly leaves are pinnate to pinnatifid. Violet to violet-blue flowers grow in terminal spikes. Zone 7.

Salvia scabiosifolia is a woolly, bushy native of the Crimean region that grows to a height of 24 to 30 inches (60 to 75 cm). The leaves are elliptical and pinnate to pinnatifid. Summer flower spikes bear 1.5-inch (3.75-cm) flowers of violet, violet-blue, or lilac. Zone 6.

Salvia sclarea (clary, cleareye, muscatel sage) is an erect perennial or biennial herb. A tall plant with flower stalks up to 36 inches (90 cm) in height, clary has large, rugose, hairy gray-green leaves up to 9 inches (22.5 cm) long that grow in a large rosette at the base of the plant. Small creamy white or lavender flowers appear in spring to summer and have showy bracts of white to pink or mauve. Zones 4–9.

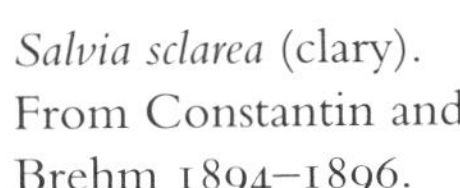
Salvia sclarea (clary). From Constantin and Brehm 1894–1896.

Salvia sonomensis (creeping sage) is a creeping, mat-forming perennial up to 12 inches (30 cm) tall and native to California. The woolly leaves are elliptic-obovate, crenulate, and up to 2 inches (5 cm) long. Violet to blue-violet flowers grow in terminal spikes. Zone 8.

Salvia spathacea (pitcher sage), also native to California, is a coarse perennial herb with creeping rhizomes. It has oblong, hairy leaves 4 to 8 inches (10 to 20 cm) long. Reddish purple 1.5-inch (3.75-cm) flowers grow in dense flower spikes. Zone 9.

Salvia splendens (scarlet sage) is a tall annual or perennial subshrub native to Brazil that reaches 36 inches (90 cm) or more in height. Leaves are ovate, smooth to slightly hairy, notched, and grow to 3.5 inches (8.75 cm) in length. Scarlet flowers growing in terminal spikes bloom in summer to fall. This species and its cultivars are often grown as annuals. Zones 9–10.

Salvia ×superba, which was first described in 1961, appears to be a naturally occurring hybrid of *S. sylvestris* and *S. villicaulis.* It has also been referred to as *S. nemorosa,* yet another case of confusion within the family and particularly within this genus. The leaves are lanceolate to oblong and scalloped. The plants are vigorous, well-branched, erect, and grow up to 24 inches (60 cm) tall by 24 inches wide. Among the many cultivars are 'Blue Queen', 'May Night', and 'Rose Queen', with flowers ranging from violet to pink. Zones 5–9.

Salvia tiliifolia, native to Mexico through Ecuador, is a well-branched annual that grows to 48 inches (120 cm) or more in height. Broad, oval leaves up to 4 inches (10 cm) long are slightly scalloped to toothed. Summer flowers of white, blue, or lilac grow in interrupted spikes or panicles of interrupted spikes up to 10 inches (25 cm) long. Zone 10.

Salvia uliginosa (bog sage) is a 6-foot (1.8-m) perennial native to southern Brazil, Uruguay, and Argentina. Oblong-lanceolate leaves grow to a length of 4 inches (10 cm) and are serrate and glabrous to

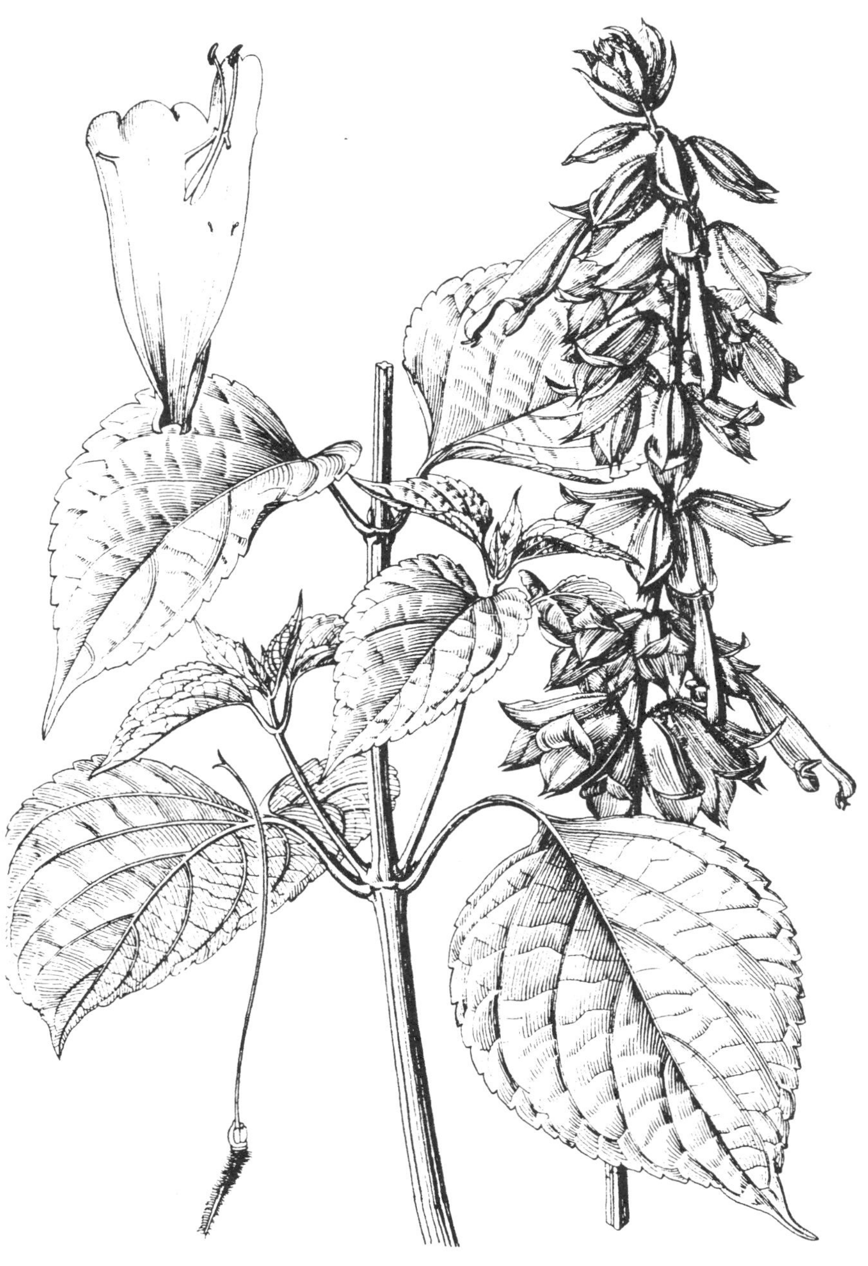

Salvia splendens (scarlet sage). From Flora of China 1998.

pubescent. Blue flowers with white markings, each up to 0.75 inch (1.9 cm) long, appear in summer to fall growing densely in whorled spikes. Zones 6–10.

Salvia vaseyi is a 54-inch (135-cm) shrub native to the deserts of southern California and northern Baja California. The woolly leaves are oval to oblong-lanceolate, notched, and grow to a length of 1.5 inches (3.75 cm). White flowers grow in interrupted terminal spikes. Zone 8.

Salvia verbenaca (vervain, wild clary) is native to Bulgaria through Israel and Syria, and widely naturalized. This erect 24-inch (60-cm) perennial has oblong to oval 4-inch (10-cm) leaves with undulate edges. Summer to fall flowers of blue, lavender, or purple grow in simple or branched whorled spikes. Zone 6.

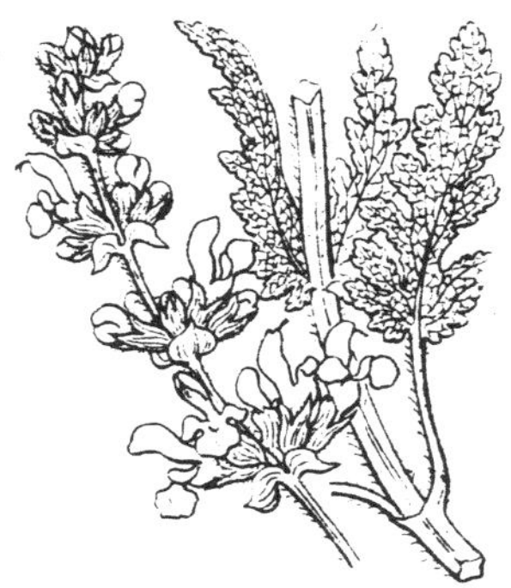

Salvia verbenaca (vervain). From Heukels 1909–1911.

Salvia verticillata (lilac sage) is native to central and southern Europe through Asia Minor. An erect perennial that grows to a height of 36 inches (90 cm), it has 3-inch (7.5-cm) leaves that are simple to lyrate.

Salvia verticillata (lilac sage). From Heukels 1909–1911.

Violet, lilac, or white flowers appear in summer in branched terminal verticillasters. Zones 5–8.

Salvia villosa is a perennial native of Mexico. It grows 15 inches (37.5 cm) or more in height and is more or less procumbent. Notched leaves grow to a length of 1.5 inches (3.75 cm). Summer flowers of violet, lilac, or white grow in simple terminal spikes. Zone 9.

Salvia viridis (annual clary, bluebeard, Joseph sage, painted sage, red-topped sage; synonym *S. horminum*) is an annual or biennial herb native to southern Europe. It grows up to 18 inches (45 cm) in height and about 12 inches (30 cm) wide. Oblong to oval leaves are pubescent and somewhat notched. Plants display pink, bluish purple, or white bracts and whitish flowers growing in simple racemes.

Salvia wagneriana is a tall perennial, reaching 3 to 10 feet (0.9 to 3 m) in height. The species is native to Guatemala, Costa Rica, and Panama. The 2- to 4-inch (5- to 10-cm) leaves are notched. Scarlet-red flowers up to 3 inches (7.5 cm) long grow in dense terminal spikes. Zone 10.

Satureja

Satureja (savory, savory calamint) includes about thirty species of annual herbs or perennial subshrubs native to temperate and warm temperate regions of the Northern Hemisphere. Lipped flowers grow in loose spikes. Several species are grown as culinary herbs, the most common being *S. hortensis* and *S. montana*. Propagation is by seeds, divisions, or cuttings of young growth.

Satureja douglasii (yerba buena) is native to California and the southwestern United States. It is a tender, creeping perennial valued for its minty fragrance and taste. Zone 8.

Satureja hortensis (summer savory) is a very aromatic, slightly pubescent annual species native to southern Europe. Plants grow 12 to 18 inches (30 to 45 cm) in height with linear leaves about 0.5 inch

(1.25 cm) long and entire. White to purple flowers appear in summer in whorled spikes.

Satureja montana (winter savory), also native to southern Europe, is an aromatic, smooth to very slightly pubescent perennial. It grows to about 12 inches (30 cm) tall with 1-inch (2.5-cm) leaves that are linear to obovate and entire. Summer to fall flowers of white or pale lavender grow in whorled spikes. Zones 5–8.

Scutellaria

Scutellaria (helmet flower, skullcap) includes some three hundred nonaromatic species native to most temperate and tropical montane regions of the world, with the exception of South Africa. Leaves are simple and flowers may be axillary, either singly or in pairs, or grow densely in terminal spikes.

Scutellaria albida is a vigorous, erect perennial native to southern Europe through central Asia. Plants grow up to 30 inches (75 cm) tall and have triangularly oval, coarsely scalloped, more or less hairy 1.5-inch (3.75-cm) leaves. White, cream, or mauve flowers have lower lips streaked with mauve and grow in dense, one-sided racemes. Zone 7.

Scutellaria alpina is native to mountains from southern Europe to Siberia. It is a spreading, sprawling perennial, often rooting at the nodes. Plants grow to 10 inches (25 cm) in height with hairy, oval, crenate leaves 1 inch (2.5 cm) in length. The 1-inch (2.5-cm) flowers appear in dense terminal racemes. Zones 4–7.

Scutellaria baicalensis is native to eastern Asia, from Siberia to Japan. This perennial reaches 15 inches (37.5 cm) in height but is decumbent at its base. Lanceolate, entire leaves grow to about 1.5 inches (3.75 cm) long. Blue-purple 1-inch (2.5-cm) flowers grow in one-sided racemes that are sometimes branched. Zones 4–8.

Scutellaria brittonii is a rhizomatous perennial native to Wyoming through Colorado and northern New Mexico. Plants grow 6 to 10

Scutellaria baicalensis.
From Flora of China 1998.

inches (15 to 25 cm) tall. The ovate-elliptical leaves are 1.25 inches (3.1 cm) long and entire to crenate-serrate. Violet-blue to white flowers grow in leaf axils, mostly on upper stems. Zone 5.

Scutellaria californica is native to California and Oregon. It is basally branched and grows 6 to 10 inches (15 to 25 cm) in height. This hairy perennial species has oblong-elliptic 1.25-inch (3.1-cm) leaves that are entire to crenate-serrate. Yellowish white to creamy white flowers up to 0.75 inch (1.9 cm) long grow in leaf axils, mostly on the upper parts of stems. Zone 7.

Scutellaria columnae is an erect perennial with oval, crenate-serrate leaves up to 2 inches (5 cm) in length. It is native to southeastern Europe and grows 24 to 36 inches (60 to 90 cm) tall. White to purple flowers with whitish lower lips are 1 inch (2.5 cm) long and grow in 8-inch (20-cm) one-sided racemes. Zone 6.

Scutellaria costaricana is a slender, erect, tender perennial native to Costa Rica. It grows to 36 inches (90 cm) or more with elliptical to ovate-elliptical leaves that are toothed to shallowly scalloped. The 2.5-inch (6.25-cm) scarlet-orange flowers are deep yellow inside and grow crowded on one-sided racemes. Zone 9.

Scutellaria galericulata is considered cosmopolitan, meaning that it grows in most temperate regions of the world. Reaching 12 to 24 inches (30 to 60 cm) in height, it has 2.5-inch (6.25-cm) leaves that are oval to oblong and scalloped to toothed. Violet-blue flowers grow singly in leaf axils or on one-sided terminal racemes. Zone 5.

Scutellaria hirta is an erect, densely pubescent, shrubby 10-inch (25-cm) perennial with oval to deltoid, scalloped leaves. Cream-colored flowers have upper lips tinged with red and grow in racemes that each bear only a few flowers. Zone 6.

Scutellaria incana is a very hairy, dense, shrubby perennial native to Ontario through Virginia and Missouri. Plants grow to a height of 48 inches (120 cm) with ovate, crenate-serrate leaves 2.5 to 5 inches

Scutellaria galericulata.
From Flora of China 1998.

(6.25 to 12.5 cm) in length. Blue-gray pubescent flowers up to 0.75 inch (1.9 cm) in length grow in showy panicles. Zone 5.

Scutellaria indica is a slender, procumbent perennial that grows to 12 inches (30 cm) tall and is native to China, Korea, and Japan. Oval 1-inch (2.5-cm) leaves are crenate-serrate. Pale purplish blue flowers are 0.75 inch (1.9 cm) long and grow in dense racemes. Zone 5.

Scutellaria integrifolia is an erect, hairy perennial native to Connecticut through Florida and Missouri. It grows 12 to 24 inches (30 to 60 cm) in height. The leaves are oval to narrowly elliptical, up to 2.5 inches (6.25 cm) long, and usually entire. Blue to white 1-inch (2.5-cm) flowers grow in racemes that are 2 to 4 inch (5 to 10 cm) long. Zone 5.

Scutellaria longifolia is native to Mexico through El Salvador. This erect 20-inch (50-cm) perennial has oval to ovate-lanceolate, sinuate-serrate leaves that grow to a length of 3 to 4 inches (7.5 to 10 cm). Scarlet 1.25-inch (3.1-cm) flowers grow in branched racemes 2 to 4 inches (5 to 10 cm) in length. Zone 9.

Scutellaria orientalis is a decumbent, woody, woolly species native to southeastern Europe from southern Greece to Iran. The oblong to oval leaves are up to 0.75 inch (1.9 cm) long and toothed. Flowers are usually yellow but may also be pink, red, or purple, are sometimes spotted with red, and grow in dense racemes or spikes. Zone 7.

Scutellaria parvula is a small species, growing only 4 to 12 inches (10 to 30 cm) in height. It is native to Quebec through Virginia and west through Minnesota and Texas. Plants are densely hairy and have small 0.5-inch (1.25-cm) leaves that are slightly toothed. Blue flowers are 0.5 inch (1.25 cm) long and grow singly in leaf axils. Zone 5.

Scutellaria resinosa is native to Kansas through Texas and Arizona. This heavily branched perennial grows from woody stems to a height of 9 inches (22.5 cm). Oval to nearly round leaves are up to

0.75 inch (1.9 cm) long, covered with minute hairs, and resinous. Deep blue-violet flowers grow to a length of almost 0.75 inch (1.9 cm) on one-sided racemes. Zone 5.

Scutellaria scordiifolia is a basally branched 18-inch (45-cm) annual or perennial native to eastern Europe and Asia. The oblong 1-inch (2.5-cm) leaves are entire to slightly toothed. Blue flowers are 0.5 inch (1.25 cm) long and grow in leaf axils or in short, one-sided spikes. Zones 6–8.

Scutellaria tuberosa is a hairy, rhizomatous perennial native to Oregon, California, and Baja California. It forms mats, creeps by means of tubers, and grows about 5 inches (12.5 cm) tall. The oval 0.5-inch (1.25-cm) leaves are coarsely toothed. Violet-purple to blue flowers grow singly in leaf axils, nearly to the bases of the stems. Zone 5.

Sideritis

Sideritis includes about one hundred perennials, subshrubs, and shrubs native to northern temperate Europe and Asia, the Canary Islands, and Madeira. Sometimes these plants are grown in perennial beds and borders. In the wild they thrive on sunny, rocky, dry hillsides. Propagation is by seeds, divisions, or cuttings.

Sideritis argosphacelus is a woolly, low-growing shrub native to the Canary Islands. It grows 6 to 18 inches (15 to 45 cm) tall with oval, scalloped leaves 2 to 4 inches (5 to 10 cm) long. Yellow flowers tipped with brown grow in dense terminal spikes that are somewhat pendulous. Zone 10.

Sideritis candicans, another native of the Canary Islands, is a bushy, white, hairy shrub up to 36 inches (90 cm) tall. It has oval to linear-lanceolate, slightly notched leaves 2 inches (5 cm) in length. Yellow flowers tipped with red to brown grow in spikes up to 12 inches (30 cm) long. Zone 10.

Sideritis hyssopifolia is a perennial shrub native to the mountains of southeastern Europe through Switzerland. Plants are nearly smooth to shaggy with thick hairs and grow 15 to 30 inches (37.5 to 75 cm) tall. The 1.5-inch (3.75-cm) leaves are linear to ovate to obovate and entire to coarsely toothed. Yellow flowers, occasionally flecked with purple, grow in dense spikes. Zone 8.

Sideritis libanotica is very slightly hairy to very woolly and grows 18 to 36 inches (45 to 90 cm) in height. This perennial is native to the eastern Mediterranean region from Syria to Israel and has linear to lanceolate leaves that are serrate and grow to a length of 2.5 inches (6.25 cm). Terminal verticillasters bear flowers that are yellow to purple with interior stripes of brown. Zone 8.

Sideritis macrostachys is a 36-inch (90-cm) shrub native to the Canary Islands. Oval to round, crenate leaves are bright green on top and tomentose beneath. White flowers tipped with brown grow in dense, branched spikes. Zone 9.

Sideritis montana is an annual species native to southern Europe and the Mediterranean region. Plants are slightly to very woolly and grow to about 15 inches (37.5 cm) in height. Linear to elliptic to oblong leaves are dentate and 0.75 inch (1.9 cm) long. Yellow or brown flowers grow in dense spikes.

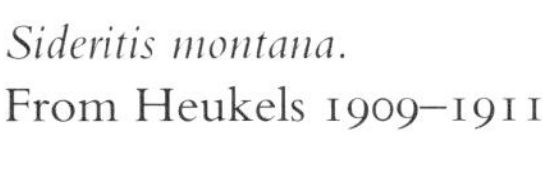

Sideritis montana.
From Heukels 1909–1911.

Sideritis syriaca is a 20-inch (50-cm) woolly perennial with leaves that are linear to oblong to ovate and either entire or dentate. Yellow flowers with brown-striped interiors grow in mostly terminal spikes. Zone 8.

Solenostemon

Solenostemon (synonym *Coleus*) includes ten to sixty shrubby, often succulent and hairy, often variegated species native to tropical Africa and Asia. The well-known ornamental annual commonly called coleus used to be classed in its own genus but is now classified as the best-known species of *Solenostemon*.

Solenostemon scutellarioides (coleus, flame nettle, painted leaves, painted nettle; synonyms *Coleus hybridus, C.* ×*hybridus, S. blumei;* Plate 56) is an aromatic, tender perennial to subshrub native to the tropics of the eastern hemisphere. It may be erect or procumbent. Toothed, scalloped, or incised leaves are variable in size—up to 6 inches (15 cm) long—and shape, depending on the cultivar. The species has been bred and selected into a wide variety of ornamental cultivars in a rainbow of variegations, sizes, and leaf forms that are useful as bedding plants and borders in shady to sunny sites. Zone 10.

Stachys

Stachys (betony, hedge nettle, lamb's ear, woundwort) includes about three hundred hairy to woolly herbs and subshrubs native to tropical mountains and temperate and tropical regions throughout much of the world, especially the Eastern Hemisphere. Some of these plants are grown as ornamentals. One species is grown in eastern Asia for its edible tubers. Flowers appear in summer. Propagation is by seeds or divisions.

Stachys affinis (Chinese artichoke, chorogi, crosnes du Japon, Japanese artichoke, knotroot) is a perennial species native to China and widely cultivated in Japan for its abundant, tasty, slender white tubers. It is an erect, hairy 24-inch (60-cm) plant with rough, lanceolate to oval leaves. Flowers are white or light red. Zone 5.

Stachys alopecuros is an erect, hairy 24-inch (60-cm) perennial herb native to the limestone mountains of southern to central Europe. It has 3.5-inch (8.75-cm) oval leaves that are coarsely crenate to dentate. Pale yellow flowers grow in dense spikes. Zone 5.

Stachys bullata, a California species, is a procumbent perennial with stems up to 18 to 36 inches (45 to 90 cm) long. Oval to oblong leaves up to 8 inches (20 cm) long are scalloped to toothed. Purple flowers grow in interrupted spikes. Zone 5.

Stachys byzantina (lamb's ear, lamb's tail, lamb's tongue, woolly betony; synonyms *S. lanata, S. olympica;* Plate 58) is an erect, densely tomentose perennial native to Turkey through southwestern Asia. The flower stalks grow 12 to 15 inches (30 to 37.5 cm) in height. Whitish, woolly leaves up to 4 inches (10 cm) long are oblong to elliptic and entire to lightly scalloped. Pink to purple flowers are woolly and grow in dense spikes. Zones 4–7.

Stachys ciliata is a 36- to 48-inch (90- to 120-cm) smooth to pubescent perennial native to British Columbia through Oregon. It has oval leaves up to 3.5 inches (8.75 cm) long and dentate. Reddish purple flowers grow in terminal verticillasters. Zone 5.

Stachys corsica is a procumbent, creeping, mat-forming, short-lived perennial often grown as an annual. The species grows to just 6 inches (15 cm) tall and is only sparsely hairy. It is native to the mountains of Sardinia and Corsica. The leaves are broad, oval, and broadly crenate. The 0.5-inch (1.25-cm) flowers are white, purple, or pink and grow singly or widely spaced on whorled spikes. Zone 5.

Stachys germanica (downy woundwort) is a densely woolly 48-inch (120-cm) perennial native to Europe, northern Africa, and central Asia. The plant is woody at its base and the oval 4-inch (10-cm) leaves are slightly serrate. Rose, pink, or purple flowers grow widely spaced on whorled spikes. Zone 5.

Stachys hyssopifolia is a stoloniferous, smooth to lightly hairy perennial native to bogs and the shores of ponds from Massachusetts to Georgia. Plants grow to a height of 30 inches (75 cm) with linear to

Stachys germanica (downy woundwort). From Heukels 1909–1911.

oblong leaves up to 1.5 inches (3.75 cm) long. Pink flowers grow in terminal verticillasters. Zone 5.

Stachys lavandulifolia is a sprawling, densely hairy, gray-green subshrub native to Asia Minor. It grows up to 5 inches (12.5 cm) tall. The leaves are entire to slightly serrate, narrowly oblong-lanceolate, and up to 2 inches (5 cm) long. Purple, mauve, or rose-purple flowers grow widely spaced on whorled spikes. Zone 5.

Stachys macrantha (big betony; synonyms *Betonica macrantha, S. grandiflora;* Plate 59) is a hardy, herbaceous perennial native to the Caucasian Mountains and Iran. It grows up to 24 inches (60 cm) in height and displays whorls of large purple-pink flowers in summer. The soft green leaves are crinkled and lanceolate to cordate with coarsely toothed edges. Cultivars include 'Alba', 'Robusta', and 'Violacea'. Zone 5.

Stachys officinalis (common betony, woody betony; synonym *S. betonica*) is an erect, rosette-forming perennial up to 36 inches (90 cm) tall and native to Europe and Asia. Ovate to oblong-ovate leaves are up to 5 inches (12.5 cm) long and crenate to crenate-dentate. White, pink, or red-purple flowers growing in dense spikes appear in spring. Zone 5.

Stachys riddellii is a tuberous perennial native to shady locations with rich soil from Maryland to Illinois and south to North Carolina and Tennessee. Plants grow 20 to 48 inches (50 to 120 cm) or more in height. Ovate leaves up to 3.5 inches (8.75 cm) long are scalloped to toothed. Purple flowers with darker spots grow widely spaced on slender spikes. Zone 5.

Stachys tenuifolia is a creeping perennial with erect stems up to 40 inches (100 cm) tall. The species is smooth to very slightly hairy and native to New York through Minnesota and south to Alabama and Texas. Leaves are narrow, toothed, oval to lanceolate, and grow to a length of 3.5 inches (8.75 cm). Purple flowers grow widely spaced on whorled spikes. Zone 5.

Tetradenia

Tetradenia includes five aromatic perennial shrubs native to southern Africa and Madagascar. Plants are somewhat succulent with roundish, scalloped leaves.

Tetradenia riparia is a southern African species that grows up to 10 feet (3 m) tall and has oval to round leaves about 3 inches (7.5 cm) or more in length. It is slightly pubescent with white to mauve flowers. Zone 10.

Teucrium

Teucrium (germander, wood sage) includes some three hundred often aromatic herbs, perennials, subshrubs, and shrubs. Though native to many parts of the world, these plants are most particularly found from the Mediterranean region through western Asia. Propagation is by seeds, cuttings, or divisions.

Teucrium aroanum is a tomentose, evergreen 12-inch (30-cm) shrub native to the mountains of Greece. Plants are bushy, procumbent, and stoloniferous with oval, elliptical, or oblong and entire leaves about 0.5 inch (1.25 cm) long. Bluish flowers grow in racemes. Zone 8.

Teucrium bicolor is a native of Peru, Chile, and Argentina. It grows 3 to 6 feet (0.9 to 1.8 m) tall. The 0.5-inch (1.25-cm) leaves are leathery, lanceolate to ovate-lanceolate, slightly hairy, and often have two lateral lobes near the middle. Summer flowers are up to 0.75-inch (1.9-cm) in length and grow in leaf axils or loose spikes. Flower color is white, pink, or violet with flecks of purple. Zone 9.

Teucrium canadense (American germander, wood sage) is a rhizomatous perennial native to eastern North America. It grows up to 36 inches (90 cm) tall with erect, stiff stems. Leaves up to 3 inches (7.5 cm) long are ovate or lanceolate to oblong, serrate, and woolly on the undersides. Summer flowers of cream, pink, or purple grow in flower spikes up to 8 inches (20 cm) long. Zone 4.

Teucrium chamaedrys (wall germander; Plate 32) is a dwarf, rhizomatous shrub native to Europe through western Asia. It grows 12 to 24 inches (30 to 60 cm) tall and has oblong to oval leaves that are 0.75 inch (1.9 cm) long and deeply toothed, notched, or lobed. Purple to purple-pink or rose-colored flowers grow in terminal spikes that are loose to dense. Zone 5.

Teucrium chamaedrys (wall germander). From Fiori et al. 1895–1904.

Teucrium flavum is a 24-inch (60-cm) perennial with a woody base. It is native to rocky slopes in the Mediterranean region. Leathery, oval leaves are notched. Yellow summer flowers grow in long interrupted spikes. Zone 8.

Teucrium fruticans (tree germander) is a tomentose, evergreen 48-inch (120-cm) shrub native to sunny places in the western Mediterranean region. Oval to lanceolate, entire leaves up to 1.25 inches (3.1 cm) in length are smooth above and woolly beneath. Summer flowers up to 1 inch (2.5 cm) long are blue or lilac and grow in leaf axils or loose terminal whorls. Zone 8.

Teucrium heterophyllum is a densely bushy 4- to 6-foot (1.2- to 1.8-m) shrub native to the Canary Islands. The species is tomentose and yellowish. The leaves of young growth are oval and crenate-dentate, while the leaves of older growth are oblong, usually entire, densely white to yellowish, and woolly. Pink to rose-purple to purple flowers grow in terminal whorls. Zone 9.

Teucrium krymense is a Crimean native. This 18-inch (45-cm) perennial or subshrub is nearly erect and densely pubescent. Ovate-oblong, finely notched leaves grow up to 1.5 inches (3.75 cm) in length. Summer flowers are red-purple to purple and grow in loose, simple racemes. Zone 6.

Teucrium lucidum is a 24-inch (60-cm) perennial native to the Alps. Plants are nearly hairless with 1.5-inch (3.75-cm) oval to oblong leaves that are lobed to deeply toothed. Pink to purple flowers grow in loose whorled spikes. Zone 6.

Teucrium lucidum. From Fiori et al. 1895–1904.

Teucrium marum (cat thyme) is a gray, woolly, erect, bushy shrub native to the western Mediterranean islands. It may grow to 12 to 18 inches (30 to 45 cm) or more in warm climates. Oval to linear-lanceolate to linear leaves are entire to toothed. Summer flowers are purplish to purple-pink, 1 to 3 inches (2.5 to 7.5 cm) long, and grow in dense racemes. Zone 9.

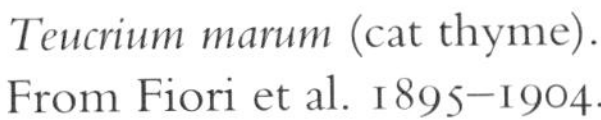

Teucrium marum (cat thyme).
From Fiori et al. 1895–1904.

Teucrium massiliense is a gray, hairy perennial or subshrub with notched, oval to oblong 0.5-inch (1.25-cm) leaves. It is native to Crete and the western Mediterranean region. Plants grow to 12 inches (30 cm) tall and bear pink to purple flowers in whorled spikes. Zone 6.

Teucrium montanum is a 12-inch (30-cm) shrub to subshrub native to southern and central Europe through western Asia. Plants are decumbent, whitish, and hairy. The leaves are entire, narrow, elliptic, and up to 0.75 inch (1.9 cm) long. Yellow, cream, or white blooms grow in dense terminal flower heads. Zone 6.

Teucrium occidentale (hairy germander) is a stoloniferous 36-inch (90-cm) perennial native to the northern United States through California and New Mexico. Pubescent leaves are ovate to lanceolate to oblong, 3 to 4 inches (7.5 to 10 cm) in length, and whitish and hairy underneath. Purple flowers grow in dense to interrupted spikes. Zone 7.

Teucrium orientale is an erect 18-inch (45-cm) subshrub or shrub native to southwestern Asia. The 2-inch (5-cm) leaves are ovate to roundish, entire to notched, and pinnatifid, with linear segments. Summer flowers of blue to blue-violet grow in loose, whorled spikes. Zone 7.

Teucrium polium is native to southern Europe through western Asia. This dwarf 18-inch (45-cm) shrub is procumbent and tomentose, covered with white, golden, or greenish hairs that are branched. Narrow, oblong leaves are 1 inch (2.5 cm) in length and entire to scalloped. White, yellow, pink, red, or purple flowers appear in summer in dense terminal whorls. Zone 7.

Teucrium polium. From Fiori et al. 1895–1904.

Teucrium pyrenaicum is a slender creeping plant with 8-inch (20-cm) stems. This perennial is pubescent and woody at its base. It is a native of the Pyrenees Mountains. The leaves are nearly round, about 1 inch (2.5 cm) long, scalloped, and hairy. Summer flowers up to 0.75 inch (1.9 cm) long are white or yellow tipped with purple and grow in dense terminal flower heads. Zone 6.

Teucrium scorodonia (wood germander, wood sage) is a dwarf, pubescent, rhizomatous shrub that grows up to 20 inches (50 cm) or more in height. Native to Europe, this species has naturalized in Ontario and Ohio. The triangular-ovate leaves are crenate and woolly. Cream to pale yellow flowers grow in loose, simple, or branched 6-inch (15-cm) racemes. Zone 6.

Teucrium subspinosum is a small shrub about 12 inches (30 cm) in diameter and 20 inches (50 cm) in height. This tomentose native of the Balearic Islands has sturdy branches and is dense and spiny. Deltoid, lanceolate, or linear leaves are woolly on their undersides. Summer flowers are purple or pink and grow in loose spikes. Zone 9.

Thymbra

Thymbra is made up of just two to three species of small, low-growing shrubs native to southeastern Europe and southwestern Asia. Leaves are overlapping and entire. Flowers grow in terminal spikes that are dense and narrow. Propagation is by cuttings or seeds.

Thymbra spicata is a sturdy shrub native to sunny slopes from Greece to Israel. It grows about 22 inches (55 cm) tall and has smooth, linear leaves that are entire and about 0.5 inch (1.25 cm) long. Pink to mauve flowers appear in spring to summer growing in spikes up to 4 inches (10 cm) long. Zone 8.

Thymus

Thymus (thyme; Plate 34) is comprised of three to four hundred aromatic perennial herbs, subshrubs, and shrubs native to Europe and Asia. Members of this genus have been among the best-known and best-loved culinary and medicinal herbs for thousands of years. They are often creeping and woody at the base, and flowers frequently appear crowded in terminal verticillasters. Many species are grown as ornamentals in paths and along walkways as well as in beds, borders, and rock gardens. Some species, especially *T. vul-*

garis, are grown as potherbs for seasoning foods. Propagation is by cuttings or divisions. The many cultivars include a wide variety of growth habits, flower color, and foliage color.

Thymus broussonettii is an erect, bushy perennial subshrub or shrub native to Morocco with shoots that are fully hairy or hairy on just two opposite sides. The plant grows 5 to 12 inches (12.5 to 30 cm) tall and has 0.75-inch (1.9-cm) leaves that are narrow and oval to elliptic. Flowers are rose red. Zone 9.

Thymus caespititius is a dwarf, mat-forming subshrub with upright flower stems 2 inches (5 cm) tall. It is native to the Azores, Portugal, and northwestern Spain. Narrow, smooth leaves are only about 0.75 inch (1.9 cm) in length. White, pink, rose, or lilac flowers appear in late spring to summer growing in loose flower heads or singly in axils. Zone 7.

Thymus camphoratus is a camphor-scented, shrubby herb 6 to 12 inches (15 to 30 cm) tall and native to southern Portugal. The small leaves are only 0.125 inch (0.3 cm) long and woolly above. Rose-colored flowers grow in rounded inflorescences. Zone 7.

Thymus carnosus is native to southern Portugal. This stiffly erect dwarf shrub grows 5 to 9 inches (12.5 to 22.5 cm) tall and is narrow in its growth habit. The elliptical, fleshy leaves are smooth above and woolly underneath, reaching only 0.25 inch (0.6 cm) in length. Flowers are white, pink, or lilac. Zone 7.

Thymus cimicinus is a procumbent, woody species from southern Russia with 0.25-inch (0.6-cm) leaves that are entire and glabrous. Reddish leaves grow in leaf axils. Zone 5.

Thymus ×*citriodorus* (lemon thyme) is believed to be a cross between *T. pulegioides* and *T. vulgaris.* The plant grows up to 12 inches (30 cm) in height and has small, oval to slightly lanceolate leaves. It is grown in many forms including 'Aureus', 'Golden King', and 'Silver Queen' (Plate 35). Zone 7.

Thymus comosus is a mat-forming species with flowering stems that grow to a height of 6 inches (15 cm). This pubescent plant, native to the mountains of Romania and central Europe, has smooth to slightly hairy, ovate to almost round leaves that grow to about 0.5 inch (1.25 cm) long. Pink or purple flowers in round to cylindrical heads appear in midsummer. Zone 5.

Thymus comptus is native to Bulgaria, Greece, and Turkey. This densely hairy, procumbent subshrub has erect flower stems 2 to 6 inches (5 to 15 cm) tall. The 0.5-inch (1.25-cm) leaves are smooth, stiff, and linear to lanceolate. Rose-colored flowers are spaced apart on 4-inch (10-cm) whorled spikes. Zone 5.

Thymus doerfleri is a dwarf shrub native to Albania. Flowering stems grow to a height of only 4 inches (10 cm). The densely hairy leaves are linear and very small. Pink or purple flower spikes appear in early summer. This plant makes a good ground cover. Zone 5.

Thymus glabrescens is a subshrub native to central and southeastern Europe. It forms low mats and has flower stems up to 6 to 12 inches (15 to 30 cm) tall. The smooth leaves are more or less 0.5 inch (1.25 cm) long. Purple flowers, often spaced apart, grow on whorled spikes. Zone 6.

Thymus herba-barona (caraway thyme; Plate 36) is a dwarf, procumbent subshrub that grows in loose carpets with flower stalks 2 to 5 inches (5 to 12.5 cm) in height. The smooth, oval to lanceolate leaves grow to about 0.5 inch (1.25 cm) in length and may smell like caraway, lemon, or nutmeg when crushed. Bright pink flowers grow in whorled spikes. Zone 7.

Thymus hyemalis is an erect, hairy 12-inch (30-cm) shrub native to southeastern Spain. Linear to lanceolate gray-green leaves are 0.25 inch (0.6 cm) long. Appearing in winter and spring, deep rose to mauve flowers grow in almost round heads. Zone 5.

Thymus mastichina is a native of northern Africa and the Iberian Peninsula. This erect, hairy shrub grows 6 to 12 inches (15 to 30 cm) tall. Elliptical 0.5-inch (1.25-cm) leaves may be pubescent and scalloped. White to off-white flowers grow in nearly round heads. Zone 7.

Thymus membranaceus is a hairy, nearly round 4- to 8-inch (10- to 20-cm) shrub native to southeastern Spain. The leaves are linear to somewhat lanceolate and hairy on both sides. White flowers grow in somewhat oval heads. Zone 7.

Thymus nummularius is a spreading subshrub with a woody base. It reaches 8 to 12 inches (20 to 30 cm) in height and grows from the Caucasus to Asia Minor, including Iran. The stems are hairy on two sides. Leaves are broad, ovate to elliptical, usually smooth, and up to 0.75 inch (1.9 cm) in length. Rose, pink, mauve, or lilac-purple flowers appear in summer on oblong terminal spikes. Zone 7.

Thymus pannonicus is native to eastern and central Europe through the Caucasus. This usually herbaceous, hairy perennial with flower stems 4 to 8 inches (10 to 20 cm) tall has ascending branches and a woody base. The leaves are lanceolate and up to 0.75 inch (1.9 cm) long. Pink, rose, or red flowers grow in simple spikes. Zone 5.

Thymus praecox (creeping thyme, red creeping thyme, wild thyme; Plate 37) is native to the northern and central Balkan Peninsula. It is a creeping, mat-forming, somewhat woody perennial herb. The leaves are obovate to almost round and quite leathery. Flowers are purple to mauve, sometimes white. The pubescent *T. praecox* subsp. *arcticus* has been selected or bred into white-flowered and dark green forms. Zone 5.

Thymus pseudolanuginosus (woolly thyme; Plate 38) is hairy, creeping, and mat-forming. This prostrate perennial rises less than 1 inch (2.5 cm) above the soil and spreads as much as 12 to 18 inches (30 to 45 cm) in diameter. It is woody at its base. Hairy gray leaves are elliptical and only about 0.125 inch (0.3 cm) long. Rosy purple flowers are few and grow in leaf axils. This plant is a good choice for growing in flagstone terraces and walks. Zone 6.

Thymus pulegioides (broad-leafed thyme) is a very aromatic, bushy, spreading shrub native to Europe. It grows just 4 to 12 inches (10 to 30 cm) tall. It is hairy only in axils and sometimes on opposite sides of the stems. The oval to elliptical leaves are under 0.5 inch (1.25 cm) long and mostly smooth. Pink, mauve, or purple flowers grow in interrupted spikes. The cultivar 'Oregano-scented' has been named for obvious reasons. Zone 5.

Thymus quinquecostatus is a prostrate, wiry shrub with pubescent stems. It grows only 4 inches (10 cm) tall and is native to the desert regions of Mongolia and Japan. Narrow to broad oval leaves are glabrous and only about 0.25 inch (0.6 cm) long. Pink to rose to purple flowers grow in terminal spikes. Zone 5.

Thymus richardii is a prostrate, creeping perennial with flower stems that grow only 4.5 inches (11.25 cm) tall. It is native to Sicily. Leaves are gray, ovate, and about 0.5 inch (1.25 cm) long. Pink to lilac flowers grow profusely in cymes. Zone 7.

Thymus serpyllum (creeping thyme, mother of thyme, wild thyme; Plate 39) is a creeping herb that forms matlike growth only 3 to 6 inches (7.5 to 15 cm) tall. The species is native to northwestern Europe. Linear to oval leaves are pubescent. Pink or purple flowers grow in rounded heads. A great deal of variation exists in the many cultivars of this species. Among the better-known varieties are 'Albus', 'Annie Hall', 'Coccineus', and 'Elfin'. Zone 5.

Thymus serpyllum (mother of thyme). From Blytt and Dahl 1906.

Thymus vulgaris (common thyme, English thyme, French thyme, garden thyme) is a potherb known to herb gardeners in its many forms and cultivars. A woody, erect plant that grows 6 to 15 inches (15 to 37.5 cm) tall, it has linear to elliptical leaves that are tomentose. Lilac, white, or pale purple flowers grow in terminal heads. Among the many cultivars are 'Erectus', 'Lavender', 'Narrow-Leaf French', and 'Orange Balsam'. 'Narrow-Leaf French' is the most common culinary variety and includes several variations. Zones 5–8.

Thymus zygis grows only 4 to 7 inches (10 to 17.5 cm) tall. Nonetheless, this Iberian species is a sturdy, erect shrub. It is slightly pubescent and has linear leaves about 0.25 inch (0.6 cm) long. White flowers grow in interrupted spikes. Zone 7.

Trichostema

Trichostema (blue curls) includes some sixteen aromatic herbs and shrubs native to North America. The leaves are usually entire. Flowers grow densely in whorled spikes or axillary cymes. Blue curls make good subjects for rock gardens and wild gardens.

Trichostema lanatum (California romero, woolly blue curls) is an erect shrub native to California. It grows up to 42 inches (105 cm) tall. Narrow, linear 2.5-inch (6.25-cm) leaves are smooth on top and tomentose underneath. Blue to violet, woolly flowers appear in spring growing densely on interrupted whorled spikes.

Trichostema lanceolatum (vinegar weed) is a strongly scented 24-inch (60-cm) annual native to the western United States. Lanceolate leaves are up to 0.25 inch (0.6 cm) in length. Light blue flowers appear in late summer growing in axillary racemes. Zones 7–10.

Trichostema ovatum (alkali blue curls), another native of California, is an erect 24-inch (60-cm) annual with oval to nearly round leaves. Light blue flowers appear in late summer.

Westringia

Westringia includes twenty to twenty-seven species of Australian shrubs. The plants are often hairy and bear flowers growing either singly in leaf axils or in terminal heads. Propagation is by seeds or cuttings. There is some disagreement on the taxonomy of one species cultivated in California. From what I can tell, this species is *W. rigida*. Zone 10.

Westringia rigida is a 36-inch (90-cm) shrub native to Australia and Tasmania. Its flowers are white or violet and flecked with purple. The cultivar 'Variegata' was chosen for its green and white variegated leaves. Zone 10.

USDA Hardiness Zone Map

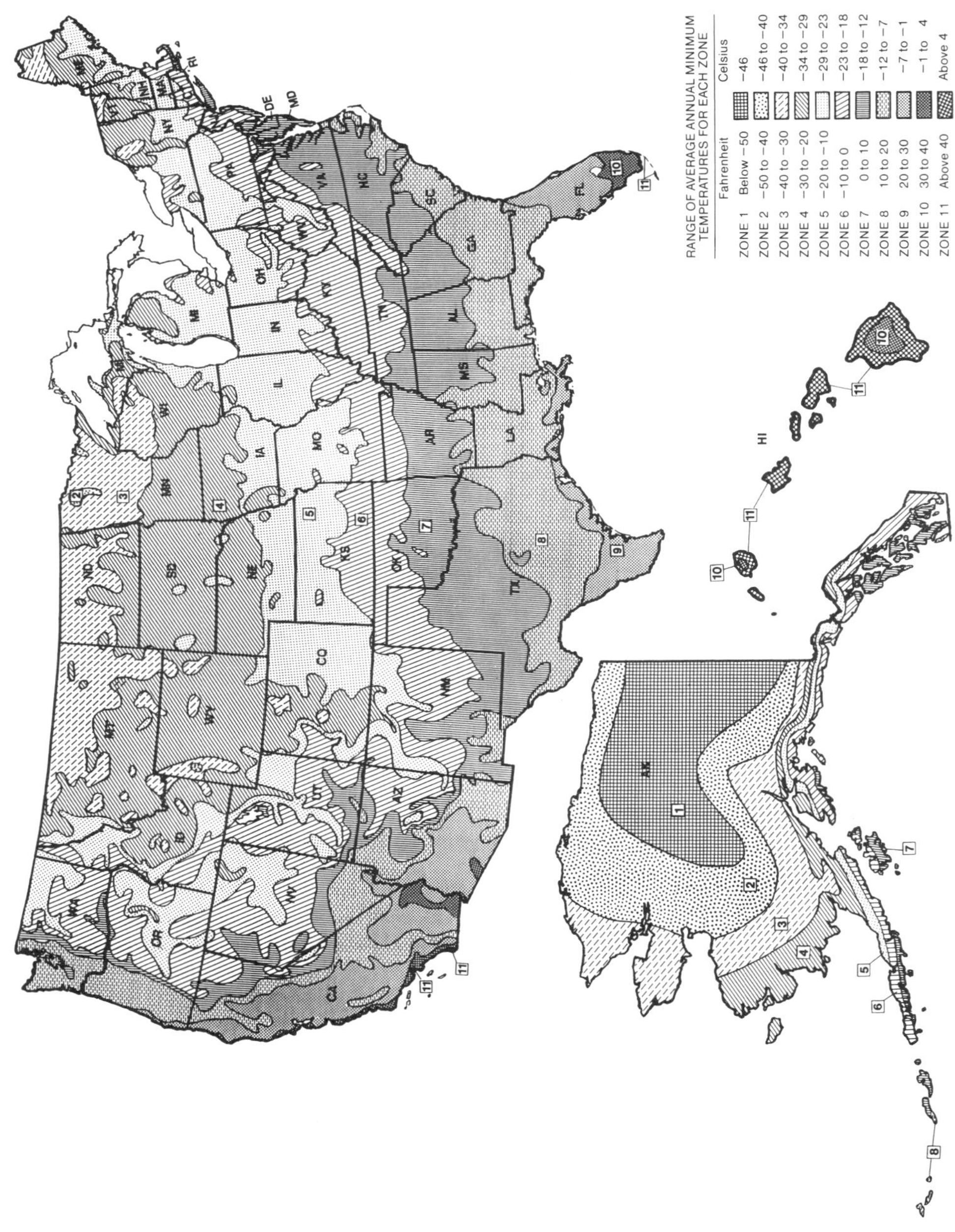

Further Reading

Anderson, Frank J. 1977. *An Illustrated History of the Herbals.* Columbia University Press, New York.

Armitage, Allan M. 1997. *Herbaceous Perennial Plants,* Second Edition. Stipes Publishing, Champaign, Illinois.

Bailey Hortorium. 1976. *Hortus Third.* Macmillan, New York.

Bender, Steve, editor. 1999. *Southern Living Garden Problem Solver.* Oxmoor House, Birmingham, Alabama.

Blackwell, Elizabeth. 1737. *A Curious Herbal.* John Nourse, London.

Blunt, Wilfrid, and William T. Stearn. 1994. *The Art of Botanical Illustration.* Antique Collectors' Club, Woodbridge, Suffolk, England.

Blytt, Axel Gudbrand, and Ove Dahl. 1906. *Haandbog i Norges Flora.* A. Cammermeyer, Oslo.

Bock, Hieronymus. 1546. *Kreuter Buch.* Strassburg.

Bown, Deni. 1995. *Encyclopedia of Herbs.* Dorling Kindersley, New York.

Brunfels, Otto. 1530. *Herbarum Vivae Eicones ad Nature Imitationem.* Ioannem Schottum, Argentorati.

Clebsch, Betsy. 1997. *A Book of Salvias.* Timber Press, Portland, Oregon.

Clifford, Derek. 1963. *A History of Garden Design.* Frederick A. Praeger, New York.

Constantin, Paul, and Alfred Edmund Brehm. 1894–1896. *Le Monde des Plantes.* J. B. Baillière et Fils, Paris.

Culpeper, Nicholas. 1652. *The English Physitian.* Peter Cole, London.

DiSabato-Aust, Tracy. 1998. *The Well-Tended Perennial Garden.* Timber Press, Portland, Oregon.

Dobelis, Inge N., editor. 1986. *Magic and Medicine of Plants.* Readers Digest, Pleasantville, New York.

Fiori, Adriano, Giulio Paoletti, and Francois Crepin. 1895–1904. *Iconographia Florae Italicae.* Tipografia del Seminario, Padua.

Flora of China Editorial Committee. 1998. *Flora of China Illustrations,* Volume 17. Missouri Botanical Garden Press, St. Louis.

Foster, Gertrude B., and Rosemary F. Louden. 1980. *Park's Success with Herbs.* Park Seed, Greenwood, South Carolina.

Fuchs, Leonhart. 1542. *De Historia Stirpium Commentarii Insignes.* Officina Isingriniana, Basileae.

Garland, Sarah. 1979. *The Complete Book of Spices and Herbs.* Viking Press, New York.

Gerard, John. 1597. *The Herball.* John Norton, London.

Goebel, Karl, and Isaac Bayley Balfour. 1900–1905. *Organography of Plants.* Clarendon Press, Oxford, England.

Griffiths, Mark. 1995. *Index of Garden Plants.* Timber Press, Portland, Oregon.

Heukels, Hendrik. 1909–1911. *De Flora van Nederland.* E. J. Brill, Leiden.

Hughes, Roberta L. Summer. 1980. The language of herbs. *The Herb Quarterly* 2 (6): 32–34.

Karsten, Hermann. 1895. *Flora von Deutschland, Österreich und der Schweiz.* Fr. Eugen Köhler, Gera-Untermhaus, Germany.

Kourik, Robert. 1998. *The Lavender Garden.* Chronicle Books, San Francisco.

Mattioli, Pietro Andrea. 1583. *Commentarij in VI, libros Pedacij Dioscoridis Anazarbei de Medica materia.* Felicem Valgrisium, Venetijs.

Muenscher, Walter Conrad. 1955. *Weeds,* Second Edition. Macmillan, NewYork.

Newcomb, Lawrence. 1977. *Newcomb's Wildflower Guide.* Little, Brown, Boston.

Ober, Richard, editor. 1996. *The National Herb Garden Guidebook.* Potomac Unit, Herb Society of America, Springfield, Vermont.

Parkinson, John. 1629. *Paradisi in Sole Paradisus Terrestris.* Humfrey Lownes and Robert Young, London.

Parkinson, John. 1640. *Theatricum Botanicum.* Tho. Cotes, London.

Pickthall, Mohammed Marmaduke. 1993. *The Meaning of the Glorious Koran.* Penguin Books, New York.

Pirone, Pascal P. 1978. *Diseases and Pests of Ornamental Plants.* John Wiley, New York.

Rollins, Elizabeth, and Arthur O. Tucker. 1992. The other origanums. *The Herb Companion.* Interweave Press, Loveland, Colorado.

Schöffer, Peter. 1484. *Herbarius Latinus.* Mainz.

Schöffer, Peter. 1485. *Der Gart der Gesundheit.* Mainz.

Still, Steven M. 1994. *Manual of Herbaceous Plants,* Fourth Edition. Stipes, Champaign, Illinois.

Swenson, Allan A. 1981. *Your Biblical Garden.* Garden City, Doubleday, New York.

Thomas, Graham Stuart. 1990. *Perennial Garden Plants,* Third Edition. Timber Press, Portland, Oregon.

Tucker, Arthur O. 1992a. The truth about mints. *The Herb Companion.* Interweave Press, Loveland, Colorado.

Tucker, Arthur O. 1992b. Will the real oregano please stand up? *The Herb Companion.* Interweave Press, Loveland, Colorado.

Turner, William. 1551–1568. *A New Herball.* Steven Mierdman, London.

Walsh, Huber M. 1997. The Elizabeth Blackwell story. *Missouri Botanical Garden Bulletin.*

Youngkin, Heber W. 1946. Japanese mint. *The Herbarist* (12).

Glossary

Acuminate. Tapering to a point, often with somewhat concave sides.

Ascending. Rising upward, usually from a horizontal or slanting position.

Axil. The upper angle of the joint between a stem or axis and a leaf, branch, or stalk.

Basal. At the base or arising from the base.

Bract. A modified leaf, often small and scalelike, that is usually part of an inflorescence and that encloses the stem and flower bud.

Calyx. The outer whorl of a flower consisting of separate or joined sepals.

Cordate. Heart-shaped.

Corolla. The inner circle or second circle of the perianth, composed of either separate or fused petals.

Corymb. A short, broad, rather flat-topped inflorescence that is indeterminate, meaning that the outer flowers open first.

Crenate. Scalloped, with shallow, rounded teeth.

Crenulate. Minutely crenate.

Cultivar. A cultivated variety.

Cyme. A broad, rather flat-topped inflorescence that is determinate, meaning the central flower opens first.

Deciduous. Having leaves that fall off periodically, usually once a year in fall.

Deltoid. Triangular.

Dentate. Toothed.

Dissected. Deeply divided or cut.

Downy. Covered with short, soft hairs.

Elliptic. Oblong and widest at the middle with narrowed or rounded ends.

Entire. Having a continuous, unbroken margin; not toothed, notched, or scalloped in any way.

Erect. Perpendicular to level ground or another point of attachment.

Evergreen. Having foliage that remains green throughout more than one growing season.

Filament. A threadlike part or organ, especially the stalk of the stamen that bears the anther.

Genus (pl. **genera**). The taxonomic rank between family and species.

Glomerule. A cluster of flowers generally rising from a single conspicuous bract.

Habit. The general appearance and characteristics of a plant.

Habitat. The type of locality in which a plant grows naturally.

Hair. An outgrowth of the plant epidermis that may be one of several types according to its form, branching, and attachment.

Herb. A plant without above-ground woody stems or a plant with aromatic, medicinal, or savory qualities.

Herbaceous. Having stems and foliage that die back to the ground each year.

Hirsute. Covered with long, coarse, rough hairs.

Hoary. Densely covered with whitish hairs.

Hybrid. A plant resulting from a spontaneous or purposeful cross-breeding of parents that are genetically unlike, usually belonging to different species.

Lanceolate. Lance-shaped, several times longer than wide, widest below the middle, and tapering to a spearlike tip.

Lyrate. Pinnatifid but with a large, round, terminal lobe and smaller lateral lobes that diminish in size toward the leaf base.

Obovate. Egg-shaped, round at both ends, broader above the middle, and more narrow below the middle.

Opposite. On opposite sides of an axis, such as two leaves at the same level.

Orbicular. Round or nearly round.

Ovate. Egg-shaped, round at both ends, and most broad below the middle.

Panicle. An indeterminate, branched, more or less flat-topped inflorescence the length of which is not circumscribed by having the center flower open first and the branches of which are usually elongated or short and broad.

Perianth. The part of a flower consisting of the calyx and the corolla, especially when they are not greatly differentiated. Also known as the floral envelope.

pH. A measure of hydrogen-ion concentration in the soil in which a value of 7 indicates neutrality, higher numbers indicate alkalinity, and lower numbers indicate acidity.

Pinnate. Featherlike, with leaflets (pinnae) arranged in two rows along the axis or rachis.

Pinnatifid. Pinnate with deep clefts, nearly to the rachis or midrib of the leaf.

Procumbent. Having stems that trail along the ground without rooting.

Pistil. The female reproductive organ of a plant consisting of ovary, style, and stigma.

Pubescent. Covered with short, fine hairs.

Raceme. An unbranched, indeterminate, usually elongated inflorescence with stemmed flowers.

Racemose. Bearing flowers in racemelike inflorescences.

Revolute. Rolled backward or toward the underside.

Rhizome. A ground-level or underground, specialized stem that produces roots, leaves, and stems.

Rosette. A cluster of leaves radiating from a plant crown usually near or at ground level.

Rugose. Wrinkled, with irregular lines and veins that appear impressed into the surface.

Serrate. Saw-toothed.

Simple. Unbranched, rather than compound or divided.

Sinuate. Having a wavy margin.

Solitary. Occurring singly, usually referring to a flower borne alone on a stem or in an axil.

Species. The taxonomic rank below genus.

Spike. An indeterminate, elongated, unbranched inflorescence with sessile flowers.

Stamen. The pollen-bearing male organ of a seed-bearing plant consisting of anther and filament, sometimes reduced to anther only.

Stigma. The apical part of the pistil that receives pollen.

Stolon. A trailing shoot or stem that runs along the ground and takes root, giving rise to plantlets at the tip or the nodes.

Stoloniferous. Having or producing stolons.

Style. The more or less elongated portion of the pistil between the ovary and the stigma, absent if the stigma is sessile.

Subshrub. A perennial herb with a woody base and somewhat soft stems, or a very low shrub treated as a perennial.

Terminal. At the tip, apical.

Tomentose. Covered with densely matted, short, rigid, woolly hairs.

Tuber. A short, thick, usually subterranean modified stem or branch that bears buds and is used for storage.

Tuberous. Having tubers.

Variety. A subdivision of species.

Verticil. A whorl or ring of three or more parts at one node.

Verticillaster. A false whorl with opposite cymes appearing to surround the stem.

Viscid. Covered with sticky or gelatinous exudate.

Whorl. A circle of three or more leaves, flowers, or other organs arranged at one node or loosely around a single axis.

Woolly. Having long, soft, somewhat matted hairs.

Index of Plant Names

Acinos, 116
Acinos alpinus, 116
Acinos arvensis, 116
Acinos thymoides. See *Acinos arvensis*
African sage. See *Salvia aethiopis*
Agastache, 85, 86–87, 117–118
Agastache barberi, 87, 117
Agastache barberi 'Firebird', 117
Agastache barberi 'Tutti-frutti', 117
Agastache foeniculum, 86, 117, Plate 41
Agastache rugosa, 86, 117, 118
Ajuga, 87–88, 119–120
Ajuga genevensis, 88, 119, 120
Ajuga genevensis 'Alba', 119
Ajuga genevensis 'Pink Beauty', 119
Ajuga genevensis 'Robusta', 119
Ajuga genevensis 'Rosea', 119
Ajuga genevensis 'Tottenham', 119
Ajuga genevensis 'Variegata', 119
Ajuga pyramidalis, 88, 119, 120
Ajuga pyramidalis 'Metallica Crispa', 120
Ajuga reptans, 87, 119, 120, 121, Plate 42
Ajuga reptans 'Alba', 88, 120
Ajuga reptans 'Atropurpurea', 87, 88, 120
Ajuga reptans 'Bronze Beauty', 88, 120
Ajuga reptans 'Burgundy Glow', 88, 120
Ajuga reptans 'Catlin's Giant', 88, 120
Ajuga reptans 'Gray Lady', 88, 120
Ajuga reptans 'Jungle Beauty', 88, 120
Ajuga reptans 'Multicolor', 88, 120
Ajuga reptans 'Pink Elf', 88, 120
Ajuga reptans 'Pink Spire', 88, 120
Ajuga reptans 'Purple Brocade', 88, 120, Plate 43
Ajuga reptans 'Purple Torch', 87, 120
Ajuga reptans 'Rosea', 88, 120
Ajuga reptans 'Silver Carpet', 88, 120
Ajuga reptans 'Tricolor'. See *Ajuga reptans* 'Multicolor'
Ajuga reptans 'Variegata', 88, 120
Alehoof. See *Glechoma hederacea*
Alkali blue curls. See *Trichostema ovatum*
Alpine calamint. See *Acinos alpinus*
American dittany. See *Cunila origanoides*
American germander. See *Teucrium canadense*
American mountain mint. See *Pycnanthemum*
American pennyroyal. See *Hedeoma pulegioides*
Amethysteya, 120
Amethysteya caerulea, 120
Anise hyssop. See *Agastache foeniculum*
Anise mint. See *Agastache foeniculum*
Annual clary. See *Salvia viridis*

Annual marjoram. See *Origanum majorana*
Anthriscus cereifolium, 49
Apple mint. See *Mentha suaveolens*
Archangel. See *Lamium album*
Artemisia drancunculus, 50
Australian mint bush. See *Prostanthera*
Autumn sage. See *Salvia greggii*
Azure sage. See *Salvia azurea*

Baby sage. See *Salvia microphylla*
Ballota, 121–122
Ballota nigra, 52, 121–122
Balm. See *Melissa*
Balm mint bush. See *Prostanthera*
Balm of Gilead. See *Cedronella canariensis*
Basil. See *Ocimum*
Basil mint. See *Mentha arvensis*
Basil thyme. See *Acinos arvensis, Calamintha nepeta*
Bastard balm. See *Melittis melissophyllum*
Bay leaf. See *Anthriscus cereifolium*
Bee balm. See *Melissa officinalis, Monarda*
Beefsteak plant. See *Perilla frutescens*
Bee nettle. See *Lamium amplexicaule*
Bee sage. See *Salvia apiana*
Bells of Ireland. See *Moluccella laevis*
Bergamot. See *Mentha aquatica, Monarda didyma*
Bergamot mint. See *Mentha ×piperita* 'Citrata'
Betonica macrantha. See *Stachys macrantha*
Betony. See *Stachys*
Big betony. See *Stachys macrantha*
Black horehound. See *Ballota nigra*
Black peppermint. See *Mentha ×piperita* var. *piperita*
Bladder sage. See *Salazaria mexicana*
Blephilia, 122
Blephilia hirsuta, 54, 122
Blind nettle. See *Lamium amplexicaule*
Bluebeard. See *Salvia viridis*
Blue bugle. See *Ajuga genevensis*
Blue curls. See *Trichostoma*
Blue sage. See *Salvia clevelandii, Salvia azurea*
Bog sage. See *Salvia uliginosa*
Brazilian coleus. See *Plectranthus oertendahlii*
Broad-leafed thyme. See *Thymus pulegioides*
Bugle. See *Ajuga*
Bugle weed. See *Ajuga*
Bugleweed. See *Ajuga, Lycopus virginicus*
Bush basil. See *Ocimum basilicum, Ocimum Indicum*

Calamint. See *Calamintha*
Calamintha, 88, 116, 122
Calamintha grandiflora, 88, 122
Calamintha nepeta, 88, 122, Plate 44
Calamintha sylvatica, 122
California romero. See *Trichostema lanatum*
California white sage. See *Salvia apiana*
Canary balm. See *Cedronella canariensis*
Cancerweed. See *Salvia lyrata*
Candle plant. See *Plectranthus oertendahlii*
Caraway thyme. See *Thymus herba-barona*
Carpenter's square. See *Scrophularia marilandica*
Carpet bugleweed. See *Ajuga reptans*
Caspian perovskia. See *Perovskia abrotanoides*
Catharanthus, 100
Catmint. See *Nepeta*
Catnip. See *Nepeta cataria*

Cat's foot. See *Glechoma hederacea*
Cat's whiskers. See *Orthosiphon stamineus*
Cat thyme. See *Teucrium marum*
Cedronella, 123
Cedronella canariensis, 123
Chaparral sage. See *Salvia leucophylla*
Chia. See *Salvia columbariae*
Chinese artichoke. See *Stachys affinis*
Chorogi. See *Stachys affinis*
Cinnamon basil. See *Ocimum basilicum* 'Cinnamon'
Citronella. See *Collinsonia canadensis*
Clary. See *Salvia sclarea*
Cleareye. See *Salvia sclarea*
Cleveland sage. See *Salvia clevelandii*
Clinopodium, 123
Clinopodium chinense, 123, 124
Clinopodium georgianum, 123
Clinopodium vulgare, 123
Clover. See *Trifolium*
Colebrookea, 123
Colebrookea oppositifolia, 123
Coleus. See *Solenostemon*
Coleus hybridus. See *Solenostemon scutellarioides*
Coleus ×*hybridus.* See *Solenostemon scutellarioides*
Collinsonia, 123–125
Collinsonia canadensis, 125
Colquhounia, 125
Colquhounia coccinea, 125
Common basil. See *Ocimum basilicum*
Common betony. See *Stachys officinalis*
Common bugleweed. See *Ajuga reptans*
Common calamint. See *Calamintha sylvatica*
Common horehound. See *Marrubium vulgare*
Common sage. See *Salvia officinalis*
Common thyme. See *Thymus vulgaris*
Conradina, 125
Conradina canescens, 125
Conradina grandiflora, 125
Conradina verticillata, 125
Corn mint. See *Mentha arvensis*
Corsican mint. See *Mentha requienii*
Country borage. See *Plectranthus amboinicus*
Coyote mint. See *Monardella villosa*
Creeping Charlie. See *Glechoma hederacea*
Creeping mint. See *Meehania cordata*
Creeping rosemary. See *Rosmarinus officinalis*
Creeping sage. See *Salvia sonomensis*
Creeping thyme. See *Thymus praecox, Thymus serpyllum*
Crème-de-menthe plant. See *Mentha requienii*
Cretan oregano. See *Origanum onites*
Crosnes du Japon. See *Stachys affinis*
Cuban oregano. See *Plectranthus amboinicus*
Cunila, 125–126
Cunila origanoides, 54, 126
Curled mint. See *Mentha cruciata*
Curly mint. See *Mentha* ×*piperita* 'Crispa'
Cushion calamint. See *Clinopodium vulgare*

Dead nettle. See *Lamium*
Desert sage. See *Salvia dorrii*
Digitalis, 28
Digitalis purpurea, 28
Dittany of Crete. See *Origanum dictamnus*
Dog mint. See *Clinopodium vulgare*
Dotted mint. See *Monarda punctata*
Downy woundwort. See *Stachys germanica*
Dracocephalum, 126–129
Dracocephalum argunense, 126, 127

Dracocephalum austriacum, 126
Dracocephalum botryoides, 126
Dracocephalum calophyllum, 126
Dracocephalum moldavicum, 126
Dracocephalum moldavicum 'Album', 126
Dracocephalum nutans, 128
Dracocephalum parvifolium, 128
Dracocephalum peregrinum, 128
Dracocephalum purdomii, 128
Dracocephalum renatii, 128
Dracocephalum rupestre, 128, 129
Dracocephalum ruyschianum, 128
Dragonhead. See *Dracocephalum*
Dragon mouth. See *Horminum pyrenaicum*
Dumb nettle. See *Lamium album*
Dwarf sage. See *Salvia officinalis* 'Nana'
Dwarf thyme. See *Thymus serpyllum* 'Elfin'

Eau de cologne mint. See *Mentha* ×*piperita* 'Citrata'
Egyptian marjoram. See *Origanum maru*
Elsholtzia, 130
Elsholtzia ciliata, 130
Elsholtzia stauntonii, 130
Elsholtzia stauntonii 'Alba', 130
English lavender. See *Lavandula angustifolia*
English pennyroyal. See *Mentha pulegium*
English thyme. See *Thymus vulgaris*
Eremostachys, 130–131
Eremostachys laciniata, 130
Eremostachys superba, 130–131
European corn mint. See *Mentha arvensis*

False dragonhead. See *Physostegia*
Field balm. See *Glechoma hederacea*
Field mint. See *Mentha arvensis*
Figwort. See *Scrophularia*
Flame nettle. See *Solenostemon scutellarioides*
Foxglove. See *Digitalis*
Fragrant giant hyssop. See *Agastache foeniculum*
French lavender. See *Lavandula dentata, Lavandula stoechas*
French thyme. See *Plectranthus amboinicus, Thymus vulgaris*
Fringed lavender. See *Lavandula dentata*
Fruit-scented sage. See *Salvia dorisiana*

Galeopsis, 131
Galeopsis pubescens, 131
Galeopsis segetum, 131
Galeopsis speciosa, 131
Garden sage. See *Salvia officinalis*
Garden thyme. See *Thymus vulgaris*
Geneva bugleweed. See *Ajuga genevensis*
Gentian sage. See *Salvia patens, Salvia purpurea*
Germander. See *Teucrium*
Giant hyssop. See *Agastache*
Gill-over-the-ground. See *Glechoma hederacea*
Ginger mint. See *Mentha arvensis* 'Variegata'
Glechoma, 100–101, 132
Glechoma hederacea, 99, 100–101, 132, Plate 60
Glechoma hederacea 'Rosea', 101, 132
Glechoma hederacea 'Variegata', 101, 132
Golden lemon balm. See *Melissa officinalis* 'Aurea'
Golden marjoram. See *Origanum vulgare* 'Aurea'
Goldenrod. See *Solidago*

Gray ball sage. See *Salvia dorrii*
Gray sage. See *Salvia leucophylla*
Greasewood. See *Salvia apiana*
Greek basil. See *Ocimum basilicum* var. *minimum* 'Fine Leaf'
Greek mountain oregano. See *Origanum vulgare* subsp. *hirtum*
Greek oregano. See *Origanum onites*
Ground ivy. See *Glechoma hederacea*
Gypsywort. See *Lycopus europaeus*

Hairy germander. See *Teucrium occidentale*
Hairy wood mint. See *Blephilia hirsuta*
Hardy marjoram. See *Origanum* ×*majoricum*
Heal-all. See *Prunella*
Hedeoma, 132
Hedeoma pulegioides, 54, 132
Hedge nettle. See *Stachys*
Helmet flower. See *Scutellaria*
Henbit. See *Lamium amplexicaule*
Hidcote lavender. See *Lavandula angustifolia* 'Hidcote'
Hoary basil. See *Ocimum americanum*
Holy basil. See *Ocimum tenuiflorum*
Hop marjoram. See *Origanum dictamnus*
Horehound. See *Marrubium*
Horminum, 132
Horminum pyrenaicum, 132–133
Horminum pyrenaicum 'Album', 133
Horminum pyrenaicum 'Grandiflorum', 133
Horminum pyrenaicum 'Roseum', 133
Horse balm. See *Collinsonia*
Horsemint. See *Mentha longifolia, Monarda*
Horseweed. See *Collinsonia*
Hypericum, 28
Hyssop. See *Hyssopus*
Hyssopus, 66–67, 85, 88–89, 133
Hyssopus officinalis, 19, 43, 53, 54, 66–67, 88, 133
Hyssopus officinalis 'Alba', 133
Hyssopus officinalis 'Grandiflora', 133
Hyssopus officinalis 'Rosea', 133
Hyssopus officinalis 'Rubra', 133
Hyssopus officinalis 'Sissinghurst', 133

Indian mint. See *Plectranthus amboinicus*
Italian basil. See *Ocimum basilicum* var. *minimum* 'Fine Leaf'
Italian oregano. See *Origanum* ×*majoricum*

Japanese artichoke. See *Stachys affinis*
Japanese dead nettle. See *Meehania*
Japanese mint. See *Mentha arvensis* var. *piperascens*
Jerusalem sage. See *Phlomis fruticosa*
Jim sage. See *Salvia clevelandii*
Joseph sage. See *Salvia viridis*
Judean sage. See *Salvia judaica*
Jupiter's staff. See *Salvia glutinosa*

Knotroot. See *Stachys affinis*
Knotted marjoram. See *Origanum majorana*
Knotweed. See *Polygonum*
Korean mint. See *Agastache rugosa*

Lady-in-the-bath. See *Moluccella laevis*
Lallemantia, 134
Lallemantia canescens, 134
Lallemantia iberica, 134
Lallemantia peltata, 134
Lallemantia royleana, 134, 135
Lamb's ear. See *Stachys byzantina*
Lamb's tail. See *Stachys byzantina*
Lamb's tongue. See *Stachys byzantina*
Lamiastrum galeobdolon. See *Lamium galeobdolon*

Lamium, 85, 89–90, 101–102, 134–139
Lamium album, 134, 136, 137
Lamium album 'Friday', 136
Lamium album 'Goldflake', 136
Lamium album 'Pale Peril', 136
Lamium amplexicaule, 100, 101–102, 136, 138
Lamium galeobdolon, 89, 136, Plate 45
Lamium galeobdolon 'Herman's Pride', 89, 136
Lamium galeobdolon 'Silver Angel', 136
Lamium galeobdolon 'Silver Carpet', 136
Lamium galeobdolon 'Variegatum', 136
Lamium garganicum, 136
Lamium garganicum 'Golden Carpet', 136
Lamium maculatum, 89–90, 102, 139
Lamium maculatum 'Beacon Silver', 89, 102, 139
Lamium maculatum 'Pink Pewter', 89, 139
Lamium maculatum 'White Nancy', 89, 102, 139, Plate 46
Lamium purpureum, 102, 139, Plate 61
Large-flowered calamint. See *Calamintha grandiflora*
Lauris nobilis, 49
Lavandula, 23, 34, 43, 45, 46, 47, 49, 51, 55, 56, 57, 67–68, 112, 139–141
Lavandula angustifolia, 54, 67, 140, 141
Lavandula angustifolia 'Alba', 67, 140
Lavandula angustifolia 'Hidcote', 67, 140, Plate 14
Lavandula angustifolia 'Jean Davis', 68, 140, Plate 15
Lavandula angustifolia 'Munstead', 68, 140, Plate 16
Lavandula angustifolia 'Nana', 68, 140
Lavandula angustifolia 'Rosea', 68, 140
Lavandula angustifolia 'Vera', 68, 140
Lavandula dentata, 140, Plate 4, Plate 17
Lavandula multifida, 140
Lavandula pinnata, 140
Lavandula stoechas, 67, 68, 140
Lavandula stoechas 'Alba', 68, 140
Lavandula stoechas 'Papillon', 68, 140
Lavender. See *Lavandula*
Lavender hyssop. See *Agastache foeniculum*
Lemon balm. See *Melissa officinalis*
Lemon basil. See *Ocimum basilicum* var. *citriodorum*
Lemon mint. See *Mentha ×piperita* 'Citrata', *Monarda citriodora*
Lemon thyme. See *Thymus ×citriodorus*
Leonotis, 142
Leonotis leonurus, 142
Leonotis nepetifolia, 142
Leonotis ocymifolia, 142
Leonurus, 142–143
Leonurus cardiaca, 54, 142–143
Lepechinia, 143
Lepechinia calycina, 143
Lesser calamint. See *Calamintha nepeta*
Lettuce leaf basil. See *Ocimum basilicum* var. *crispum*
Licorice basil. See *Ocimum basilicum* 'Anise'
Lilac sage. See *Salvia verticillata*
Lion's ear. See *Leonotis*
Lion's heart. See *Physostegia*
Lycopus, 143–144
Lycopus americanus, 144
Lycopus europaeus, 144
Lycopus virginicus, 144
Lyre-leafed sage. See *Salvia lyrata*

Macbridea, 144–145
Macbridea alba, 145
Macbridea pulchra, 145
Majorana. See *Origanum*
Majorana hortensis. See *Origanum majorana*
Majorana onites. See *Origanum onites*
Marjoram. See *Origanum majorana*
Marrubium, 68, 112, 145
Marrubium album, 41
Marrubium album. See *Marrubium vulgare*
Marrubium incanum, 145
Marrubium leonuroides, 145
Marrubium vulgare, 43, 54, 68, 80, 100, 145, 146
Marvel. See *Marrubium vulgare*
Meadow clary. See *Salvia pratensis*
Meadow sage. See *Salvia pratensis*
Mealycup sage. See *Salvia farinacea*
Mealy sage. See *Salvia farinacea*
Meehan's mint. See *Meehania*
Meehania, 145–148
Meehania cordata, 148
Meehania fargesii, 147, 148
Meehania urticifolia, 148
Melissa, 23, 68, 148
Melissa officinalis, 31, 43, 45, 46, 51, 54, 64, 68–69, 109, 148, Plate 18
Melissa officinalis 'All Gold', 69
Melissa officinalis 'Aurea', 69, Plate 19
Melittis, 149
Melittis melissophyllum, 149
Mentha, 24, 51, 59, 75, 149–155
Mentha aquatica, 47, 54, 61, 64, 149–150
Mentha arvensis, 60, 61, 62–63, 150, 151
Mentha arvensis 'Banana', 63
Mentha arvensis 'Coconut', 63
Mentha arvensis var. *piperascens,* 59, 63
Mentha arvensis 'Variegata', 63
Mentha austriaca. See *Mentha arvensis*
Mentha canadensis. See *Mentha arvensis*
Mentha cervina, 59, 150
Mentha cruciata, 37
Mentha gentilis. See *Mentha arvensis*
Mentha hirsuta. See *Mentha aquatica*
Mentha incana. See *Mentha longifolia*
Mentha insularis. See *Mentha suaveolens*
Mentha longifolia, 150
Mentha macrostachya. See *Mentha suaveolens*
Mentha ×*piperita,* 20, 23, 43, 46, 47, 54, 60, 62, 63–64, 100, 150, 152
Mentha ×*piperita* 'Chocolate Mint', 64, Plate 11
Mentha ×*piperita* var. *citrata.* See *Mentha* ×*piperita* and *Mentha aquatica*
Mentha ×*piperita* 'Citrata', 64
Mentha ×*piperita* var. *crispa.* See *Mentha* ×*piperita*
Mentha ×*piperita* 'Crispa', 64
Mentha ×*piperita* 'Lime', 64
Mentha ×*piperita* var. *officinalis,* 64
Mentha ×*piperita* var. *piperita,* 64
Mentha ×*piperita* var. *piperita* 'Micham', 64
Mentha pulegium, 23, 45, 48, 53, 59, 60, 61, 65, 132, 150, 152, 153
Mentha requienii, 56, 59, 60, 61, 65, 152
Mentha rotundifolia. See *Mentha suaveolens*
Mentha spicata, 23, 43, 46, 47, 48, 53, 54, 59, 60, 61, 63, 64, 65–66, 100, 150, 152, 154, Plate 12
Mentha spicata 'Crispa', 60, 65
Mentha spicata 'Kentucky Colonel', 65
Mentha suaveolens, 61, 62, 65, 154–155
Mentha suaveolens 'Variegata', 47, 65, 155, Plate 9, Plate 13

Mentha sylvestris. See *Mentha longifolia*
Menthella. See *Mentha requienii*
Mexican bush sage. See *Salvia leucantha*
Mexican hyssop. See *Agastache*
Mexican mint. See *Plectranthus amboinicus*
Micromeria, 155–156
Micromeria chamissonis, 155
Micromeria croatica, 155
Micromeria dalmatica, 155
Micromeria graeca, 155
Micromeria juliana, 155
Micromeria thymifolia, 156
Mint. See *Mentha*
Mint bush. See *Prostanthera*
Mint shrub. See *Elsholtzia ciliata*
Molucca balm. See *Moluccella laevis*
Moluccella, 90, 156
Moluccella laevis, 90, 156
Monarda, 90–91, 156–159
Monarda citriodora, 156, 158
Monarda clinopodia, 158
Monarda coccinea. See *Monarda didyma*
Monarda didyma, 53, 90, 91, 109, 111, 112, 158
Monarda didyma 'Cambridge Scarlet', 90, 114, 158
Monarda didyma 'Marshall's Delight', 90, 158, Plate 47
Monarda didyma 'Scorpio', 91, 158
Monarda didyma 'Violet Queen', 91, 158
Monarda fistulosa, 54, 90, 91, 157, 158
Monarda pectinata, 158
Monarda punctata, 54, 158–159
Monardella, 159–160
Monardella lanceolata, 159
Monardella linoides, 159
Monardella macrantha, 159
Monardella odoratissima, 159–160
Monardella villosa, 160
Mother of thyme. See *Acinos arvensis, Thymus serpyllum*
Motherwort. See *Leonurus*
Mountain mint. See *Calamintha nepeta, Pycnanthemum*
Munstead lavender. See *Lavandula angustifolia* 'Munstead'
Muscatel sage. See *Salvia sclarea*

Nepeta, 69, 91, 160–163
Nepeta camphorata, 160
Nepeta cataria, 41, 53, 100, 111, 160, 161
Nepeta ×faassenii, 69, 91, 160, 162, Plate 48
Nepeta ×faassenii 'Blue Beauty'. See *Nepeta ×faassenii* 'Souvenir d'André Chaudron'
Nepeta ×faassenii 'Blue Wonder', 91, 162
Nepeta ×faassenii 'Six Hills Giant', 91, 162
Nepeta ×faassenii 'Snowflake', 91, 162
Nepeta ×faassenii 'Souvenir d'André Chaudron', 91, 162
Nepeta ×faassenii 'Superba', 91, 162
Nepeta grandiflora, 162
Nepeta hederacea. See *Glechoma hederacea*
Nepeta melissifolia, 162
Nepeta mussinii. See *Nepeta ×faassenii*
Nepeta nepetella, 160, 162
Nepeta nervosa, 162
Nepeta nuda, 162
Nepeta racemosa, 160, 162–163
Nepeta raphanorhiza, 163
Nepeta sibirica, 163
Nepeta tuberosa, 163
Nepeta ucranica, 163

Obedience. See *Physostegia*
Obedience plant. See *Physostegia virginiana*

Obedient plant. See *Physostegia*
Ocimum, 69–72, 111, 163–165
Ocimum americanum, 163, 165
Ocimum americanum 'Spicy Globe'. See *Ocimum basilicum* × *Ocimum americanum* 'Spicy Globe'
Ocimum basilicum, 23, 25, 38, 45, 49, 50, 54, 70, 164, 165
Ocimum basilicum 'Anise', 71, 165
Ocimum basilicum 'Cinnamon', 71, 165, Plate 20
Ocimum basilicum var. *citriodorum,* 71
Ocimum basilicum var. *citriodorum* 'Mrs. Burns', 71
Ocimum basilicum var. *citriodorum* 'Sweet Dani', 71
Ocimum basilicum var. *crispum,* 71
Ocimum basilicum 'Dark Opal', 71, Plate 21
Ocimum basilicum 'Fino Verde Compatto', 71
Ocimum basilicum 'Genovese', 165
Ocimum basilicum var. *minimum* 'Fine Leaf', 71
Ocimum basilicum 'Napoletano', 71
Ocimum basilicum 'Purple Ruffles', 49, 72, 165, Plate 22
Ocimum basilicum 'Red Rubin', 72
Ocimum basilicum 'Siam Queen'. See *Ocimum basilicum* 'True Thai'
Ocimum basilicum 'Sweet Thai', 72, 165
Ocimum basilicum 'True Thai', 49, 72, 165, Plate 23
Ocimum basilicum × *Ocimum americanum* 'Spicy Globe', 70, 72
Ocimum canum. See *Ocimum americanum*
Ocimum gratissimum, 165
Ocimum Indicum, 38
Ocimum micranthum. See *Ocimum americanum*
Ocimum sanctum. See *Ocimum tenuiflorum*
Ocimum tenuiflorum, 72, 165
Ocimum tenuiflorum 'Red and Green', 72
Orange mint. See *Mentha aquatica*
Oregano. See *Origanum*
Oregano-scented thyme. See *Thymus pulegioides* 'Oregano-scented'
Organy. See *Origanum vulgare*
Origanum, 48, 49, 72–74, 75, 133, 165–167
Origanum dictamnus, 53, 73, 166, Plate 24
Origanum majorana, 24, 45, 47, 48, 49, 51, 53, 54, 72, 73, 165
Origanum ×*majoricum,* 54, 74, 166
Origanum maru, 19, 166
Origanum onites, 54, 73, 166–167
Origanum onites 'Aureum', 73
Origanum sipyleum, 167
Origanum vulgare, 47, 48, 49, 53, 72, 74, 100, 167
Origanum vulgare 'Alba', 74
Origanum vulgare 'Aurea', 74
Origanum vulgare 'Aureum Crispum', 74
Origanum vulgare 'Compactum', 74
Origanum vulgare subsp. *hirtum,* 48, 53
Orthosiphon, 85, 115, 167–168
Orthosiphon aristatus. See *Orthosiphon stamineus*
Orthosiphon stamineus, 85–86, 115, 168, Plate 40
Oswego tea. See *Monarda didyma*

Pachysandra, 100
Painted leaves. See *Solenostemon scutellarioides*
Painted nettle. See *Solenostemon scutellarioides*
Painted sage. See *Salvia viridis*
Parsley. See *Petroselinum crispum*

Patchouli. See *Pogostemon cablin*
Peach sage. See *Salvia dorisiana*
Pennyroyal. See *Mentha cervina, Mentha pulegium*
Peppermint. See *Mentha ×piperita*
Perilla, 91–92, 168–170
Perilla frutescens, 91–92, 168–170, Plate 49
Perilla frutescens 'Fancy Fringe', 92
Periwinkle. See *Catharanthus*
Perovskia, 85, 92–93, 170
Perovskia abrotanoides, 93, 170
Perovskia artemesioides, 170
Perovskia atriplicifolia, 53, 92–93, 170, Plate 7, Plate 50
Perovskia atriplicifolia 'Blue Haze', 93
Perovskia atriplicifolia 'Blue Spire', 93
Petroselinum crispum, 49
Phlomis, 170–172
Phlomis alpina, 171
Phlomis cashmeriana, 171
Phlomis fruticosa, 53, 171
Phlomis herba-venti, 171
Phlomis russeliana, 171
Phlomis samia, 171
Phlomis tuberosa, 171, 172
Physostegia, 85, 93, 112, 172–173
Physostegia digitalis, 172
Physostegia parviflora, 172
Physostegia virginiana, 93, 172–173, Plate 51
Physostegia virginiana 'Alba', 93
Physostegia virginiana 'Nana', 93
Physostegia virginiana 'Rose Pink', 93
Physostegia virginiana 'Variegata', 93
Physostegia virginiana 'Vivid', 93, Plate 8
Pineapple mint. See *Mentha suaveolens* 'Variegata'
Pineapple sage. See *Salvia elegans*
Pineapple-scented sage. See *Salvia elegans*
Pitcher sage. See *Lepechinia calycina, Salvia spathacea*
Pitcher's salvia. See *Salvia azurea*
Plains lemon monarda. See *Monarda pectinata*
Plectranthus, 173–174
Plectranthus amboinicus, 54, 173
Plectranthus fruticosa, 173
Plectranthus madagscariensis, 173
Plectranthus oertendahlii, 174
Plectranthus thyrsoideus, 174
Plectranthus verticillatus, 174
Pogostemon, 74, 174
Pogostemon cablin, 74, 174
Poison ivy. See *Toxicodendron radicans*
Polygonum, 99
Pot marjoram. See *Origanum onites, Origanum vulgare*
Prairie hyssop. See *Pycnanthemum virginianum*
Prairie sage. See *Salvia azurea*
Prostanthera, 174–175
Prostanthera lasianthos, 175
Prostanthera melissifolia, 175
Prostanthera nivea, 175
Prostanthera rotundifolia, 175
Prostanthera sieberi, 175
Prostrate coleus. See *Plectranthus oertendahlii*
Prunella, 102, 112, 175–177
Prunella grandiflora, 177
Prunella lancineata, 177
Prunella vulgaris, 53, 102–103, 176, 177
Purple sage. See *Salvia dorrii, Salvia leucophylla*
Pycnanthemum, 74, 177–178
Pycnanthemum flexuosum, 177
Pycnanthemum muticum, 74, 177–178
Pycnanthemum pilosum, 178
Pycnanthemum virginianum, 54, 74, 178
Pycnostachys, 178

Pycnostachys dawii, 178
Pycnostachys stuhlmannii, 178
Pycnostachys urticifolia, 178
Pyrenean dead-nettle. See *Horminum*

Red creeping thyme. See *Thymus praecox*
Red dead nettle. See *Lamium purpureum*
Red-topped sage. See *Salvia viridis*
Richweed. See *Collinsonia canadensis*
Rosemary. See *Rosmarinus officinalis*
Rose sage. See *Salvia pachyphylla*
Rosmarinus, 75–76
Rosmarinus officinalis, 17, 23, 26, 43, 45, 46, 47, 50, 51, 53, 54, 55, 56, 75–76, 107, 110, 112, 179, Plate 4
Rosmarinus officinalis var. *albiflorus,* 76
Rosmarinus officinalis 'Arp', 76, 179
Rosmarinus officinalis 'Aureus', 76, 179
Rosmarinus officinalis 'McConnell's Blue', 76, 179
Rosmarinus officinalis 'Pinkie', 76, 179
Rosmarinus officinalis 'Roseus', 76, 179
Rosmarinus officinalis 'Sissinghurst Blue', 76, 179
Rosy leaf sage. See *Salvia involucrata*
Round-leaf mint. See *Prostanthera rotundifolia*
Runaway robin. See *Glechoma hederacea*
Russian sage. See *Perovskia atriplicifolia*

Sage. See *Salvia*
Salazaria, 180
Salazaria mexicana, 180
Salvia, 23, 76–79, 85, 93–96, 112, 180–193
Salvia aethiopis, 180
Salvia apiana, 180
Salvia argentea, 93, 180–181
Salvia azurea, 94, 181
Salvia azurea var. *grandiflorum,* 94, 181
Salvia barrelieri, 181
Salvia bracteata, 181
Salvia brandegei, 181
Salvia broussonetii, 181
Salvia canariensis, 182
Salvia carduacea, 182
Salvia clevelandii, 76, 182
Salvia coccinea, 94, 182, Plate 52
Salvia columbariae, 182
Salvia costaricensis, 182
Salvia divinorum, 44, 183
Salvia dorisiana, 77, 183
Salvia dorrii, 183
Salvia elegans, 54, 77, 183, Plate 25
Salvia eremostachya, 183
Salvia farinacea, 94–95, 183–184
Salvia farinacea 'Argent', 95, 183–184
Salvia farinacea 'Blue Bedder', 95, 184
Salvia farinacea 'Cirrus', 95, 184, Plate 53
Salvia farinacea 'Victoria', 95, 184, Plate 10, Plate 54
Salvia farinacea 'Victoria Blue', 184
Salvia fruticosa, 184
Salvia glutinosa, 184
Salvia greggii, 94, 95, 184
Salvia greggii 'Cherry Red', 95
Salvia greggii 'Furman's Red', 95
Salvia greggii 'Purple Pastel', 95
Salvia guaranitica, 184
Salvia hispanica, 184–185
Salvia horminum. See *Salvia viridis*
Salvia interrupta, 185
Salvia involucrata, 185–186
Salvia judaica, 20, 186
Salvia leucantha, 186
Salvia leucophylla, 186
Salvia lyrata, 54, 186
Salvia major, 33

Salvia mexicana, 186
Salvia microphylla, 186
Salvia minor, 33
Salvia munzii, 187
Salvia nemorosa, 95, 187
Salvia nemorosa 'East Friesland', 95, Plate 55
Salvia nemorosa 'Rose Queen', 95
Salvia officinalis, 17, 23, 43, 47, 48, 51, 53, 54, 55, 77, 78, 111, 187, Plate 26
Salvia officinalis 'Aurea', 78, 187, Plate 33
Salvia officinalis 'Berggarten', 78, 187, Plate 28, Plate 33
Salvia officinalis 'Icterina', 78, 187, Plate 10, Plate 29
Salvia officinalis 'Nana', 57, 78, 187, Plate 27
Salvia officinalis 'Purpurescens', 78, 187, Plate 9, Plate 30
Salvia officinalis 'Tricolor', 78, 187, Plate 31
Salvia pachyphylla, 187
Salvia patens, 187
Salvia pitcheri. See *Salvia azurea* var. *grandiflorum*
Salvia pratensis, 95–96, 187–188
Salvia purpurea, 188
Salvia reflexa, 188
Salvia ringens, 188
Salvia Romana, 39
Salvia rutilans. See *Salvia elegans*
Salvia scabiosifolia, 188–189
Salvia sclarea, 53, 78–79, 189
Salvia sonomensis, 190
Salvia spathacea, 190
Salvia splendens, 96, 190, 191
Salvia ×superba, 95, 96, 190
Salvia ×superba 'Blue Queen', 190
Salvia ×superba 'May Night', 190
Salvia ×superba 'Rose Queen', 190
Salvia sylvestris, 96
Salvia tiliifolia, 190
Salvia uliginosa, 190, 192
Salvia vaseyi, 192
Salvia verbenaca, 192–193
Salvia verticillata, 192–193
Salvia villicaulis, 96
Salvia villosa, 193
Salvia viridis, 52, 96, 193
Salvia viridis 'Alba', 96
Salvia viridis 'Bluebeard', 96
Salvia viridis 'Pink Sunday', 96
Salvia viridis 'Rose Bouquet', 96
Salvia wagneriana, 193
San Luis purple sage. See *Salvia leucophylla*
Satureja, 48, 79–80, 193–194
Satureja douglasii, 79, 193
Satureja hortensis, 47, 48, 51, 54, 79, 193–194
Satureja montana, 24, 47, 48, 51, 53, 54, 79, 193–194
Savory. See *Micromeria juliana, Satureja*
Savory calamint. See *Satureja*
Saw-toothed lavender. See *Lavandula dentata*
Scarlet sage. See *Salvia splendens*
Scophularia, 112
Scrophularia marilandica, 112
Scutellaria, 43, 85, 194–199
Scutellaria albida, 194
Scutellaria alpina, 194
Scutellaria baicalensis, 194, 195
Scutellaria brittonii, 194, 196
Scutellaria californica, 196
Scutellaria columnae, 196
Scutellaria costaricana, 196
Scutellaria galericulata, 196, 197
Scutellaria hirta, 196
Scutellaria incana, 196, 198
Scutellaria indica, 198
Scutellaria integrifolia, 198
Scutellaria longifolia, 198

Scutellaria orientalis, 198
Scutellaria parvula, 198
Scutellaria resinosa, 198–199
Scutellaria scordiifolia, 199
*Scutellaria tuberosa*199
Self-heal. See *Prunella*
Shellflower. See *Moluccella laevis*
Sideritis, 199–200
Sideritis argosphacelus, 199
Sideritis candicans, 199
Sideritis hyssopifolia, 199–200
Sideritis libanotica, 200
Sideritis macrostachys, 200
Sideritis montana, 200
Sideritis syriaca, 200
Silver sage. See *Salvia argentea*
Skullcap. See *Scutellaria*
Snow flake. See *Lamium album*
Solenostemon, 96–97, 201
Solenostemon blumei. See *Solenostemon scutellarioides*
Solenostemon scutellarioides, 96–97, 201, Plate 56
Solenostemon scutellarioides 'Alabama Sunset', 97
Solenostemon scutellarioides 'Burgundy Sun', 97
Solenostemon scutellarioides 'Copper Queen', 97
Solenostemon scutellarioides 'India Frills', 97
Solenostemon scutellarioides 'Inky Fingers', 97
Solenostemon scutellarioides 'Japanese Brocade', 97
Solenostemon scutellarioides 'Kiwi Fern', 97
Solenostemon scutellarioides 'Max Levering', 97
Solenostemon scutellarioides 'Rusty', 97, Plate 57
Solenostemon scutellarioides 'Super Sun Plum Parfait', 97
Solenostemon scutellarioides 'Yellow in Sun', 97
Solidago, 99
Soup mint. See *Plectranthus amboinicus*
Spanish lavender. See *Lavandula stoechas*
Spanish sage. See *Salvia barrelieri*
Spanish thyme. See *Plectranthus amboinicus*
Spearmint. See *Mentha spicata*
Spotted dead nettle. See *Lamium maculatum*
Spur flower. See *Plectranthus*
Stachys, 97–98, 201–204
Stachys affinis, 201
Stachys alopecuros, 201–202
Stachys betonica. See *Stachys officinalis*
Stachys bullata, 202
Stachys byzantina, 97–98, 202, Plate 6, Plate 58
Stachys byzantina 'Cotton Ball', 98
Stachys byzantina 'Primrose Heron', 98
Stachys byzantina 'Sheila McQueen'. See *Stachys byzantina* 'Cotton Ball'
Stachys byzantina 'Silver Carpet', 98
Stachys ciliata, 202
Stachys corsica, 202
Stachys germanica, 202, 203
Stachys grandiflora. See *Stachys macrantha*
Stachys hyssopifolia, 202–203
Stachys lanata. See *Stachys byzantina*
Stachys lavendulifolia, 203
Stachys macrantha, 98, 203, Plate 59
Stachys macrantha 'Alba', 98, 203
Stachys macrantha 'Robusta', 98, 203
Stachys macrantha 'Violacea', 98, 203
Stachys officinalis, 53, 98, 203
Stachys olympica. See *Stachys byzantina*
Stachys riddellii, 203–204
Stachys tenuifolia, 204

Stay-in-place. See *Physostegia virginiana*
St. John's wort. See *Hypericum*
Stone mint. See *Cunila originoides*
Stoneroot. See *Collinsonia canadensis*
Summer savory. See *Satureja hortensis*
Swedish begonia. See *Plectranthus*
Swedish ivy. See *Plectranthus*
Sweet balm. See *Melissa officinalis*
Sweet basil. See *Ocimum basilicum*
Sweet horsemint. See *Cunila origanoides*
Sweet marjoram. See *Origanum majorana*
Syrian marjoram. See *Origanum maru*

Tarragon. See *Artemisia drancunculus*
Tetradenia, 80, 204
Tetradenia riparia, 204
Teucrium, 204–209
Teucrium alterum, 35
Teucrium aroanum, 204
Teucrium bicolor, 204–205
Teucrium canadense, 205
Teucrium chamaedrys, 53, 80, 205, Plate 32, Plate 33
Teucrium flavum, 205
Teucrium fruticans, 206
Teucrium heterophyllum, 206
Teucrium krymense, 206
Teucrium lucidum, 206
Teucrium marum, 80, 207
Teucrium massiliense, 207
Teucrium montanum, 207
Teucrium occidentale, 207–208
Teucrium orientale, 208
Teucrium polium, 53, 208
Teucrium pyrenaicum, 208
Teucrium scorodonia, 209
Teucrium subspinosum, 209
Texas sage. See *Salvia greggii*
Thistle sage. See *Salvia carduacea*
Thymbra, 209
Thymbra spicata, 209
Thyme. See *Thymus*
Thymus, 46, 47, 49, 52, 80–83, 209–214, Plate 5, Plate 34
Thymus broussonettii, 210
Thymus caespititius, 210
Thymus camphoratus, 210
Thymus carnosus, 210
Thymus cimicinus, 210
Thymus ×citriodorus, 45, 54, 56, 81, 82, 210
Thymus ×citriodorus 'Aureus', 82, 210
Thymus ×citriodorus 'Golden King', 82, 210
Thymus ×citriodorus 'Silver Queen', 49, 82, 210, Plate 35
Thymus comosus, 211
Thymus comptus, 211
Thymus doerfleri, 211
Thymus glabrescens, 211
Thymus herba-barona, 49, 82, 211, Plate 36
Thymus hyemalis, 211
Thymus mastichina, 211–212
Thymus membranaceus, 212
Thymus nummularius, 212
Thymus pannonicus, 212
Thymus praecox, 49, 82, 212, Plate 37
Thymus praecox subsp. *arcticus,* 53, 54, 82, 211
Thymus pseudolanuginosus, 49, 82, 212, Plate 38
Thymus pseudolanuginosus 'Hall's Variety', 82
Thymus pulegioides, 82, 213
Thymus pulegioides 'Oregano-scented', 54, 213
Thymus quinquecostatus, 213
Thymus richardii, 213
Thymus serpyllum, 49, 56, 82, 213, Plate 39

Thymus serpyllum 'Albus', 82, 213
Thymus serpyllum 'Annie Hall', 82–83, 213
Thymus serpyllum 'Coccineus', 83, 213
Thymus serpyllum 'Elfin', 83, 213
Thymus vulgaris, 17, 23, 25, 49, 51, 53, 54, 54, 55, 81, 82, 209–210, 214
Thymus vulgaris 'Erectus', 83, 214
Thymus vulgaris 'Lavender', 83, 214
Thymus vulgaris 'Narrow-Leaf French', 83, 214
Thymus vulgaris 'Orange Balsam', 83, 214
Thymus zygis, 214
Toxicodendron radicans, 99
Tree germander. See *Teucrium fruticans*
Trichostema, 214
Trichostema lanatum, 214
Trichostema lanceolatum, 214
Trichostema ovatum, 214
Tropical sage. See *Salvia coccinea*

Upright bugle. See *Ajuga genevensis*
Upright bugleweed. See *Ajuga pyramidalis*
Upright rosemary. See *Rosmarinus officinalis*

Vervain. See *Salvia verbenaca*
Victoria dogwood. See *Prostanthera lasianthos*
Victorian Christmas bush. See *Prostanthera lasianthos*
Vinegar weed. See *Trichostema lanceolatum*
Violet sage. See *Salvia nemorosa*
Virginian mint. See *Pycnanthemum virginianum*

Wall germander. See *Teucrium chamaedrys*
Water horehound. See *Lycopus americanus*
Water mint. See *Mentha aquatica, Mentha* x*piperita* var. *citrata*
Westringia, 215
Westringia rigida, 215
Westringia rigida 'Variegata', 215
White dead nettle. See *Lamium album*
White horehound. See *Marrubium vulgare*
White peppermint. See *Mentha* x *piperita* var. *officinalis*
Wild basil. See *Clinopodium vulgare, Pycnanthemum virginianum*
Wild bergamot. See *Monarda*
Wild clary. See *Salvia verbenaca*
Wild marjoram. See *Origanum vulgare*
Wild thyme. See *Thymus praecox, Thymus serpyllum*
Winter savory. See *Satureja montana*
Wood germander. See *Teucrium scorodonia*
Wood mint. See *Blephilia hirsuta*
Wood sage. See *Teucrium*
Woody betony. See *Stachys officinalis*
Woolly betony. See *Stachys byzantina*
Woolly blue curls. See *Trichostema lanatum*
Woolly mint. See *Mentha suaveolens*
Woolly thyme. See *Thymus pseudolanuginosus*
Woundwort. See *Stachys*
Wrinkled great hyssop. See *Agastache rugosa*

Yellow archangel. See *Lamium galeobdolon*
Yerba buena. See *Micromeria chamissonis, Satureja douglasii*

3 1221 06822 7409